Genius Unmasked

Genius Unmasked

ROBERTA B. NESS

OXFORD
UNIVERSITY PRESS

OXFORD
UNIVERSITY PRESS

Oxford University Press is a department of the University of Oxford.
It furthers the University's objective of excellence in research, scholarship,
and education by publishing worldwide.

Oxford   New York
Auckland   Cape Town   Dar es Salaam   Hong Kong   Karachi
Kuala Lumpur   Madrid   Melbourne   Mexico City   Nairobi
New Delhi   Shanghai   Taipei   Toronto

With offices in
Argentina   Austria   Brazil   Chile   Czech Republic   France   Greece
Guatemala   Hungary   Italy   Japan   Poland   Portugal   Singapore
South Korea   Switzerland   Thailand   Turkey   Ukraine   Vietnam

Oxford is a registered trademark of Oxford University Press in the UK and certain other
countries.

Published in the United States of America by
Oxford University Press
198 Madison Avenue, New York, NY 10016

Library of Congress Cataloging-in-Publication Data
Ness, Roberta B.
Genius unmasked / Roberta B. Ness.
   pages cm.
Includes bibliographical references.
ISBN 978–0–19–997659–1
1. Genius—Case studies.   2. Creative ability in science—Case studies.
3. Creative ability.   I. Title.
BF412.N46 2013
153.9′8—dc23   2013003365

9 8 7 6 5 4 3 2 1
Printed in the United States of America
on acid-free paper

To David, Joel, and Sara to whom I am forever indebted
for keeping me thinking

CONTENTS

Genius Unmasked

Hero Worship

My first encounter with inspirational thinking occurred when I was a medical intern at Bellevue Hospital in New York City. I was taking care of a 16-year-old prostitute. She came in for treatment of an infection in her heart valve that had resulted from shooting up heroin. What distinguished her from the other intravenous drug users with endocarditis that I had admitted was her unusual cleverness and optimism. She seemed eager to mend her ways. Perhaps I could convince her to escape her wayward lifestyle—to be one of the rare ones to get off the street and back to school. We talked about life and hope each day as I delivered her intravenous antibiotics. I felt sure that I was having an impact. One day, about halfway through her course of treatment, when I arrived with my miracle drugs she was gone, intravenous catheter still embedded in her arm. "A great way to shoot up," a wiser resident informed me.

Her treatment had been working—the fever had come down and the white blood count had normalized. Yet completion of such a short course of antibiotics could not have eliminated the bacteria. Going back to her pimp and the drugs meant that it was only a matter of time before she landed right back in the emergency department. Her next visit would be brutal. The unencumbered pestilence that was still inside her heart valve would have eaten away the tissue leaving only a gaping hole. The surgical residents at Bellevue had a rule in those days—they would replace a value once but never twice. An unsuccessful course of antibiotics fated the young prostitute to her first strike. And it fated me to my first failure. Hadn't my good intentions been enough?

The only person who seemed to fathom what had happened was Lewis Goldfrank, chairman of Bellevue's famed Department of Emergency Medicine. Goldfrank was, simply put, the smartest guy in the room. I remember once waking him at home at 2 A.M. because I knew he would council me through the management of a patient whose twitching muscles and dilated pupils I feared had resulted from a poisonous adventure with forest mushrooms. But Goldfrank was not just stimulating because he knew a lot. He was remarkable because he reasoned in a way that was surprising.

Goldfrank saw beyond the press of caring for the 110,000 patients with car crash injuries, drug overdoses, and gunshot wounds who poured into the Bellevue Emergency Department (ED) each year. "The purpose of a physician in the Emergency Department," Goldfrank once said, "should be to shut the place down." Accidents should never happen; medical calamities, according to him, were largely preventable. Rather than working to perfect the most fashionable emergency treatments, Goldfrank studied how to avert repeat emergency visits. He ran the New York City Poison Control Center, shifting the focus from mitigating the consequences of poisoning to thwarting toxins from ever reaching unsuspecting hands. New York City, Goldfrank believed, was full of toxins, both real and metaphorical. Speeding and drunk driving were toxins that predisposed to motor vehicle accidents. The trail of tears that preceded the prostitute's drug addiction was what had destroyed her valve. Thinking broadly, backward, and while walking in his patient's shoes—those were the unusual thought processes that Goldfrank embedded in the minds of us residents.

After Bellevue—after Goldfrank—my desire to deliver clinical care to individuals became replaced by a new passion. Public health. I now aspired to prevent disease before it ever took a toll. With seven years invested in training to be a physician, I went back to public health school to learn to be an epidemiologist, a scientist who, rather than treating disease in one patient at a time, seeks to understand patterns of illness among thousands. It was an unexpected and risky reversal of my life's path.

Lew Goldfrank, along with other remarkable scientific innovators I have known, instigated this book. The creators who populate these pages were chosen because they not only saw things differently, as did Goldfrank, but because they left the world so enriched, that their stories have transcended to legend.

Some are idols whom we all recognize—Edison, Pasteur, and Einstein. Their inventions and discoveries brought us light, health, and power—things more marvelous than our ancestors could have imagined. Others are less popularly iconic—for instance, Norman Borlaug, Russell Marker, and Paul Baran—yet within their own disciplines their claims to fame are no less imposing. Borlaug is the "father of the Green Revolution"; Marker first synthesized the chemical key to formulating oral contraceptives; Baran invented the brilliant network behind the Internet. We call these heroes "geniuses."

Genius—it is a word that invokes mystique. Such thinking is inscrutable, even though its results are recognizable as creativity on a revolutionary scale. Although the product of genius is, by definition, surprising, some of the routes taken were a series of predictable steps; other courses seemed to pop out of nowhere. Sometimes geniuses envisioned their terminus far off in the distance; other times, their destination was unforeseen. To date, however, no one—not even the autobiographical accounts written by geniuses themselves has produced satisfying insights into their thinking process. How did radical innovators think? Perhaps their minds, prepared through the providence of genetics, were simply lucked upon by chance. Or perhaps, as it sometimes seemed, their visionary insights were attained through divine intervention. But could there be an entirely different explanation? Could there be a more knowable process underlying genius?

This book seeks to unmask the nature of genius. It is designed to get inside a few inspirational minds and ask: Is genius really so magical, or does it, instead, consist of predictable patterns of imaginative thinking, no matter how transformative? Can the mental features of breathtaking creativity be revealed? What I hope to demonstrate in these pages is that genius is achieved through a thinking process that is less mystical than it is systematic. I hope to show that even the greatest of innovative minds has used a cognitive toolbox that can be opened and understood.

Of course, such a demonstration seems like a tall order and will have to be convincing. But let's just imagine for a moment that it is true—that the activity of prodigious creativity can be discerned. Then genius actually involves a set of strategies. And those strategies can be emulated.

What is inside the scientific genius's toolbox? As their stories unfold, we find the following devices: (1) finding the right question; (2) observation; (3) analogy; (4) juggling induction and deduction; (5) changing point of view; (6) broadening perspective; (7) dissecting the problem; (8) reversal; (9) recombination and rearrangement; (10) the power of groups; and (11) frame shifting.

These tools are not magic. Together, they are techniques that have been previously described for use in teaching children and adults to be more creative. Creativity training programs that incorporate many of these instruments, as described in my previous book, *Innovation Generation: How to Produce Creative and Unusual Scientific Ideas,* have been shown to substantially improve innovation for almost anyone. Trainees from these programs, no matter their age, gender, or even intellectual prowess, generate two- to threefold more ideas on standardized creativity tests, and their ideas are more original. Professionals who complete creativity training are more productive. Their thinking is more flexible and they have a greater preference for novel problem-solving.

What this book hopes to demonstrate, then, is that some of the most creative minds in science have used devices that any of us can learn to use, and which can improve our creative abilities. Geniuses were not omnipotent and they were not divine. They were simply particularly skilled master craftsmen of creative surprise.

As we hear these stories, it is also worth asking two other questions. The first is whether there are, in fact, two subsets of scientific creators— those who worked within the rules and those who overturned the rules. The common terms for these two types of innovation are "evolutionary" and "revolutionary." All of the innovators discussed here initiated social transformation—that is, they created a state of things that was utterly new. Yet social disruption does not always imply scientific transformation. Evolutionary innovation does not alter the very essence of science, whereas revolutionary innovation does. In business parlance, evolutionary innovations are brought about by many, incremental advances and create products that do not disrupt human (in this case, scientific) routines. Revolutionary innovations overturn the status quo; they necessitate the acceptance of radical departures from comfortable traditions.

As we shall see, the peculiarities of naming can be misleading. Darwin's evolutionary theory was not an evolutionary innovation—it was a revolutionary one that forced experts and the public to rethink assumptions about the origin of life around us and of our own human species. Conversely, the Green Revolution and the Contraceptive Revolution were not revolutionary innovations in a scientific sense but instead reflected a string of modest advances that, when applied synergistically, nonetheless produced social change on a massive scale. Naming aside, it seems reasonable to ask: Did those geniuses who contributed small steps think in the same way as those who made huge leaps?

The second question is how cognition interacts with character. Birthing radical new ideas, as we will see, is often accompanied by deep curiosity, unshakable self-belief, and dogged tenacity. Kirk Varnedoe, in his book *Fine Disregard: What Makes Modern Art Modern,* posits that the modern artists who changed art history engaged in "gratuitous rearrangement" that found the fortune to strike a cultural nerve. Modern art, he claims, was in fact instigated by people who engaged in acts that were "simple, human, and willfully contrary." Are scientific innovators also individuals with the willingness, indeed the craving, to flout convention in the service of some fascination? How common and how necessary to scientific discovery are such characteristics? Are such traits all good, or do they have an unwanted underbelly?

Every generation needs great innovators. Today, unique insights are needed to solve the greatest threats to mankind—problems such as cancer, Alzheimer's disease, obesity, emerging infections, and climate change. Yet a blue ribbon Committee of the National Academies of Science recently warned that modern American science is making slow progress toward finding solutions. Why? Because, according to the distinguished panel, the United States is not sustaining its "creative ecosystem"—its intellectual capital. Moreover, a rash of commentaries published in *Business Week, National Review,* and the *New York Times* has decried that America is in the midst of a worrisome slowdown of innovation. Tyler Cowen's influential book *The Great Stagnation* (2010), although it applauded advances in information technology, agonized about the sluggishness of invention in many other technical and science sectors. David Brooks, a nationally syndicated columnist, reminded us that a time traveler arriving in 2011 after having blasted off in 1970 would be disappointed at the pace of progress if she expected to see advancements on par with those of the first half of the twentieth century, when horse-drawn buggies transmuted into moon rockets.

To remain healthy and prosperous, society must maximize the potential in each of us. We all hope to create something interesting and original. By understanding the methods used by eminent scientists, can we work toward useful mimicry? Can we learn from geniuses to become better innovators?

To start, we need only adopt the one trait universal among geniuses—a characteristic essential to their creativity. It is the belief that we can do whatever we seriously set out to do—that our thinking can develop. Surely, with faith in ourselves and inspirational stories as our guide, we will at the very least learn something interesting. By peeking beneath the mask of genius we may even find our own surprising capacity for ingenuity.

2

Nature versus God

Charles Darwin

N ovelty often breeds controversy. If the impact of an innovative idea were ranked by its contentiousness, the theory of evolution by means of natural selection would top the list. When Charles Darwin's *On the Origin of Species* was published in 1859, it caused what has been widely described as "a sensation." Religious authorities considered it blasphemous, if not diabolical. For half a century, scientists actively contested it. Darwin himself anticipated and shied away from the maelstrom that he knew the theory could cause. With his social and scientific standing built on an impeccable record of mainstream scientific contributions, he kept the manuscript locked away in his office for 20 years, along with instructions to his wife to publish it only upon the occasion of his death. It was not until a young, entrepreneurial naturalist named Alfred Russell Wallace was about to scoop him that Darwin rushed the manuscript to press.

Darwin's theory of evolution by means of natural selection still surprises and divides the American public. Despite its profound influence on much of science—the fields of genetics, psychology, sociology, and biology, to name a few—a constant stream of books continues to challenge, tweak, or disbelieve it outright. Fewer than 20 percent of Americans surveyed in a series of recent Gallup Polls subscribe to Darwin's central tenet: human beings developed over millions of years from other life forms without the guidance of God. In contrast, about 45 percent select as true the alternative statement: "God created human beings pretty much in their present form at one time within the last 10,000 years or so." Another 35 percent believe that humans developed slowly from other life forms but that God guided the process. Thus, 150 years after its inception, Darwin's theory departs so radically from religious teachings and is so counterintuitive that most of the American public continues to reject it.

What is the theory of evolution by means of natural selection? Let us try to absorb it, recognizing its strangeness, by breaking it into two parts. First, species are not immutable. This part of the theory has been termed "evolution," and it explains the abundance of diversity in the world's plants and animals. Within that diversity, species are the simplest units of biological classification. Commonly defined, a species is a group of organisms that can breed among themselves and produce fertile offspring. Prior to Darwin, it was commonly believed that this most basic element of life had characteristics that were absolute and unchangeable. Evolutionists, including Darwin, argued that the opposite was true: within species, alterations in both body and behavior are inevitable.

The second part of Darwin's theory is more contentious, bizarre, and earth-shattering. Darwin speculated that the driver of evolution is natural selection. "Natural selection" means that traits change because the ones that provide a reproductive advantage become more common in the population.

Random variations, Darwin argued, were the result of the mixing of traits inherited from each parent. Although "like breeds like," offspring traits were an admixture of those from each parent, which made them utterly unique. Those inherited traits that were better adapted to the environment benefitted the organism in its survival and benefitted their ability to reproduce. In the case of Galápagos finches, for example, the shape of beaks was one such trait; some beaks worked best for certain seeds, and other beaks worked better for others. A finch whose beak was most successful at opening the most common seed type was most likely to thrive. However, nature is not kind. Environmental resources are inadequate to feed or support all progeny of all species. Those individuals whose characteristics were best adapted to their environment, such as the finches with the best seed-opening beaks, were most likely to win the struggle for survival and to produce more offspring. Over successive generations, the advantageous trait became dominant—it was selected.

Imagine that reproduction is Mother Nature's way of dealing random cards from the species deck. If a card is dealt for some characteristic that enhances the holder's hardiness in the particular environment, then that card gets dealt again to more players in the next round. On the other hand, cards that reduce hardiness get discarded. Eventually, the hardiness card becomes the most dominant in the game.

Had Darwin's logic stopped there, perhaps his theory would not have been so controversial. But he further proposed that species undergoing lengthy natural selection morphed into other species. From apes sprang man.

Darwin's later book, *The Descent of Man and Selection in Relation to Sex* (1871), argued that while humankind trended evolutionarily toward a smaller and weaker habitus, it also evolved toward superior cognition, providing complex behavioral strategies to attract mates. The image of a brute luring a beauty back to his cave was, in Darwin's mind, more literal than figurative. It was an idea almost perfectly designed to be objectionable to Victorian society.

How did Darwin hatch such a disruptive concept? Although we may remember him as a retiring aristocrat, as he was in his later years, he was anything but conventional. Early on, he rejected the upper-class expectations of his family. Rather than becoming a medic like his father, Charles dropped out of the University of Edinburgh Medical School and spent his days hunting, beetle collecting, and classifying plants. Such appetites seemed of little or no use to society. His father renounced Charles's dallying, fearing that without a shift in course, his son would become "a disgrace to yourself and all your family." That is, Charles's early exploits were not conventional and they were not reinforced by accolades. Instead, they reeked of the spontaneity, curiosity, and individuality that are characteristics so common among great innovators.

Had a letter from his former botany professor John Stevens Henslow not arrived when it did, the young Darwin would have been compelled to enter the Anglican clergy. His inclination toward genius might never have been complemented by an apprenticeship in the use of the tools

of innovation. Henslow recommended Charles as a suitable gentleman companion to Captain Robert FitzRoy on an around-the-world
voyage on the *HMS Beagle*. Darwin would be the onboard naturalist
on the *Beagle*'s excursion (1831–1836), which was designed to map the
coast of South America. The work was not only unpaid but required
self-funding. Fortunately, with the help of a respected uncle, Charles
"sold" his father on the trip—giving himself five intensive years to
sharpen his thinking skills.

The most prominent tool that Darwin used was *observation*. Darwin's
boyhood exploits in beetle collection and plant classification had opened
his naturalist's eye for characterizing the minute details that categorize species. During the voyage of the *Beagle*, his powers of observation
were enhanced by the development of patience, persistence, and discipline. Crate loads of flora and fauna from South America and the South
Seas arrived back in England, representing a collection whose vastness
was historic. Upon disembarking from the trip in Falmouth, he was an
instant scientific celebrity. He was, after all, the man who had found the
fossilized bones of huge extinct mammals, including the Megatherium, a
giant sloth-like creature from Patagonia.

But observation did not resolve Darwin's curiosity. Surely he had
encountered a fantastic range of diversity. But how did it all fit together?
Ultimately, a question took shape. It was massively ambitious—a question
far more bold than those any naturalist had previously asked. "By what
means," Darwin queried, "do all living things in nature come to be?"

The tool of *asking the right question* was a second fundamental step in
Darwin's cognitive maturation. But his question's scope was so huge that
it could only be embraced over time. In a series of notebooks that Darwin
initiated soon after he arrived home, he recorded his embryonic intellectual struggles. He called his thinking on evolution "[a] most labori-
ous, & painful effort of the mind." In these notebooks, a unique cognitive
record emerges. Remarkably, Darwin documents the use of every tool in
the innovator's chest.

The most sweeping of these tools was *frame shifting*. Traditionally,
the accepted belief was that all living things are replicas of perfect

creations produced by God. Since there could be no alteration from this perfection, to ask how species change over time made no sense. Notably, Darwin's question about how all species originated necessarily eliminated any assumption about divine intervention. It gave him the freedom to ask whether species vary and how they vary. It gave him the freedom to produce the breakthrough that species variation occurs, and that change is driven by randomness. Rather than resulting from a perfect plan designed by a loving deity, Darwin proposed, beauty and monsters alike are created by an environment whose harshness is arbitrary.

Had Darwin trained as an Anglican minister, it is unlikely that he would have conceptualized natural selection. Prominent biologists of Darwin's time were trained first as theologians, then as scientists. God, they believed, has a hand throughout nature. In his 1802 book, *Natural Theology: Evidences of the Existence and Attributes of the Diety, Collected from the Appearances of Nature,* William Paley popularized the analogy between God and a watchmaker. His argument was: if any of us found a watch lying on the ground, we would assume that it had been made by an expert craftsman. Similarly, when we observe the perfection and variety of flora and fauna in nature, we appreciate it as the work of a master creator. Underlying this logic was the even more ancient idea, popularized by Plato, that all of life derives from a limited number of prototypes, called "natural kinds." In Plato's view, species are separate and distinct: a cat is a cat and a dog is a dog and never the twain shall meet. David Quammen, in his book *The Reluctant Mr. Darwin,* comments about creationism, "To believe otherwise was to reject an assumption that was interwoven with ecclesiastic teachings and ideas of civil order."

This is not to say that radical, anti-sectarian thinkers had not preceded Darwin. Earlier thinkers had, indeed, been so bold as to propose evolution of species and to reject creationism. Among the infamous group were Jean-Baptiste Lamark, his protégé Geoffrey Saint-Hilaire, and even Darwin's grandfather, Erasmus Darwin. Unfortunately, the brand of evolution they put forth had been forcefully refuted. In particular, these early evolutionists proposed that evolved characteristics result from use. For example, a giraffe stretches its neck to nip at the uppermost leaves of a tree, and the act of stretching causes a somewhat longer neck. The next generation of giraffes then inherits longer necks. This was a more purposeful—and in many ways more appealing—explanation than was Darwin's. It attributed characteristics in the next generation to the hard work of parents. Unfortunately, it also led to some fairly crazy ideas, for example, that the architecture of mollusks and invertebrates had to be the same. Such extrapolations quite quickly put an end to not only Lamarkian evolution but the whole notion of variability and its origins. To make matters worse, evolution as a social construct was quickly embraced by violent social anarchists. To mainstream thinkers, evolution was a dangerous idea.

Darwin, then, did *not* propose the frame of evolution—that had already been done. He used the tool of *rearrangement* to combine the best of what had been suggested: species variability. But he replaced Lamark's notion that inherited characteristics arise out of use with his own, less self-evident idea of natural selection. Natural selection, with its randomness and arbitrariness, was Darwin's radical frame shift.

Who wouldn't be nervous, proposing an idea that opposed "ecclesiastic teachings and ideas of civil order?" Darwin struggled mightily with the development of his ideas. Early in his notebooks, he sometimes wrote down an insight and then countered it. It was his own internal battle between an emerging David and an existing Goliath. Indeed, despite having transcribed in his notebook the essence of his theory as far back as 1838, it was not until 1844 that he cautiously hinted its outline to anyone. In a letter to a new friend, the young botanist Joseph Dalton Hooker, he begins, "I have been now ever since my return engaged in a very presumptuous work that species are not (it is like confessing a murder) immutable."

The fact that, after his return home from the voyage of the *Beagle*, Darwin became a conventional landed aristocrat makes his intellectual ferment all the more extraordinary. Married to his cousin Emma in 1839, the two moved to Down House in the Kent countryside and had 10 children (two of whom died in infancy). Darwin inherited a princely sum and invested it wisely. The family became comfortable, and their lives became routine; Darwin never again ventured far from home partially due to recurrent stomachaches, vomiting, heart palpitations, and even boils, apparently made worse by social contact. Only a strict regimen of eating, sleeping, and exercise seemed to prevent recurrences. By all appearances, Darwin had become the most tedious traditionalist.

But beneath the external trappings, an innate curiosity and intellectual independence boiled. Once Darwin had started down the path toward his theory, there was no turning back. He had already uttered the earth-shattering question and broken the existing frame. Now he took the vastness of his pondering and *dissected* it into brain-size pieces. It was like a tree, the first two branches of which constituted evolution and natural selection: (1) Do flora and fauna vary? and (2) What process orchestrates natural variability? Indeed, in his notebook, Darwin drew a tree to help visualize his theory. Further dividing the first question, he asked himself, "Why is sex so important?" The answer provided the clue that sexual assortment allows for variation. In his words, "According to this view animals, on separate islands, ought to become different if kept long enough." Thus, each question was separated into sub-questions, and each divide led to the next.

One of the sentinel characteristics of Darwin's thinking was, again, his brilliance as a keen observer. In both *On the Origin of Species* and *The Descent of Man*, he uses reams of examples, each the result of his own clear and unbiased visualizations. But Darwin also drew on the observations of others. Strongly connected to like-minded intellectuals through avid discussion and correspondence, the *power of these contemporaries* greatly influenced Darwin's thinking. For example, shortly after his return to England in 1837, he consulted with ornithologist John Gould about a collection of brown birds he had brought back from the isolated Galápagos Islands. To Darwin's surprise, Gould identified the assortment—which the collector had assumed were a mixture of orioles, grosbeaks, and wrens—all as finches. Despite a great variety of beak sizes and shapes, Gould was telling Darwin that these birds were closely related cousins. It reinforced a line of reasoning that Darwin had considered while still on the *Beagle*: If related birds lived on separate, neighboring islands, could they all have originated from a common ancestor? Gould's observation suggested that the answer was "yes"; they all belonged to the same species.

Analogies were yet another tool central to Darwin's thinking, two in particular: selective breeding and population explosion. Farmers breed animals for certain characteristics—why wouldn't Mother Nature do the same, Darwin asked. "Can the principle of selection which we have seen is so potent in the hands of man, apply to nature?" he queried, "…Can it, then, be thought improbable, seeing that variations useful to man have undoubtedly occurred, that other variations useful in some way to each being in the great and complex battle of life, should sometimes occur in the course of thousands of generations?"

Another analogy that strongly influenced Darwin's thinking was Thomas Malthus's provocative essay on population explosion. Population growth, Malthus noted, is geometric. Two Englishfolk reproduce to make 4 offspring; 4 make 8; 8 make 16. Within a few generations, the world is overrun with Englishmen. In contrast, Malthus posited, increases in the food supply are arithmetic. Thus, in the absence of war and pestilence to contain population growth, population will always outstrip agricultural production. The result, according to Malthus, is inevitable mass starvation. Only crowding and resource competition checks population growth. This, for Darwin, was the missing piece—the explanation for the selection of more adapted traits. Humans are constrained by resources and competition, Malthus proposed. Traits become dominant in the population through survival of the fittest, Darwin explained.

Darwin's construction of the concept of survival of the fittest also benefitted from his use of imagining his question from a *different point of view*. In *Origin*, he writes, "It is good thus to try in our imagination to give any form some advantage over another.…All that we can do, is to keep steadily in mind that each organic being is striving to increase at a geometrical ratio; that each at some period of life, during some season of the year, during each generation or at intervals, has to struggle for life, and to suffer great destruction." Thus, Darwin imagined himself as a plant or other organic being. In this fantasy of himself as a plant, he was buffeted by storms, eaten by predators, forced to suffer the killing freeze of a long winter.

A final and perhaps the most striking tool that is evident in Darwin's thinking is *reversal*. He literally flips two widely held contemporary views: (1) that God created species that are eternally fixed; and (2) that these painstaking creations are one more excellent than the next, with the most perfect being man. In contrast, Darwin posits that: (1) species evolved from common progenitors; and (2) Mother Nature cares nothing for the variations created—their final forms represent only competitive fitness and not any hierarchy. When, ultimately, Darwin extended his theory to human beings in *The Descent of Man,* he wrote, "Unless we willfully close our eyes, we may, with our present knowledge, approximately recognize our parentage; nor need we feel ashamed of it...an unbiased mind cannot study any living creature, however humble, without being struck with enthusiasm at its marvelous structure and properties." Thus, according to Darwin, creatures evolved from each other, and no creature (including humankind) is more awe-inspiring than another.

Darwin left a voluminous trail of writing that reflected his thinking. His use of the tools of innovation is thus perhaps the most clearly documented in the history of radical scientific innovation. He started by building on extensive observations, crafting an audacious question, and then dissecting it. Long and hard he pondered the solution—formulating and reformulating his arguments over two decades. His thinking shifted continuously between opposites. He used *deduction* to construct the logical argument that evolution by way of natural selection necessarily followed from *observations* such as species variation and ecological diversity. *Induction* allowed him to make generalizations from his extensive observations. His remarkably original theory was shaped by denying the conventional frame, building on the work of others, and using analogy, a changing perspective, rearrangement, expansion, deduction/induction, and reversal.

A century and a half after its publication and now bolstered by major insights from genetic research, Darwin's theory of evolution by means of natural selection generally rings true. No other explanation for the origin of life on earth has emerged to replace its elegance and breadth. Nonetheless, the idea's surprising originality continues to attract incredulity, which apparently no amount of proof will completely dispel. Perhaps the greatest irony regarding Darwin's work is this: many have called *On the Origin of Species* the most influential book since the Bible.

3

Darwin Annotated: The Use of Tools of Innovation

D id Darwin actually rely so solidly on the tools of innovation to support his genius? Or is such a contention simply a post hoc rewriting of history? To find out, let's open the tool chest and dig inside. Diderot's pithy reflection on science in 1753 although it does not enumerate all of the tools, captures an important aspect of their use:

> There are three principal means of acquiring knowledge available to us: observation of nature, reflection, and experimentation. Observation collects facts, reflection combines them, and experimentation verifies the result of that combination. Our observation of nature must be diligent, our reflection profound, and our experiments exact. We rarely see these three means combined.

For each of us, the use of a subset of the devices of innovation can enhance observations and reflection. Every time we say "he was big as a bear" or "her hair was the color of sunshine," we are employing analogy. Therein observations and reflection more readily create knowledge. But what most of us rarely do is to authoritatively use tools in combination. In this chapter, we will see that geniuses such as Darwin were Diderot's rare breed.

Tool 1: Finding the right question. To generate an innovative answer requires asking the right question. Curiosity, a characteristic inherent to innovators, stimulated them to ask reams and reams of questions. Random questions, however, are like throwing darts blindfolded. Somehow innovators found their way to asking the right question in the right way. How did they do it?

Important questions that lend themselves to purposeful creativity are not as enigmatic as they might seem. A convergence of technology, on the one hand, and theory and evidence, on the other, make at least some questions "obvious." Without the correct technology, innovators cannot "see" what is there. Without the appropriate theory, there is no basis for developing the device that allows visualization. Darwin built his question about the origin of species upon the theory proposed by previous evolutionists, as well as on his own data collection from the *Beagle*. For him, technology was not terribly critical. In contrast, Thomas Edison, the subject of chapter 9 of this volume, required the technology of the first electric power generator, the "dynamo" invented by Michael Faraday, in order to ask how to create a system of residential lighting, a major feature of which became the light bulb. Edison's lighting system, in turn, clarified and elaborated the fundamental scientific theory linking electric current, resistance, and voltage. Science created technology, and technology created science. Both aligned to produce salient questions.

Questions that were "ripe" for the asking were often so apparent that they initiated great rivalries. Einstein, to whom chapter 5 is devoted, was one of the most unique thinkers in science, publishing (among other classic papers) the first to use Brownian motion to legitimize the physical existence of atoms. But an Austrian physicist, Marian Smoluchowski, had previously suggested but not published the idea. Alexander Graham Bell submitted his patent for the telephone only hours before his competitor, Elisha Gray, did. Had Gray been first, Bell Telephone might have been called Gray Telephone instead. On the other hand, eminent minds were particularly attuned to ripe questions. Theirs was not simple destiny. As Pasteur noted, "Chance favors the prepared mind."

A more unique characteristic of the questions asked by creative scientists is that they were big. Most scientists restrict their curiosity to precisely limited elaborations of existing theory. Iconic innovators (to turn a phrase) asked big, hairy, audacious questions. (The term "big hairy audacious goals", otherwise known as BHAGs was created by James Collins and Jerry Porras to describe ideologies that are visionary and compelling.) The student-run organization AIESEC (Association Internationale des Étudiants en Sciences Économiques et Commerciales) has a goal of engaging and developing every young person in the world. Twitter aspires to become "the pulse of the planet."

In the cases presented in this book, big questions—such as, How did all species come to be? What is the nature of matter? How does a poor country gain agricultural self-sufficiency?—led to big answers.

Tool 2: Observation. Darwin's theory of evolution by means of natural selection was deeply rooted in observation. After his intensive data collection on the voyage of the *Beagle*, Darwin surveyed plants and animals around the English countryside. He studied selective breeding. He puzzled about plant coexistence within a single ecosystem. From these observations came the inescapable realization that life's diversity stemmed from its struggle for survival.

Exacting observations require overcoming barriers. The first is habituation. Anyone who lives in the country and spends a night in the city finds it difficult to sleep through the street noise. After several days or weeks, however, the clamor seems to have blissfully faded. Repeated sensory stimulation results in a process called habituation. The firing of fewer and fewer neurons results when we are exposed over and over to the same stimulus—a fact demonstrated even in experiments on the microscopic roundworm, *C. Elegans* (with only 302 neurons). Habituation is the physiologic underpinning of complacency. To overcome this natural tendency, discoverers had to tenaciously attend to what often appeared to be mundane and nonessential details.

The second barrier to observation is the tendency to see only what we expect. Overwhelmed by more sensory information than we can process, we selectively attend through the filter of our assumptions. Seeing what others missed was a particular skill among illustrious innovators. Ernest Rutherford, father of nuclear physics, discussed in chapter 10 noticed that alpha particles (later realized to be helium) that were shot out of a microscopic "gun" and onto a target did not quite form a clean, straight line. The denser the element coating the target, the greater their scatter.

Indeed, when alpha particles hit against a layer of gold, the particles deflected backward. This anomaly was one that no one else seemed to have much noticed. Rutherford was so astonished by it that he famously remarked, "It was almost as incredible as if you had fired a 15 inch shell at a piece of tissue paper and it came back and hit you." The observation led Rutherford to infer that the alpha particles and target must each be composed of cores of a single charge that mutually repelled each other. This then became the basis for Rutherford's revolutionary conception of the shape of the atom.

Tool 3: Analogy. Analogy is one of the most commonly used tools to create scientific novelty. It entails the application of lessons from one situation to another. Elementary school students conceptualize the spatial relationship between the sun and the planets by surrounding a suspended baseball with ping pong balls. Blood vessels are equated to road systems or waterways. Light is understood to behave like a wave on a pond. The human mind readily constructs associations. The wider our webs of association, the more likely two associative networks are to overlap and form an analogy.

Highly creative individuals characteristically conjure up broad patterns of similarity. Darwin realized that when farmers practiced selective breeding, they were simply using an artificial form of natural selection. Paul Baran, the subject of chapter 12, who created the computing backbone behind the Internet, related a web of computers to neuronal pathways in the brain. Moreover, he imagined messages traveling through the network to be like letters placed in a mailbox. Metchnikoff, father of immunology and a subject of chapter 11, envisioned the white blood cells defending against foreign invaders like organisms in evolution battling for survival.

Tool 4: Juggling induction and deduction. Inductive reasoning makes generalizations based on individual instances—that is, on patterns of observations. Gregor Mendel, for instance, built the theory of classical genetics on the basis of thousands of crosses between pea plants. However, not all knowledge can be based on the collection of data. Our senses are not always capable of detecting the essence of things. The fact that we have not found all the evolutionary intermediaries between apes and man does not disprove Darwin's theory of evolution. The fact that we cannot directly see atomic particles does not negate electromagnetic theory.

Deductive reasoning uses logic to move inexorably from assumptions, stated as axioms or givens, to a conclusion. Whereas induction moves from a series of observations to the development of a theory, deduction moves from theory to validation through observation. Induction requires sharp observation. Deduction is the permission to use pure imagination.

Creativity often arises at the intersection of the two ways of knowing. Hans Eysenck, a pioneer in creativity research, suggests that "perhaps the incongruity itself is the sign of a creative person, combining [in this case, different logical strategies] in an unusual manner."

Darwin based his theory of natural selection on multitudes of observations, but its essence derived from progressive layers of logic. Einstein used deduction, aided by thought experiments that were mental scenes in which he contemplated the physics of various events, such as a man walking while inside a moving train. Yet these only provided a framework for the empiric, data-gathering knowledge already accumulated by others. "It is the theory that describes what we can observe," Einstein believed. Movement back and forth between observation and theory, between experimental evidence and pure reasoning, was their winning strategy.

Tool 5. Changing point of view. "Don't judge a man until you have walked a mile in his shoes" is a powerful maxim that encourages us to see as another sees. In their book *Poor Economics*, Abhijit Banerjee and Esther Duflo put forth a "radical rethinking of the economics of poverty" based on field experiments that show a clear logic behind decisions made by the desperately poor. For instance, the suburbs of Tangiers, Morocco, are filled with unfinished houses. Why? Because in a society where the poor have insufficient capital to avoid excessive banking fees, this is the safest and most effective way to save money—one brick at a time. If the rich could think like the poor, Banerjee and Duflo argue, they might help the world's most disenfranchised find novel solutions to scarcity. In other words, Banerjee and Duflo suggest that the most informed philanthropy springs from changing one's point of view.

Foreign points of view can seem odd or even illogical. In Sweden, most citizens pay taxes to the church, yet no political party would even consider advocating for teaching any theory of evolution other than Darwin's. The United States takes pride in its sectarian separation of church and state. Yet, as recently as 2005, a School Board in York County, Pennsylvania, required teachers to instruct children in a close cousin of creationism, termed "intelligent design." How reasonable such internal contradictions can seem from the inside and how irrational from the outside!

Breakthroughs by Darwin involved imagining himself as a plant. Einstein imagined traveling at the speed of light. Maria Montessori, the great scientist-educator featured in chapter 4, imagined herself as a child. The more alien the alternative viewpoint, the greater the insight.

Tool 6. Broadening perspective. When Nike launched its advertising campaign "Just Do It," its leadership hoped that the campaign would enlarge Nike's brand recognition. Company legend has it that the idea came from the last words of a convicted murderer who said, as he was strapped to the electric chair, "Let's do it." A more mundane (and less captivating) story is that the slogan came out of the mouth of a Nike corporate executive. Whatever the origin, Wieden and Kennedy, Nike's advertising agency, say that they never imagined its expansive impact. "Just Do It" tripled Nike's market share by growing the brand's clientele from athletes to anyone who moves. Millions interpreted "Just Do It" as an appeal that transcended running. It was a call to spiritual liberation.

Take a scientific question, such as, How can we provide more nutritious foods in America's lunchrooms? An obvious answer might be to provide wholesome foods wrapped up as things kids like to eat (think zucchini fries). But what if we broaden the perspective and instead ask, How do we get America to eat better? Then the trickle of associations becomes a raging river that might lead to further questions: What is the role of price, culture, and convenience? Why do low-income families buy less nutritious foods? Why are foods of high nutritional value often more expensive? What effect do agricultural subsidies have on food pricing? Broadening the perspective generates curiosity and novelty.

Broad perspectives were inherent in the big questions asked by geniuses. Darwin's question was: By what means do all living things in nature come to be? Broad perspectives also underscored wide-reaching approaches. To understand the links between diet and heart disease, Ancel Keys, subject of chapter 8, conceptualized the Mediterranean diet when he expanded his research network internationally. Russell Marker, the chemist whose synthesis of progesterone legitimized the oral contraceptive pill, analyzed 400 species and 40,000 kilograms of plant material and found the perfect chemical precursor. Bold thinking brought vast scientific rewards.

Tool 7: Dissecting the problem. Big questions are complex. And science does not blithely accept answers until they have been subjected to an extensive and rigorous process of validation. When confronted by an underground leak, a plumber finds its location by shutting off one pipe segment after another. Similarly, proof of a whole theory often requires certifying the correctness of each of its pieces.

In 1950, with 40 million cars on the road, over 33,000 people died in traffic accidents. Sixty years later, while the number of cars had exploded to 248 million, the number of highway fatalities had fallen below that 1950 mortality statistic. These statistics underscore the triumph of improving highway safety. How did it happen? It took dissecting the root causes of driving fatalities and eliminating them.

Consider the basic physics of a two-car crash. Impact depends on each car's speed and change in velocity. In turn, change in velocity is composed of features that include each vehicle's mass and the distances between centers of gravity. After testing various ways to improve each of these components, automotive engineers successfully employed more durable materials, considered appropriate centers of gravity, and designed safer bumpers. Highway engineers recommended appropriate speed limits. Seat belts and air bags, too, came from dissecting aspects of the problem of motor vehicle deaths.

Successful innovators dissected problems until they had been separated into testable and answerable components. Darwin's approach to answering the question of whether there was intraspecies variability generated sub-questions, such as, Why is sex so important? and, What happens to species separated into disconnected ecological niches? and, Does one species arise from another? Stanley Milgram, a famed social psychologist who is the subject of chapter 7 in this volume, dissected his questions by systematically adjusting parameters and then repeating his experiments. For instance, he tested the strength of conformity in studies requiring subjects to choose between an answer that they knew to be correct versus an answer that was incorrect but conformist by telling subjects that their answers would be used to design safety signals on airplanes.

Tool 8: Reversal. Reversal works either by flipping assumptions or by realizing the import of a serendipitous turn of events. Reversals twist our minds around. A funny and heart-warming song by Brad Paisley tells the tale of an apologetic suitor who tries to gain the forgiveness of his true love by sending her serial gifts of flowers. Rather than begging her directly to re-ignite her love for him, he argues the opposite: "Stop the senseless killing; can't you hear those roses cry? Tell me, how many flowers have to die?"

Serendipity, appreciating a "happy accident," is a particularly potent trigger for innovation. Not everyone grasps the implications of finding the *un*expected—but innovators do. Alexander Fleming, father of antibiotics, is the poster child for serendipity. Upon returning to his laboratory from a vacation in 1928, he noticed mold growing on one of his petri dishes. Unfortunately, it had ruined his experiment by killing the *Staphylococcus* sp. bacteria he was studying. In retrospect, others had experienced the same problem and had simply discarded their failed bacterial plates. But Fleming recognized the mold not as a calamity but an opportunity. He turned the course of his career to focus on how the mold inhibited bacteria. Ultimately, he identified the mold as *Penicillium* sp., and he called its extract penicillin, which became the first antibiotic.

Serendipity also initiated the era of cancer chemotherapeutics. Mustard gas, a World War I and World War II agent of chemical warfare, was known to cause incapacitating burns of the eyes, skin, and respiratory tract. Its effects were so horrible that production and stockpiling were eventually prohibited by international treaty. Dr. Stewart Alexander, while treating victims of a vast mustard gas spraying by the Germans in Bari, Italy, noticed something unforeseen. Victims' white blood cells were suppressed—a fact that most scientists would have simply added to a list of mustard's effects. But Dr. Alexander flipped it. Cancers are the most quickly dividing of all cells. If mustard gas arrested the division of rapidly growing white blood cells, he reasoned, perhaps the agent could be used as a cancer treatment. Indeed, the mustard derivative Mustine, after animal and human testing, became the first chemotherapeutic agent used to combat leukemia.

Serendipity is an accidental reversal. An equally potent creative strategy is to create a purposeful reversal. Darwin lived at a time when the main belief about how life came to be was creationism. God, it was thought, created all species as perfect embodiments of his care and love. Darwin turned this idea on its head. In the theory of natural selection, he posited that the variations that gained dominance by out-competing others in a vicious struggle for survival were initially random. Caring had nothing to do with Mother Nature's arbitrary mechanism for evolving species.

Tool 9: Recombination and rearrangement. "Rearranging the deck chairs on the Titanic" is a flippant aphorism for doing something useless. But reorganizing, combining, or finding unusual uses for previous ideas is far from useless. Humans have a tendency toward what gestalt psychologist Karl Duncker called "functional fixedness." Once we are taught a use for a particular object, we are fixed to that particular usage or function. A classic demonstration is this: Given a candle, a book of matches, and a box of thumbtacks, experimental subjects are told to attach the candle to a wall. Most people try to fix the candle with a thumbtack or to melt it to the wall (neither of which work). The trick is to take the thumbtacks out of the box, put the candle in the box, and attach the box to the wall with a thumbtack. The need to alter the function of the box so that it becomes a candle base stumps most subjects. Innovators, in contrast, seem remarkably free of fixedness.

Edison was the master of combination and rearrangement. One of his signature technological revolutions, the phonograph, entailed little more than taking previous inventions and combining them.

The telegraph repeater was an invention that Edison patented to record, store and later play back telegraphic messages. The phonautograph was an invention by Leon Scott that recorded the vibration of a diaphragm moving to waves of sound. Scott's invention used a sheet of paper coated with lampblack and fixed to a rotating cylinder to record sound's visual pattern. Edison's phonograph joined the two: the recording on a rotating cylinder and the storage and later playback of messages. A stylus attached to a diaphragm recorded auditory vibrations onto the phonograph's rotating cylinder, which was covered with a sheet of tin foil. A second diaphragm played sound back just as it was originally recorded. It was the phonoautograph version of the telegraph repeater—a technological sensation.

Combining disciplines can also create unusual insights. When urban planners, geographic information experts, and nutritionists came together to catalog locations of food outlets, they realized that poor city neighborhoods are often deserts for nutritious foods, a fact that has been identified as a link between poverty and obesity. Nanoparticle engineers interacting with pharmacologists have designed novel systems for drug delivery. Cross-disciplinary interactions have spawned whole new fields: bioengineering, genetic epidemiology, astrophysics, neuropsychopharmacology, and many more.

Tool 10: The power of groups. Scientists, even when they appear to be lone wolves, work within a network of colleagues, mentors, and role models. Thus, although a single mind is generally credited for a given discovery or invention, that person almost always built on the work of others.

The discovery of the structure of DNA, ascribed to James Watson and Francis Crick, was actually group science. The two could never have worked it out had they not seen X-ray crystallography photographs taken by Rosalind Franklin. In a conference that Watson and Crick convened only months before they "broke the code," scientists who were all reaching for the holy grail of DNA's structure convened to share data and insights. Franklin's photographs of DNA's hazy helical outline gave Watson and Crick (and Franklin—she published the crystallography data concurrently with their *Nature* article) a critical clue.

Even Einstein, a singular genius of unitary stature, built his theories squarely on the shoulders of others: giants such as Galileo, Newton, Plank, and Maxwell. Without the experimental knowledge amassed by others, Einstein could not have devised his shocking theories of the workings of nature.

In the twenty-first century, the power of social networks, self-organizing collectives, and open sources have brought communal scholarship and creativity to a pinnacle. Wikipedia, the online encyclopedia, written by thousands of volunteer contributors and editors, has become a source of global information. YouTube has become the arbiter for creative talent. Linux is an open-source operating system fashioned out of something like $1 billion free man-hours of work. As we will see later, it turns out that the Internet, the vehicle for this cooperative fervor, was also the product of group invention.

Tool 11: Frame shifting. Normal thinking is constrained by habitual patterns that linguists call "frames." Frames are a structure of expectations that we use to interpret new information. They allow us to think and speak in a common and highly efficient shorthand consisting of assumed norms. Without frames, scientists would constantly have to check their suppositions before every thought or action. Working within a frame-free scientific world would mean having to start every experiment from first principles. For all practical purposes, it would be paralyzing.

At the same time, frames are intrinsically constraining. In a recent experiment, subjects were asked to devise solutions to rising crime in a community after reading a brief description. When the narrative characterized crime as a contagion, respondents proposed social solutions such as reducing poverty and increasing education. When crime was described metaphorically as a beast, subjects selected punitive legal interventions. This and other experiments show us that our beliefs, attitudes, and actions are guided by the way in which situations are framed.

Consider what it would have been like to be a scientist working before Robert Koch, Louis Pasteur, and others formalized germ theory in the 1860s and 1870s. Microscopy had been available since 1670 when Anton Van Leeuwenhoek visualized cells within plants and animals and discovered bacteria. But what did the presence of such bacteria mean? Today, of course, we would immediately know that the microorganisms within diseased tissues were pathogenic agents. Yet scientists working prior to the development of germ theory had no frame for such an interpretation. Instead, they were steeped in the idea of bacterial spontaneous generation. If bacteria mysteriously arose in fetid meat, wouldn't the same agents simply arise without a source in human organs? Only after Pasteur and Koch established that specific diseases are caused by specific bacteria did scientists and clinicians have a frame for understanding the genesis and spread of infectious diseases. Before that revolutionary innovation, disease seemed to appear out of nowhere and thus could never be prevented. Afterward, Joseph Lister spearheaded antisepsis.

Darwin overturned the frame (in science also called a "paradigm") of creationism and replaced it with evolution. Rutherford shattered the paradigm that atoms are immutable and replaced it with evidence of a world of subatomic particles. Montessori upended the assumption that elders must dispense knowledge to children and instead demonstrated that children can be their own best teachers.

In his classic discussion of the process of science, *The Structure of Scientific Revolutions*, Thomas Kuhn distinguished between "normal science" and "scientific revolutions." What the great majority of scientists engage in, he argued, is a process of refining and elaborating agreed-upon theories. Said another way, Kuhn argued that in normal science, the frame is sacrosanct. Kuhn called revolutionary innovations "paradigm shifts." He imagined them as infrequent, periodic disruptions, representing insights that fundamentally altered the scientific worldview. We would call these frame breaks, but either terminology suggests upending fundamental assumptions about nature, a prospect with unknown, even alarming consequences.

Not everyone agrees with Kuhn's monolithic view of frame shifts. Other scholars, including Stephen Toulmin in his book *Human Understanding*, have argued that normal science, too, is textured with innovation. Advances, according to Toulmin, may occur through the slow erosion of beliefs rather than by the sudden obliteration of convictions. In subsequent chapters, we will see that both processes—the revolutionary innovation (à la Kuhn) that entails frame shifts and the evolutionary innovation (à la Toulmin) that does not require breaking frames—have been powerful forces for societal change. However, the debate opens an interesting question. Is frame-shifting innovation fundamentally different from non-frame-shifting innovation? This is a question we will examine within the following chapters.

In summary, Darwin did, indeed, employ the full range of the tools of innovation, (see Figure 3.1) each of which was beneficial and which together were transformative. Many of the tools in the innovation toolbox are used every day by the average scientist. The use of many, particularly when used masterfully and in combination, can be an engine for genius. How common and consistent were the use of these strategies by other genius scientists and inventors? The stories in the following chapters tell the tale.

	Question	Groups	Analogy	Rearrange	Observation	Deduction / Induction	Change Point of View	Expand	Narrow/ Dissect	Reverse	Break Frames	Autonomy	Openness	Persistence
Darwin	⚸	⚸	⚸	⚸	⚸	⚸	⚸	⚸	⚸	⚸	⚸	⚸	⚸	⚸

Figure 3.1. Darwin: Tools and Characteristics

4

The Miracle Worker

Maria Montessori

Scientific historians believe that there are golden periods when the pace of scientific progress—and with it the pace of societal transformation—is at a fever pitch. Surely one of these was the turn of the twentieth century. In Switzerland, Albert Einstein was only a few years away from publishing his *Annus Mirabilis* papers. Sigmund Freud in Austria was developing a new and revolutionary method called psychoanalysis. Italy's Guglielmo Marconi was about to receive the first radio signals from across the Atlantic and grow a communications empire. Wilhelm Roentgen's discovery of X-rays in Germany had provided a peephole into nuclear physics. And the Americans Thomas Edison (two decades earlier) and Henry Ford (a decade later) had invented the light bulb and would produce the first assembly-line automobile.

Meanwhile, a newly minted doctor in a psychiatric clinic in Rome was puzzling about how to improve the lives of developmentally disabled children. It was a problem that no one else much wanted to contemplate—surely, such children were simply retarded, and nothing could be done to change that. But under the scrutiny of this most unique innovator, observations about mental abnormality would lead to transformational insights about education writ large. And "Montessori" would become a household name.

Maria Montessori was born in Ancona, Italy, in 1870. Her family, although willing after moving to Rome, to allow her to continue into higher education, hoped to see Maria become a teacher, the traditional profession considered suitable for a bright and energetic "modern" woman. But Maria had other ideas. Despite everyone's objections, of professors and family, she opted to take classes at a boys' technical school for engineers. When she decided to go on to become a physician, her aspiration was considered scandalous; indeed, both her father and the professor of clinical medicine at the University of Rome told her it would be impossible. Nevertheless, Maria enrolled at the University to study math, physics, and the natural sciences. When she excelled in everything, the institution finally capitulated. In those days, the pursuit of a medical degree involved not only completing a curriculum, but engaging in scholarship. Maria's thesis, presented in 1896, was of such exemplary quality that the Board of Review could do nothing other than award her a full medical degree. With this, she became Italy's first woman physician. Indeed, not only did the University of Rome award her a degree but it recognized her tenacity and intelligence by offering her the opportunity to stay on as an assistant physician at the Psychiatric Clinic.

At the time, mental health had no subcategorizations: insanity and developmental disability were treated equally (and terribly). Children, like adults, were locked away in bleak facilities where they suffered privation and isolation. Part of Montessori's responsibilities was to travel to each of the asylums around Rome to choose suitable patients for the university clinic. The conditions that confronted Montessori induced in her great sympathy for these poor souls. Among the children, the thing that struck her in particular was their desire for stimulation. They would reach out for things to grasp, even searching the ground for crumbs of food after they were fed, just to have something to manipulate. The young doctor jumped to a daring *deduction*: that the developmental delays associated with retardation might be not only a function of temperament but also of environment.

Montessori began with this *bold question*: Could retardation, in part, be a problem not only of children's inherent mental deficits but also of the way in which they are taught? If so, could education be the means of improving their development? Since sequestering retarded children in sterile institutions was normative, the question probed fundamental assumptions or *frames*. It courageously challenged an uncaring medical system and, indeed, implied a need for sweeping change in societal attitudes.

Montessori's medical training had taught her that the first step toward answering her question was to assimilate and build on the *power of previous research*. She set about reading every major thesis on educational theory over the prior 200 years. Although today we take it as a given that education influences behavior, at the time, that concept had garnered little attention and even less systematic study. Only a few educators had researched the physiological and psychological consequences of educational methods, and these few—including Froebel, Pestalozzi, and Seguin—were practically unknown. But the embryonic work that Montessori uncovered suggested the very possibility she sought. The rehabilitation of the insane through instruction, she learned, was possible.

Montessori decided that she had found her calling. After spending so much effort to get a degree in medicine, she leapt from medical practice into the uncharted territory of educational research. The physician-turned-educator became co-director of the country's first state "Orthophrenic" school. Developmentally disabled children from around Italy were brought to live and learn under a theory and methods that Montessori was then employing and refining. By the end of their instruction, most of the students had attained a remarkable number of developmental milestones—so much so that many could successfully pass state examinations to public education taken by normal children.

What were Montessori's magical methods? How could children, many of them neglected and untaught their entire lives, perform at the level of children with normal intellects and from traditional schools? The answer lies in Montessori's use of innovation tools to develop transformational educational theory and practice.

Montessori's most pervasive and influential tool was *observation*. She spent hours, days, weeks, simply and methodically watching children interact with their environment. Young children, Montessori discovered, when left to their own devices, spontaneously concentrated with great attention on particular objects or activities. A child would repeat an activity over and over, sometimes with agitation, until she seemed to reach competence; this was then followed by a state of pleased relaxation and even by attempts to help other children with the same work. It was as if the child had flipped a switch. Montessori believed that what she was seeing was something previously unimaginable. Children were teaching themselves. Self-learning by children was an observation that countered all historical beliefs about the lowly position of children in society. Learning had always been assumed to be a gift handed down from adult to child.

To further test this observation and its implications, Montessori began to think from a *child's point of view*. If I were a child, Montessori thought, how would I react if every time I tried to manipulate my environment, the means to do so were taken away from me? What would it be like to be sent to school to learn but then to find that I am only allowed to sit still and watch, rather than trying things out for myself? How would it be if I were constantly controlled by those around me, like a little doll, allowed to do nothing on my own because I might act too slowly or incorrectly?

Montessori tells the story of a baby girl about six months old who, when given a rattle, dropped it again and again. The baby was not watching the rattle as she released it, but rather her own tiny hands. On closer scrutiny, Montessori noticed that the baby systematically varied the activity, dropping or not dropping the rattle as she opened a single finger at a time. Other babies burst into tears when they dropped something and it was taken away from them. Had the baby's mother taken away the rattle when it was dropped, she, too would have begun to cry, and her mother would have interpreted this as a groundless tantrum. The baby's reaction would have been judged by adult standards. Montessori realized that the baby girl was performing the task of letting go of the rattle not out of perversity, but from a desire to understand the capabilities of her own hands.

In considering the world through the eyes of a child, Montessori came to appreciate that actions are forced on children. For example, a child was obliged to live in a fantasy world because his environment was constricted to stories and toys. When a child desired to gain autonomy by learning to engage in real-life tasks, he was thwarted. Cleaning and cooking were considered inappropriate for a child. Even if an adult wanted to teach a child such skills, the environment, in which everything was built on an uncomfortable and awkward scale from a child's perspective, would make it difficult, if not impossible. The removal of everyday activities, Montessori came to believe, was not a relief to the child but a frustration.

Analogy also gave Montessori new insights. First she looked at how babies are treated in nature. She noticed that animal mothers, after giving birth, hide their offspring away for a period of time. Protection from light and from other animals helped to ensure that the transition from the womb to active life was as gentle as possible. In contrast, among humans, the post-partum mother was provided with respite and rest, but the child was placed under bright lights and exposed to a hoard of strangers. In Montessori's view, this illustrated a lack of consideration for the needs of the child.

Montessori came to believe that not only were children's needs over-looked but, even worse, they were oppressed. The second *analogy* that informed Montessori's thinking was that of servitude. "Never were the rights of man so disregarded as in the case of the child," she said. Only a few decades before, the American Civil War gained freedom for African American slaves. One of the main justifications for slavery was that slaves were not sufficiently mentally developed to survive on their own. They were, many Southerners claimed, "childlike." Montessori suggested that children, too, had been subjugated and thus needed to regain their independence and dignity.

Montessori's thinking had now progressed through several, ever enlarging stages: (1) there might be something about the environment that retarded child development; (2) education could impact advancement among normal children; (3) self-learning among children suggested an approach to instruction that was more child-centric; (4) morality evoked an educational system grounded in the child's right to respect and dignity. These conceptualizations were increasingly significant.

Montessori was now not just proposing small fixes. Her call for a child-centric curriculum rooted in respect was nothing less than earth-shattering. No longer was the child dependent and subservient—just the *opposite*. Montessori argued that children were not helpless but instead were developing; their natural impulses should not be suppressed but instead should be tapped to further their own progress and happiness.

The Montessori Method, then, arises from a *frame shift* that counters a long-held philosophy about a child's place as being "seen and not heard." In the Montessori Method, children were given direction over their own self-maturation. Children chose their own activities. They worked at their own pace. Montessori had taken control away from adults and handed it to those who had never previously had it.

Montessori's frame shift brought her full circle to an answer to her original question, Could retardation, in part, be a problem not only of children's inherent mental deficits but also of the way in which they were taught? What if everything from the outbursts so characteristic of children to the maladaptive development of mentally disabled individuals were a function of environment? Now Montessori used yet another *analogy*: psychoanalysis. Psychiatrists searched back within a patient's prior experience for the cause of behaviors. Montessori believed that children's deviance came from a cause "buried in the social subconscious of mankind." If children were not respected and treated with dignity, she contended, their only recourse was to act out. Just as every action caused a reaction, the bending by an implacable adult of a child's constructive impulses would cause pathology. After applying her child-centric methods, Montessori reported that regressing behaviors considered so much a part of childhood completely disappeared.

With such dramatic results from the State Orthophrenic School, Montessori began to wonder if she could apply her methods more *broadly*. Perhaps, she thought, the ultimate questions should be, Could the benefits accruing to mentally retarded children exposed to her method apply to normal children? Indeed, could education be the means, in general, to cultivating successful child development? With these *ambitious queries* in mind, she decided to return to the University and take up studies in anthropology and psychology in order to enlarge and enrich her approach. The translation was not easy. Invention of a comprehensive child-centric educational method for normal children took her a further half a dozen years.

San Lorenzo was a quarter of Rome that was one of the poorest in the city. To relieve overcrowding, two nondescript apartment complexes had been built; there, while parents were working, their preschool-age children ran wild, vandalizing apartments and staircases. Someone had to control these degenerates, so the parents, despite their limited resources, finally acquiesced to funding a teacher. Their choice was Montessori.

It was the chance that Montessori had been looking for: an opportunity to demonstrate that any child, if only allowed to self-actualize, could be rehabilitated. When the classroom was furnished with child-sized tables and chairs and the youngsters were allowed the freedom to explore a variety of objects at their own discretion, Montessori's theory was confirmed. She had only to let "the environment...teach the child" and the children of the Casa dei Bambini ("House of Children" in Italian, as Montessori named her school) became self-disciplined, orderly, and obedient. It was a development so unexpected that some observers claimed that the children had been hypnotized.

The full-blown Montessori Method defines the child's "job" as development. Within that job, the child is given unprecedented flexibility. However, Montessori took great care in *dissecting* which characteristics of the environment would best direct the child's learning. An extensive array of wooden materials that she developed and that practitioners of the Montessori Method call "the apparatus" enabled the child to develop specific skills. These were organized by subject and complexity. Bounds on the availability of the apparatus shaped the direction and pace of learning. For instance, a child may play with a counting tool, but that tool was not offered until there had been an explanatory lesson, and the lesson was not taught until the child showed the appropriate level of maturation.

Montessori described the teacher as an observer and guide. The authority figure neither directs nor judges but instead enables. Indeed, peersplay as much or more of a role in instruction as the teacher. Montessori classrooms typically contain mixed age groups as broad as ages 2–6. Children provide both support and challenge to each other. Pairings form naturally as less experienced children learn and more experienced learn to teach.

In traditional Montessori environments today, there are no grades or other external incentives, as these are considered demotivating. Children's desire to work comes from a curiosity to manipulate materials that are designed to be attractive and alluring. The method cultivates a sense of motivation from within.

Montessori wrote several books describing her discoveries, including *The Montessori Method* (translated into English, 1912) and *Pedagogic Anthropology* (translated into English, 1913). She postulated that there were three phases to learning in small children: preparation, interaction with an object, and inner psychological activity that leads to clarity in relation to the activity. If these phases were disrupted, she taught, the child became upset and acted out. Thus, the child did best when allowed independence within environmental constraints. From the ages of one to three years, children wanted to put things away and take them out themselves; they preferred work to play; and they viewed rewards and punishments as nothing more than distractions. At age four or five, children even began spontaneously to write.

Articles on the Casa dei Bambini began appearing all over the world. Visitors arrived to see the "miracle children" with their own eyes, and many brought Montessori's methods back to their countries. In America (introduced by Einstein), Australia, England, and in every kindergarten in New South Wales, Montessori's methods had amazing effects. By 1913, Maria Montessori's brilliance had been recognized by Freud and Alexander Graham Bell, as well as Einstein. In 1918, she displayed at the San Francisco World Exhibition a Montessori classroom that was open to the public for four months, winning the only two gold medals awarded there. Montessori's work inspired one of the most influential developmental psychologists of all time, Jean-Paul Piaget (who directed a Montessori type school in Geneva and was head of the Swiss Montessori society). She was nominated six times for the Nobel Peace Prize.

Today, Montessori's methods are used all over the world, on every continent except Antarctica. There are an estimated 20,000 Montessori schools worldwide. When strictly implemented, studies have shown that Montessori preschool students (as compared to ones from traditional pre-schools) were superior on their performance. on standardized tests of reading and math, as well as advanced social skills. Older Montessori students reported a greater sense of motivation and community than students from other schools. In a randomized comparison, Montessori pupils also wrote noticeably more creative essays.

Montessori's ideas are forever being rediscovered. The recently popular Kahn Academy expands Montessori's concept of self-directed learning into a web-based, virtual classroom. Kahn Academy has been able to demonstrate many of the same benefits as Montessori schools, for instance that children considered "slow" often catch up to and even exceed their peers when allowed to pace themselves.

MONTESSORI ANNOTATED: THE USE OF TOOLS OF INNOVATION

Montessori was neither a hypnotist nor a prodigy. She was a scientific genius who displayed an extensive capacity and impressive suppleness for using innovation tools. She called her *observations* of young children, a hallmark of her novel educational paradigm, being "obedient to events." Observations led her to intuit that children yearned for stimulation and had enormous capacity to teach themselves. Beyond her own observations, she leveraged those of predecessors and contemporaries, using the *power of groups* to teach herself skills in anthropology and psychology and to further validate her hypotheses.

Observation interacted with *deduction* as Montessori "guessed" that somehow environment vis-à-vis education was a crucial element in child development. This deduction led her to ask the *right question,* and it was a bold one: Could retardation, in part, be a problem not only of children's inherent mental deficits but also of the way in which they are taught? If so, could education be the means of improving child development?

One of Montessori's most poignant and powerful approaches was to *change her point of view.* The mind of the child became her own. Rather than envisioning discipline from an adult perspective as an essential implement in shaping the malleable adult-to-be, she considered it from the child's perspective—that beatings and beratings violated respect and dishonored dignity. From the child's point of view, violence begat violence—a child so debased would, understandably, respond with disobedience.

A master of mental flexibility, Montessori was able to both *broaden* and *dissect* elements of her program. When she moved from the concept of the State Orthophrenic School to that of early childhood education, she was broadening her perspective. Her argument was that the benefits accruing to mentally disabled children could potentially be attained by normal children. Yet she was also capable of attention to minute detail. In particular, she personally designed every element of her child-centric instructional environment.

Analogies informed Montessori's thinking, most profoundly the *analogy* to human oppression. This insight became one of the main justifications for her belief that, like slaves who had been considered "childlike," children were effectively their parents' chattel. What children needed, Montessori came to believe, was to be afforded independence.

All of these tools allowed Montessori to *reverse* and shatter *frames*. Ultimately, her disruptive transformation was to overturn the self evident notion that only adults can teach children. In Montessori schools, children benefit from environments in which they can teach themselves and others. Montessori schools not only provide strong academic environments and rich group interchanges, but they are also models for the fostering of creativity. Their support of peer-interaction and self-direction are now considered archetypes of creative ecosystems. Not only was Montessori herself innovative, but in her schools, Montessori left a legacy for incubating the next generation of creators.

	Question	Groups	Analogy	Rearrange	Observation	Deduction / Induction	Change Point of View	Expand	Narrow/ Dissect	Reverse	Break Frames	Autonomy	Openness	Persistence
Montessori	❧	❧	❧		❧	❧	❧	❧	❧	❧	❧	❧	❧	❧

Figure 4.1. Montessori: Tools and Characteristics

5

Bending Time

Albert Einstein

W ith the ability to map, track, and find directions, global positioning systems (GPS) are as common and useful in modern society as the microwave. But have you ever wondered how GPS works? It operates through ultra-accurate detection of the time it takes for signals from overhead satellites to triangulate to our cars. And for that remarkably precise ability to measure time over a distance, whom do we have to thank? Probably none of us would ever guess. It is Albert Einstein.

In the year 1905, Albert Einstein published not one but four papers that so overturned the central principles of physics that these explanations of how the world works and the modern technology that they spawned have altered our day-to-day life and have facilitated our aspiration to reach out into the universe. The accolades heaped on Einstein clarify the enormity of his influence on science and society. He has been called the father of modern physics. His name memorializes a park, a monument, several international awards, and a chemical element. Time magazine, in its final issue in the twentieth century (1999) named Einstein the "Person of the Century" over international heroes such as Mahatma Gandhi and Franklin D. Roosevelt. Indeed, metaphorically, the name "Einstein" has become so synonymous with genius that we call a person we deem remarkable "an Einstein."

Were the thought processes of this man of superhuman intellect so distinct and unusual that we can only marvel at them from a respectful distance? Or was Einstein simply another unusually successful purveyor of "normal" innovative thinking?

In Einstein's most prolific publication year, often called his *Annus Mirabilis,* or miracle year, he produced breakthroughs that spawned three distinct new areas of physics. He theorized the photoelectric effect that light is both a particle (technically, a quantum) and a wave and thus spurred the new field of quantum mechanics. Quantum mechanics, in turn, was like the children's song, "The hip bone's connected to the thigh bone and the thigh bone's connected to the knee bone...." It spawned semiconductors; semiconductors are the building blocks of transistors; transistors make up computers; computers created the Internet; and resultant applications, from Google to Facebook, have reshaped society.

Another of Einstein's papers in his *Annus Mirabilis* laid out a statistical argument for the existence of molecules (or atoms). The paper converted the concept of the atom, which physicists and chemists had previously considered to be theoretical or virtual, to something real, with an actual size. That paper both created the field of statistical physics and provided a tangible experimental method for going out and counting atoms. Perhaps of more relevance to the common person, Einstein's insights (conducted at a time when the concept of atoms was beginning to lose favor among physicists) catapulted science into the atomic age. With that new age came space travel, nuclear power, and nuclear weapons.

Einstein's third paper posited the equivalence between matter and energy in the equation for which he is most famous: $E = mc^2$. Finally, in a fourth paper, he worked out the special theory of relativity (which provides a theoretical basis for $E = mc^2$). This perhaps most mind-boggling breakthrough is not the one for which he received the 1921 Nobel Prize—the Prize focused on the discovery of the photoelectric effect. Nevertheless, special relativity was truly a seismic shift in physics, positing that distance and time shrink at the limit of the speed of light; suggesting a new dimension of space-time; and predicting that space is curved, among other almost unimaginable constructs. Such notions have brought us things both useful (GPS) and bewildering (black holes).

Despite the enormity of his contributions, Einstein's own autobiographical insights into his way of thinking provide evidence that his approach was not enigmatic, but by now remarkably familiar. Einstein asked the boldest and *most presumptuous of questions*, but he answered them using tools of innovation.

Einstein cared not that his questions were thought to be answered or unanswerable. He cared only that they were big and fundamental to understanding the nature of the universe. What is the essence of electromagnetism and thus light? Do atoms exist, and how do they behave? How can we remain loyal to Newton, who asserted that motion is relative, when we know that the speed of light in a vacuum is always constant?

Beyond this ability to ask brash questions, Einstein had a gift for answering them by taking a messy array of discordant evidence and *dissecting* its common essence. That is, he could *rearrange and combine* the best of previous constructs into a newly harmonized alternative. Although it may seem blasphemous to say so, many of the fundamental ideas and all of the experimental data that informed these rearrangements did not originate with Einstein. His genius was in blending existing evidence—but with a twist. Einstein's resolution of questions involved adding some new element. It could be an insight from another field. Often, it was a frame break in which Einstein supplanted the assumptions inherent in the question. Either way, reorganization plus Einstein's novel concept allowed the available ideas and evidence to coexist.

Physics at the beginning of the twentieth century was in a state of confusion. Accepted wisdom since the time of Newton and Galileo had collided with newer theory and experimentation about the behavior of atoms. Put another way, Newton's laws of classical mechanics appeared to conflict with the more modern laws of thermodynamics and electromagnetism, creating a set of paradoxes.

Thermodynamics had grown up during the nineteenth century as a means to describe and therefore maximize the energy flows in machines. Around that time, a growing number of industrial processes had ignited the hope for creating a perpetual motion machine, an aspiration that kindled the field of thermodynamics but was ultimately dashed by its emerging laws. In particular, the second law of thermodynamics stated that it is impossible to infinitely create work from heat without the input of new energy. This is because where there is energy, there is entropy. Atoms naturally lose energy due to entropy, always shifting from a hotter to a cooler state. A melting ice cube does not refreeze without the input of energy (such as from a freezer). The direction goes only one way. On the other hand, classical mechanics says that since heat is just kinetic energy affecting atoms, then atom A bouncing against atom B or atom B bouncing against atom A is all the same—interactions are reversible. So, thermodynamics clearly demands freezers to make ice cubes. Newtonian mechanics, in contrast, predicts that the atoms within ice cubes should be perfectly capable of freezing, just as they are capable of thawing, at room temperature.

Physics had reached a crossroads. Most experts refused to toss out the very appealing principles of thermodynamics. Could classical mechanics somehow be wrong? Or were atoms not real but a theoretical concept?

Solving the paradox was a question of fierce interest. The time and place were right to ask the question, Do atoms really exist and can that explain the tension between thermodynamics and classical mechanics? In fact, unbeknownst to Einstein, other physicists, Ludwig Boltzman and J. Willard Gibbs, had already hit upon a solution—that the second law of thermodynamics could be understood by the fact that molecules bounce around. Einstein unknowingly replicated (he had a limited library) their work in a series of papers culminating with the one in 1905. But he also extended their efforts because in the 1905 paper he took on the audacious task of newly wrapping the idea in statistics.

The proof that atoms exist drew on an *analogy* from biology. Brownian motion is the irregular movement of small organisms. It was first described by the English botanist Robert Brown to describe the movement of tiny particles floating atop a pond. Brown had described their incessant and chaotic movement as "swarming." Einstein posited that atoms, too, exhibit swarming, and his statistical model of their random interactions allowed him to explain the second law of thermodynamics without violating classical mechanics. Thrown into the bargain, Einstein calculated the size of atoms and proposed that if microscopists had powerful enough tools, atoms could simply be visualized.

Einstein, then, legitimized atoms not by discovering new physical laws or theorems. Neither did he seek to judge between rival camps. What he did, instead, was to combine the existing frames with a new piece of information (movement of atoms) and a new approach (statistical physics) that married the two existing constructs. It was a dazzling example of three distinct innovation tools: posing an audacious question, analogy, and rearrangement.

Of all Einstein's 1905 papers, one that was particularly transformational was the special theory of relativity. The two postulates that made up Einstein's special theory of relativity were: (1) the motion of objects exists relative to the frame of reference of the observer; and (2) independent of the frame of reference, the speed of light in a vacuum is constant. But surely these postulates are in conflict. How can motion be, at the same time, both relative and constant? Once again, Einstein brought into the discussion something previously unheard of, which allowed for resolution. In this case, that "unheard of" element was so *frame shifting* that it seems to be an almost unimaginable challenges to our fundamental assumptions; it was the clue needed to align the relativity postulate and the constancy of the speed of light.

The relativity postulate means that (using Einstein's own explanation in his book entitled *Relativity: The Special and General Theory*) if a stone falls to the ground, its trajectory does not exist as some fixed, true path. Indeed, different observers may see the trajectory differently. Said another way, the trajectory is relative to the reference point of the observer. Einstein takes as his example a passenger on a moving train dropping a stone onto the tracks. The passenger sees the stone as falling straight down. However, a pedestrian standing next to the tracks will see the stone's line of descent as a parabola. Who is right? They both are. Motion is relative to the point of view of an observer traveling in any inertial (non-accelerated) frame. This postulate was far from new—it was a standard feature of classical mechanics, proposed by Newton and Galileo and providing the basis for the belief that the earth revolves around the sun.

The second postulate, that the speed of light is constant, seems straightforward—most schoolchildren learn that this value is 300 million meters/second. But if you think about the meaning of a constant speed of light, the implications are bizarre. As per an example taken from James Kakalios's book *The Amazing Story of Quantum Mechanics,* imagine driving next to a truck that is going a bit faster than the car you are driving and so creeping up on you. You put your foot on the brake, but instead of the truck speeding past you, it continues to creep up. You accelerate and still the truck creeps up. This is constant motion independent of your referent frame of motion. But again, this was not a new idea devised by Einstein. The idea of the constancy of light was first thoroughly proposed by Ole Romer, a Danish astronomer, in 1676. Based on his observations of Jupiter and its moon, he noted that eclipses of these two were seen differently when that moon was farthest from earth from when it was closest to the earth, as a result of the constant time needed for the light from the eclipse to travel to the earth. The constant speed of light was subsequently established theoretically by James Maxwell, who, around 1862, had proposed that light is a form of electromagnetism.

Physics scrambled throughout the end of the nineteenth century to find a simultaneous explanation for relativity (classical mechanics) and the constancy of light (electromagnetism). But all that arose were peculiarities. Rather than trying yet another fix, Einstein went back to first principles—in fact, he backed up to assumptions that came even before first principles.

The very essence of how we measure motion is by means of time. Einstein *reversed* the notion that time is constant and replaced it with its opposite: the concept that (like the trajectory of a stone thrown from a train) time is relative. He asked us to reconsider something that we take as a given, that speed is defined as a distance traveled over a particular time. Speed changes, but time does not—when your car goes 60 miles per hour, your car is moving, but the time it takes, although measurable, does not change with the speed of the car. Einstein's theoretical breakthrough was to point out that the constancy of time is not established by observation—it is only an assumption.

Say (as Einstein explains) lightning strikes in two places along a train line (point A and point B). You are standing in the middle of the two strikes (point M), and with the clever use of mirrors you can see both A and B at the same time. In order to prove that both strikes occurred simultaneously, you propose to simply see in your mirror both bolts occurring together. But Einstein notes that, "Your [supposition] would be right if only you knew that … the lightning travels along the length A -> M with the same velocity as along the length B -> M. But an examination of this supposition would only be possible if we already had at our disposal the means of measuring time." In other words, Einstein was unwilling to assume that time is the same for each vector; he demanded that, in both cases, time be measured.

Ultimately (through a mathematical proof too complicated to reproduce here) Einstein demonstrated that, indeed, time is *not* constant. Like motion, it is relative to the reference point of the observer. Similarly, Einstein demonstrated that distance is relative to a reference. Thus the length of the train as measured from another moving train may be different from the length of the train as measured by a standing pedestrian. Einstein's initial argument was mathematical, using equations called Lorenz transformations. Subsequently, Einstein's special theory of relativity was demonstrated empirically by others through experiments and observations. Through both *deductive and inductive* reasoning, neither time nor distance, as they approach the speed of light, turn out to be invariant.

Einstein had once again broken existing frames by questioning their underlying assumptions. If, he reasoned, prevailing beliefs were incorrect and time and distance were relative, then the theories of relativity of motion and of a constant speed of light could be harmonized. There was no need to throw out preexisting observations or theories if one questioned and clarified more basic assumptions. The consequences of Einstein's frame shift, however, were mind-boggling. In our ordinary world, things move at speeds far slower than the speed of light, so we are unaware of the relativity of time and distance, but as objects gain closer-to-light-speed velocities, time and distance condense. Thus, clocks run slower and rulers get shorter. Einstein accepted these peculiarities and was undaunted.

Intellect surely drove Einstein to pursue these fearlessly imaginative ideas, but they were also propelled by his personality. Born in Germany to non-religious Jewish parents and the son of an engineer, Einstein, by his own estimation, was a curious child. As he records in autobiographical notes written as "something like my own obituary" at the age of 67, " . . . This 'wondering' seems to occur when an experience comes into conflict with a world of concepts which is already sufficiently fixed in us. . . . A wonder of such nature I experienced as a child of 4 or 5 years, when my father showed me a compass. That this needle behaved in such a determined way did not at all fit into the nature of events, which could find a place in the unconscious world of concepts. . . . Something deeply hidden had to be behind things." It is a passage that presages Einstein's tendency to probe assumptions. Curious as he was, much of Einstein's education took place outside the classroom. Traditional education, he believed, constrained inquisitiveness. "It is," he writes, "in fact, nothing short of a miracle that the modern methods of instruction have not entirely strangled the holy curiosity of inquiry, for this delicate little plant, aside from stimulation, stands mainly in need of freedom." As a child, Einstein built mechanical devices and models; by the age of 12, he was reading texts on his own in mathematics and the philosophy of science.

Einstein was also tenacious. He noted, "It's not that I'm so smart, it's just that I stay with problems longer." Indeed, his ability to shut himself off and think through problems for days and weeks at a time became legendary.

To say that Einstein was "strong willed" would not begin to characterize his intellectual autonomy. By the time he graduated from Zurich Polytechnic with a teaching degree, he had irritated so many of his professors that he was unable to find a teaching job. Einstein's belief in his scientific prowess was readily interpreted as obstinate. The constraints of scientific orthodoxy were something he would not abide. Fortunately, through the father of a friend, Einstein found a placement at the Swiss

Patent office. This turned out to be a stroke of luck, as it allowed him a front row seat at the premier of new technology (the basis for patent applications), ample free time, and access to a remarkably receptive and bright group of colleagues with whom he could share his ideas.

Einstein's irreverent approach to problem-solving involved the use of visual images. In a classic example of *changing one's point of view*, he regularly engaged in what have been called "thought experiments." These almost dream-like imaginings allowed Einstein to *break down* a complex problem into readily understood elements. Geometry, a discipline involving pictures and objects, was a particular early attraction for Einstein and may have propelled his visual method. The "lucidity and certainty [of geometry] made a great impression upon me," he notes. A thought experiment that contributed to the special theory of relatively, for example, he explained as follows. Imagine the train we discussed earlier. This time, a man is walking inside and in the same direction as the moving train. A pedestrian is watching the train and trying to figure out how far the man has walked. The pedestrian wants to know the distance the walking man travels in one second if the man and the train are each going at a certain speed per second. Distance = speed x time (e.g., we travel 60 miles by driving 60 miles per hour for one hour). According to classic Newtonian physics, the pedestrian observes the distance walked in one second as the man's walking speed (v) plus the train's traveling speed (w). Distance (D) = walking speed (v) + train speed (w) in one second.

Now Einstein asks us to visualize a ray of light moving along the train line and the train also moving along the line, although obviously at a much slower velocity. This is like the man and the train both traveling along, but here the speed of light (c) replaces the speed of the walking man. From the perspective of the pedestrian, now, $D = w + c$. Or, solving the equation for the speed of light, $c = D - w$. But this is impossible. The equation says that the speed of light is traveling a shorter distance than it should be in one second—its speed is less than c. Yet we know that the speed of light is always a constant (c). The laws of classic mechanics wherein motion (speed) is measured from the perspective of each person's relative position just collided with the constancy of the speed of light.

Einstein's thought experiment allowed him (and us) to clearly visualize the paradox.

Einstein's envisioning did not happen easily or quickly. "I think and think for months and years, ninety-nine times, the conclusion is false," he said. "The hundredth time I am right." In other words, the problems that Einstein solved in his *Annus Mirabilis* each represented years of work. Special relativity was proposed after a decade of concerted mental effort. Einstein's reflection also tells us that he dissected his questions just as did the great experimentalists. Various aspects of each problem were turned over and over in his mind until each was solved and then added back to the whole.

Of course, Einstein was no empiricist. He did not solve problems by generating data from which generalizations could be induced. Indeed, most consider him to be a deductionist, using pure logic and imagination to move from axioms to a solution. However, deduction alone scarcely describes Einstein's thinking. More correctly, the renowned scientist moved from axioms to theory but also from the *observations* of others to theory. Empirical inputs informed Einstein's thinking, as did pure logic.

Radical thinking always has its detractors, and the same was true for some of Einstein's theories. Philipp Lenard, whose experiments triggered Einstein's second 1905 paper, in which he devised the wave/particle duality of light to explain the photoelectric effect, became one of his most intense critics. So much of Lenard's reputation was devoted to denouncing Einstein and his photoelectric theory that Lenard ruined his own career. His legacy became not that of the great experimental physicist that he was but that of a viscous anti-Semite (he later became chief of physics under Hitler). Others had less personal animosity but hardly less skepticism. Robert Millikan, who was awarded the Nobel Prize for his cutting-edge observations, spent a decade trying to disprove Einstein's photoelectric theory, only to finally admit that the only explanation for his own observations was that light was both a wave and a particle, as Einstein had theorized.

Einstein made the most extraordinary ideas plausible. As Thomas Kuhn accurately points out in his book *The Structure of Scientific Revolutions*,

"Continued use makes even the strangest conception plausible, and once plausible, the new conception …becomes a basic tool for explaining and exploring nature." Indeed, Einstein's groundbreaking theories have gained acceptance in explaining the essence of nature, from its smallest components (atoms and their components) to its largest aspect (the universe). Modernity has been shaped by Albert Einstein.

EINSTEIN ANNOTATED: THE USE OF TOOLS OF INNOVATION

Was Einstein's approach to his mind-bending body of work superhuman? Albeit applied by a genius, there is good evidence that it was not. Like Darwin and Montessori, Einstein was simply more brilliant than almost anyone else in his application of the tools of innovation.

Einstein asked and answered some of the most *expansive questions* in the universe: What is the essence of light? Do atoms exist? How do we reconcile classical mechanics with thermodynamics? Reflected in all of these questions was not an overcoming of barriers—it was an utter lack of awareness that there were any barriers. Einstein's imagination knew no bounds. He was not so much a purposeful breaker of *frames* as he was so impervious to their presence that his creation of new terrain was as a tornado sweeping up houses.

Rearrangement and recombination were central elements in Einstein's genius. For example, in reconciling thermodynamics with classical mechanics, he added a new element: the swarming of atoms. Similarly, in reconciling the conflicting, preexisting notions that motion exists relative to an observer's frame of reference but that independent of the frame of reference, the speed of light in a vacuum is constant, Einstein simply abandoned the frame of reference. The paradox resolved itself when Einstein postulated that neither time nor distance is fixed.

Einstein also drew on the *work of others* and thus was influenced by his predecessors and his contemporaries in science. Brownian motion, for instance, was initially described by the English botanist Robert Brown to describe the movement of pond scum. This observation became the central thesis for Einstein's "proof" of the physical existence of atoms.

Moreover, Brownian motion was an *analogy*. Both the particles that Brown described atop the pond and the movement of atoms, Einstein posited, involved a similar kind of incessant and chaotic movement.

One of the most legendary elements of Einstein's thinking was his use of mental models. The famous "ray of light moving along with a train" is known to any student of physics, and it is a classic example of *changing point of view*. Einstein was able to imagine himself walking inside trains, traveling along with light beams, and all other manner of experiences in order to deduce solutions to problems. But these mind experiments were not concocted out of fantasy; they were based on known phenomena, that is, empiric observations, admixed with *deductive* leaps of insight. Thus, Einstein used both changing point of view and induction/deduction to great advantage.

Finally, Einstein's frame breaking sometimes involved *reversals,* such as replacing the age-old assumption that time and distance are constant with his supposition that time and distance are relative. These brilliant insights, in turn, stemmed from the realization that the constancy of time and space are not established by observation—they are only assumptions.

So there we have it—one of the greatest geniuses of the twentith century had a way of thinking that can be revealed. Surely, though, to say that any of us could thus be another Einstein is unreasonably simplistic. Einstein's ability to use the innovation toolbox, to pose just the right question, to sort through assumptions and identify the ones that could be recombined or reversed to transformational effect, truly defined his genius. Moreover, his personality characteristics—curiosity, persistence and determination, and autonomy—were far from average. Yet, the pattern of his thinking can be deconstructed. Einstein's brilliance was wondrous but not mystical.

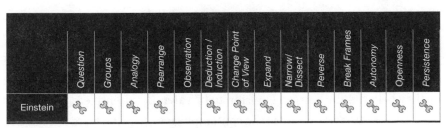

Figure 5.1. Einstein: Tools and Characteristics

6

Pick the Innovator

Did Darwin, Montessori, and Einstein have similar behavioral traits? If we spent the day with a group of scientists, knowing that one of them was considered a genius, would that person be identifiable? Most creativity experts believe so. Creativity researcher G. J. Feist, in summarizing a 1998 meta-analysis of studies on creative personalities, stated, "Empirical research over the last 45 years makes a rather convincing case that creative people behave consistently over time and situation and in ways that distinguish them from others. It is safe to say that in general a 'creative personality' does exist and personality dispositions do regularly and predictably relate to creative achievement." Let us pause here to consider the evidence suggesting that a "creative personality" facilitated genius scientists' mastery of a common mental map.

Some of the central dispositional features of brilliant innovators include: notable curiosity, self-conviction, and tenacity. And these could not be better illustrated than by a pioneer in public health before there was public health: Ignaz Semmelweis. When Semmelweis had just graduated from obstetrical residency and came to work at the Vienna General Hospital in 1846, puerperal fever, now known to be caused by a bacteria named *Staphylococcus aureus*, made hospital-based deliveries more hazardous than contemporary brain surgery. Patients begged to be admitted to the hospital ward called the Second Division, staffed by nurse midwives, over the other ward (First Division), staffed by residents at the Vienna General, as they believed the Second Division to be safer. But their pleas fell on deaf ears. In part, this was because the contemporary scientific frame precluded the notion that diseases could spread from person to person. Semmelweis was the only one who listened. He knew what he didn't know—and what he didn't know was how women acquired puerperal fever. After many months of collecting data, his first breakthrough was that the patients were correct. Deaths were far higher in the division staffed by residents (12 percent) than the one where midwives performed deliveries (4 percent).

Semmelweis burned to learn the cause. He talked to everyone, peered into everything, turned over every possibility. Even while colleagues began to keep their distance from his fanaticism to solve the puzzle, Semmelweis redoubled his campaign. But all that he could establish was that the staffing pattern in the two Divisions differed, and he simply could not make sense of that clue.

Shortly thereafter, serendipity intervened, albeit tragically. Semmelweis's friend Jacob Kolletschka was accidentally poked with a scalpel during a puerperal fever autopsy. Kolletschka became febrile and died, showing symptoms and later demonstrating pathology on autopsy that mirrored those of the dying mothers. Semmelweis's insight was immediate. "Cadaverous particles" were sticking to the hands of residents—death was accompanying doctors' best intentions to understand disease.

Semmelweis went on a hand-washing rampage. To enforce adherence, he installed concentrated solutions of chlorine water in all delivery rooms and strictly oversaw every resident's use. The maternal mortality rate in the First Division plummeted from 12 percent to 1.3 percent.

Unfortunately, as colleagues became more hesitant to wash, complaining that the chlorine chaffed and reddened their hands, Semmelweis became more rigid and goading. At the end of his first hospital term, Semmelweis was not reappointed. He moved to Pest (modern Budapest), where he worked as an unpaid obstetrician at the small St. Rochus hospital and repeated the performance of virtually eliminating puerperal fever. Again his zealotry led to his ejection. Spirit broken, mind broken, he was interned in an insane asylum, where he died prematurely.

Within two decades, Louis Pasteur and Robert Koch would codify germ theory, and Joseph Lister would introduce operating room antisepsis. Had Semmelweis been of different character, would he have intuited one of the most life-saving discoveries in modern medicine? Would he have engendered more followers and had more impact? On the other hand, would he have made such a radical breakthrough?

Creativity scientist Howard Gardner likened creative thinkers to children. In his view, both exhibit "selfishness, self-centeredness, intolerance, silliness, stubbornness..." but, more positively, "the ability to ignore convention, to follow a lead where it goes, to ask questions that adults usually have stopped asking, to go directly to the essence of an issue."

Semmelweis's story suggests that Gardner is right. The same behaviors that fired Semmelweis's genius also lay beneath his unpleasantness. Nonetheless, we learn little about how to emulate eminent scientists by concluding that being innovative is like being a child. How can we more systematically characterize innovative behaviors?

Let us conceptualize the traits distinguishing scientific virtuosi as falling in three general dimensions: autonomy, openness, and persistence. Autonomy is a characteristic that allows for independent thinking and unwillingness to conform to traditional ideals. Noted for their lack of concern for social norms, innovators are "strong willed" and are often introverts. Such characteristics can underlie useful intellectual self-dependence. But the other side of the coin is that being a loner and lacking a willingness to conform can make someone appear to be oppositional or antisocial.

Autonomy is almost synonymous with self-efficacy (self-confidence). Nothing seems to stop innovators from bringing the creative process to fruition. Einstein was a man and Montessori was a woman whose beliefs in their own abilities knew no bounds. Self-efficacy bestows upon creative thinkers the determination to carry on through years of struggle, tedium, and the negativity of skeptics. Self-confidence, too, can have an underbelly—it falls within a spectrum that can include arrogance, narcissism, and antagonism.

Curiosity and openness to experience, the second dimension of the innovative personality, is not only common but may be essential for creativity. All of the creators in this book were ravenously curious. As contrasted to individuals who are more comfortable with maintaining the status quo, innovators are intellectually restless—willing to take risks in order to quench their desire to know more. The inquisitiveness of innovators is often expansive. Einstein has been described as both a scientist and a humanist, with major interests in philosophy, politics, and literature—interests that may have spurred him to integrate across domains.

"Creativity," according to Dowd (1989), "demands that we constantly reevaluate our existing cognitive categories and remain willing to modify or even suspend them on occasion." Curiosity goes hand in hand with openness. But openness further suggests a lack of inhibition, a dearth of being limited by expectations or frames. Innovators are more observant of things that might otherwise go unnoticed. They are more willing to see things in new ways. They are more primed to find important problems and to take the risks inherent in tackling them. New facts and experiences are sought; information is viewed or combined in new ways; offbeat experiments are tried. Arguably the ability to be open to thinking in new ways is a *sine qua non* of creative thinking. At the same time (as we will see), there can be a thin line between pushing the edge of science and pushing beyond accepted ethics.

Perseverance is the final feature most consistently noted among innovators. Adelson interviewed the 2002 Franklin Institute laureates and found that their determination and dedication to problem-solving proved to be a trait most concordant with all of their successful, creative endeavors. Veena Prabhu and colleagues noted of Sir Isaac Newton that "[his] extraordinary gift may have resulted from the ability to deliberate intensely on a problem for hours, days, or weeks, if necessary, until he had solved it." Tenacity allows creative thinkers to surmount obstacles. Putting forth ideas is one thing—seeing them to fruition is quite another. Ambition and discipline are other qualities that support the kind of single-minded commitment that allows creators to find success. Isaac Newton rarely left his home and was often so consumed by his ideas that he sometimes forgot to get dressed. At the same time, the dangers of unfettered ambition are well-known in science, as they are in business and politics. Like the other traits, some is good—too much can be sociopathic.

Even though innovators must surmount what can sometimes seem like impossible odds, to them this process is invigorating and addictive.

Great creators thirst for their holy grail with superhuman tenacity. Imagine Edison surrounded by his engineering team, having just demonstrated that they are the only people on the face of the earth who have crafted a working light bulb. Imagine the excitement Darwin felt when he wrote, "Mine is a bold theory…which attempts to explain or asserts to be explicable every instinct in animals." To creative minds, transformative innovations are the jubilation of climbing Mt. Kilimanjaro, the euphoria of winning the lottery, and the triumph of achieving high office, all rolled into one.

So autonomy, openness, and persistence are almost universal among innovators. But since this book is about trying to understand the innovative mind so as to emulate it, we must ask: Can creativity traits be learned? Most research suggests that personality is manifest early in life, runs in families, and is difficult to change. Sam Gosling, renowned expert in personality, provided this answer to the question of whether the innovative personality can be acquired:

> There is some room for flexibility and learning but most traits have a very strong genetic component so the degree of flex is quite limited. What people can do is adopt strategies to improve behaviors (just like I can start writing down things if I'm not very high on conscientiousness) but they will not really change the internal personal mechanisms (I will never truly see the world like a conscientious person does).

Rather than thinking of innovative characteristics in terms of underlying personality traits that are relatively fixed, we may more usefully consider such characteristics as a function of modifiable influences. Three such influences are: social, cognitive, and motivational.

Motivation surely alters creative production. Tasks that generate high levels of excitement help individuals predisposed to be curious and persistent, to want to explore, even if the likelihood of failure is high. At a crafts table, a person who loves to make things will be more likely to engage in creative pursuit than a person who thinks that art projects are juvenile or that he/she has no artistic talent. Darwin, whose interests lay in collecting beetles and classifying plants, would not have been a passionate physician.

Social and environmental factors, such as the "open group climates" espoused by the innovative business expert Teresa Amabile, can encourage creative self-efficacy, that is, the self-confidence to engage in independent thought. In such environments, Amabile argues, novel ideas, even if constructively criticized, are supported. Individuals should be freed of restrictions that impede innovation, whether financial, social, or legal. As a counterpoint, Jonah Lehrer, in his book *Imagine*, argues that brainstorming does not work because of a deficiency of criticism. He cites research suggesting that the best ideas arise from conflict and debate. As an age-old aphorism suggests, many of us produce our best work only when we must.

In keeping with Lehrer's conceptualization that environmental conflict or stress leads to originality, it is notable that early life obstacles were common in the lives of great innovators. Montessori was a woman knocking at the male-dominated gates of science, for example. In one study of 301 geniuses, one-fifth had become orphans in childhood or adolescence. Poverty and hardship are also widespread in the life stories of geniuses. Ironically, geniuses often did not evolve from ease but from adversity. Overcoming such hurdles may reinforce the development of autonomy and persistence. Nonetheless, be it early privation or later support, environmental freedom or environmental constraint, situation seems to play a role in the nurturance of great innovators.

At its core, becoming an innovator begins with curiosity, tenacity, and a belief in oneself. For those with such personality traits, innovation may come more naturally. For others not so strongly predisposed, motivation, environment, and cognition likely interweave with and augment personality features that enhance innovative thinking.

As we read the following stories of genius, let us draw our own conclusions about their personality characteristics. For example, the next scientific celebrity was certainly not short on curiosity, autonomy, and perseverance. Was he a particularly immoderate example, or is it the case that when it comes to genius, it is not enough to have intellect and a cognitive roadmap? Do tools of innovation alone make the genius, or does a "creative personality" alone make the genius, or does genius arise out of some beautiful marriage between the two?

7

Is Psychology All in Your Head?

Stanley Milgram

Was the Holocaust, the systematic annihilation by the Nazis of 6 million Jews, an act of a few or a conspiracy of the many? Surely a whole country full of normal people could not have been complicit.

Hitler's own anti-Semitism was so rabid that perhaps the Holocaust was a nightmare attributable to one madman. In an interview a dozen years before he came to power, he said, "As soon as I have power to do so, I will have gallows built in rows.... Then the Jews will be hanged indiscriminately, and they will remain hanging until they stink.... until the last Jew in Munich has been exterminated." Or even if a single person could not have possibly carried-out murder on such an historic scale, perhaps the Holocaust "crept up" on a German populace. In 1935, Hitler passed the persecutory Nuremberg Laws, which stripped Jews of German citizenship and deprived them of basic civil rights. It was a loss of dignity but not of life. In 1938 came Kristallnacht, a Nazi organized "public outrage" against German Jews in which over 7,000 German shops and 1,600 synagogues were destroyed or vandalized. The 30,000 Jews sent to concentration camps after these pogroms were released if they agreed to emigrate or to transfer their property to the Nazis and pay an onerous "atonement tax." This escalation raised the level of violence, but stopped short of depravity.

Yet when the Nazis progressed to the "Final Solution"—the elimination of all Jews in occupied Nazi territories—there could be no denial.

The apparatus used in the Final Solution? Slave labor, torture, death camps, gas chambers, daily corpse quotas. How many thousands were involved in the enactment of such atrocities? How many others had some inkling of the scope of evil and turned a blind eye? Where were the morals and culture that define human civilization?

Historians and ethicists have debated these questions for two generations. Science, on the other hand, is not designed to provide insight into such questions—or is it?

Psychology is the field that attempts to understand the behaviors and mental processes of individuals and groups. Before World War II, the two most dominant schools of psychological thought were psychoanalysis and behaviorism. Psychoanalysis, developed by the creative genius Sigmund Freud, posited an internal psychological drama played out by the id, the ego, and the superego, each of which was influenced by childhood experiences and expressed through dreams. Behaviorists rebelled against the lack of empirical proof supporting Freud's theories and, led by greats such as John Watson, Ivan Pavlov, and B. F. Skinner, focused squarely only on physiology that could be measured. Repeated stimuli capable of eliciting pleasure or pain, they believed, resulted in entrenched behaviors. For instance, in a classic experiment by Pavlov, dogs (which, through their autonomic system, salivate to meat) were conditioned to salivate to a bell that had been linked to the offering of meat. The behavior (salivation) was measurable, but what was unknowable was the "black box" within the brain that determined not just if, but how, the choice to salivate was made.

Neither psychoanalysis nor behaviorism could explain German behavior under the Nazis, however; the choice to engage in genocide had to represent something within psychology beyond predetermined internal conflict or physiology. The inability to fathom what had happened provoked a crisis within the field and a paradigm shift; a third school of psychology emerged, proposing that subtleties of behavior could be both measured and understood on the basis of social situation. It took the name, social psychology.

Imagine Bob, a huge hockey fan who is a committed friend and a respectable citizen. Bob has never spit on the street, let alone committed an act of violence. After the Canucks lost the 2011 Stanley Cup, Bob found himself acting as part of a rebellious crowd in Vancouver vandalizing shops and burning cars. In the aftermath, no one was more surprised than Bob himself. It was the same low-key, fun-loving Bob, but his emergent behavior was less that of Bob as an individual and more one of Bob as someone swept up by the raging irrationality of the group.

Stanley Milgram, although not one of the founders of social psychology, pushed the field to a place that was so frame shattering that his experiments became among the most controversial in all of science. Milgram's predecessor was Kurt Lewin, a Jew who fled the Nazis and landed at the University of Iowa with a desire to understand the behaviors influenced by authoritarianism. Situationalism, the subfield of social psychology that he founded, was later defined by Milgram as "The ... capacity to reconstruct varied types of social experience in an experimental format, to clarify and make visible the operation of obscure social forces so that they may be explored in terms of the language of cause and effect." Lewin's classic experiments questioned how 11-year-old boys behaved when their social clubs were led by adult leaders role-playing various authority styles. He found that authoritarian and democratic leadership styles got the same level of productivity from the boys, while a laissez-faire leader got less. However, the authoritarian leader brought out the boys' aggressions. Lewin had shown that a social phenomenon as intangible and complex as leadership style elicited group conduct.

Stanley Milgram was a prodigious user of the tools of innovation—one of the most pervasive of which, in both his professional and personal life, was the *power of groups*. Milgram was born in 1933 to Jewish immigrants who, after entering the United States at Ellis Island, explored no farther than the Bronx, and he was the first in his family to attain a graduate degree. An early experience with group intelligence occurred when he attended James Monroe High School, where he was tracked into the "gifted" program upon earning a staggering 158 on the placement IQ test. There he found himself in a precocious circle that began to shape his thinking. At Monroe, Milgram encountered Philip Zimbardo, the man who would conduct the only other social psychology experiment of the era that rivaled Milgram's for infamy. Called the Stanford Prison experiment,

Zimbardo fabricated a relatively lifelike prison setting in the basement of the psychology building at Stanford, made up of six-by-nine-foot cells. He selected 21 subjects who appeared particularly normal on psychological testing and randomly assigned them to be guards and prisoners. Almost immediately, the guards became rigid martinettes. They awakened prisoners at 2 A.M. and forced them to do push-ups. When the prisoners rebelled, the guards sprayed them with fire extinguishers and threw the ring leader into solitary. By day six, the guards were consistently acting in a cruel and dehumanizing manner. Prisoners had gone from crying and rageful to docile and immobile. Zimbardo prematurely brought the experiment to an end. He had demonstrated beyond anyone's imagining the power of social setting.

In graduate school, Milgram experienced the *power of groups* in the synergy between disciplines. After earning a bachelor's degree with honors in political science from Queens College, he planned a career in the Foreign Service, but a dean suggested he investigate the Department of Social Relations at Harvard which combined the study of politics, which fascinated Milgram, with the use of hard science, which impressed him. Indeed, Harvard's department was unique. It had daringly integrated several disciplines: social psychology, clinical psychology, social anthropology, and sociology in order to capture their creative intersection.

The Ford Foundation had a fellowship program to encourage students with majors in unrelated fields to move into the social sciences, and Milgram was able to garner one of these. Unfortunately, he was not able to gain acceptance to the Department as he had never taken a course in psychology. Undaunted, he signed up for six undergraduate courses in psychology and sociology over the summer (while working at night) and aced them all. He started graduate classes in the Department of Social Relations in the fall. Harvard was Milgram's creative Garden of Eden. One of his professors recalls that when required to lead a seminar in psycholinguistics, in which students normally discussed a scholarly paper, Stanley brought in an audio tape containing every imaginable sort of speech: slips of the tongue, a child's first words, and psychotic utterings. His tendency toward doing the unexpected, as well as engaging whimsy and humor, were long remembered. What was also remembered was his disregard for norms, such as scandalously addressing younger faculty by their first names.

Milgram's dissertation, too, built squarely upon the *power of groups*, that is, upon work implemented by his mentors. Soloman Asch, Milgram's role model at Harvard had designed a classic experiment on conformity that went like this: a group of paid confederates are sitting around a table when an actual study subject enters. The study subject believes, erroneously, that he is just one of eight subjects now sitting around the table. Each participant is told to look at a picture of a line and to say out loud which of three other lines is closest to it in length. Each time the procedure is repeated, the actual subject is made the last to respond. At first, all the confederates give a correct response, as does the subject. Then a picture is passed around in which the line that each confederate chooses is clearly incorrect. Yet they have all agreed. What does the research subject do? Surely he sees the lines and knows that the one closest in size is not the one that everyone else has identified. Can every other person in the room be wrong? Could he somehow be confused? About one-third of the time, the actual subject went against his own judgment and went with the opinion of the majority. Asch believed that his results reflected not some mechanistic response to stimuli (as a behavioral psychologist would infer) but an active weighting of social alternatives.

Milgram's doctoral research was a cross-cultural examination of conformity. His application of Asch's methods to Norwegian and French society was the first social psychology research ever conducted across national borders. It mingled political science (the conformity of political systems), sociology (cross-cultural comparisons), and psychology. It was a preview of Milgram's later work—a design with transcendent implications for politics and society.

To interpret his findings, Milgram used another tool of innovation: he *changed his point of view.* In Norway a high percentage, between half and three-quarters of subjects, yielded to erroneous social assessments. Norwegians, Milgram surmised, were more conformist than Americans because, in imaging himself as a member of the culture, he noted a strong feeling of group identity. Changing his point of view to theirs, he commented, "It would not be surprising to find that social cohesiveness of this sort goes hand in hand with a high degree of conformity." In contrast, he seems to have found Frenchmen to be inscrutable. In France the proportion of subjects who conformed was lower than in Norway, although still sizeable at 34–59 percent. The French, Milgram reported, were critical and judgmental in ways that "often [seem] to go beyond reasonable bounds."

Milgram's dissertation research also reflected another tool of innovation learned from Asch: *dissection*. In what would become a hallmark of his work, Milgram conducted multiple versions of his experiment, systematically adjusting parameters so as to separate out the nature of social influence. To give weight to honesty over conformity, he told subjects that the information gleaned from the experiment would be used to design safety signals on airplanes. To even further reduce conformity, he applied these same "airplane" instructions and did not require subjects to share answers with the group—only to write each down. In both of these conditions, the rates of conformity fell but only modestly—remaining at or above 50 percent in Norway and 34 percent in France. This systematic approach allowed him to go beyond answering, How much do people conform? to intangibles such as, What is it about the social circumstance that impels people to conform?

The write-up of Milgram's dissertation demonstrated his own ambivalence about conformity. It earned him the repute of a Harvard doctoral degree, but instead of publishing in a peer review journal, he published it in the trade magazine *Scientific American*. His next experiment would take him even further from the hallowed halls of orthodoxy.

What came next was Milgram's most important and infamous work— his "Obedience to Authority" experiment. In it, he demonstrated that ordinary people will inflict shocking cruelty in response to authoritarian direction. "I was dissatisfied that the test of conformity was judgments about lines," he stated in explaining the genesis of the experiment. "I wondered whether groups could pressure a person into performing an act whose human import was more readily apparent, perhaps behaving aggressively toward another person, say by administering increasingly severe shocks to him.... At that instant, my thought shifted.... Just how far would a person go under the experimenter's orders? It was an incandescent moment...."

Milgram had used *deduction* to hit upon a remarkably *big and daring question*. An assumption or axiom that people are conformist led him to a theorem that people might do almost anything under the influence of authority. He asked, Can a situation be powerful enough to overshadow a person's own morality, indeed of humanity?

The question used the tool of *recombination* to admix inquiry from several distinct disciplines: political science in its quest to understand the Holocaust; ethics in asking about the plasticity of deeply held moral values; and situational psychology in trying to understand the power of situation. This combination and rearrangement moved Milgram past Lewin, who had asked whether group situations influence behavior, and past Asch, who had asked whether groups can influence decisions. This new question was more fundamental and more disturbing.

If there was any question as to whether Milgram's question sprang from an *analogy* to the Holocaust, the introduction to his first publication from the obedience experiments leaves no doubt. "Obedience, as a determinant of behavior is of particular relevance to our time. It has been reliably established that from 1933–45 millions of innocent persons were systematically slaughtered on command ... [these atrocities] could only be carried out on a massive scale if a very large number of persons obeyed orders." Were inhumane German actions during the Holocaust caused because authorities demanded obedience? Analogously, would anyone, even an American, behave the same way under the same circumstances?

Milgram had now settled into his first academic job at Yale, and he concentrated all his energies on getting every detail of the "Obedience to Authority" protocol right. It proceeded in this manner: Male subjects between the ages of 20 and 50 who worked in the New Haven area were recruited through ads. The subjects believed that they were participating in an experiment about how people learn. Upon arrival, each subject was greeted by the experimenter, an actor, dressed in a grey lab coat to look like a scientist but not like a physician (whom we are socialized to obey). Also in the room was a supposed fellow subject, actually a paid confederate. The experimenter explained that the purpose of the study was to see how the intensity of a punishment administered by a "Teacher" affected the ability of a "Learner" to memorize a list of words. The two men were told that they could leave the study at any time and still keep the $4.50 compensation that they had been paid for their participation. Lots were drawn by the subject and the confederate for who would be the Teacher and who the Learner but they were rigged so that the subject always became the Teacher.

The experiment's first step was that the Learner (confederate) was tied to a chair and had electrical wires hooked up to his arm as the Teacher (subject) looked on. The Learner mentioned having a minor heart condition, an off-hand detail that would later become part of the subject's harrowing dilemma. The experimenter reassured the Learner that the shocks might be painful, but not seriously harmful.

In step two, all participants took their places. The subject and experimenter moved to a room separated from the Learner by a wall. Taking a seat in front of a very real-looking machine displaying a plate marked: SHOCK GENERATOR, TYPE ZLB, DYSON INSTRUMENT COMPANY, WALTHAM, MA, the subject was introduced to the equipment. Switches lined up along the face of the machine ranged from 15 to 450 volts in 15-volt intervals. Under the switches was placed an increasingly ominous description: "slight shock, moderate shock, strong shock, intense shock, extreme intensity shock, and danger severe shock." Under the 435 and 450 volt switches was etched simply "XXX." Flipping a switch resulted in a light flashing, a sound buzzing, and a meter needle swinging to the right. In fact, it was all bogus, and the Learner was never shocked. But the realism was absolute. For all the subject knew, he was teaching word pairs to the Learner, and each incorrect response resulted in his administering an increasingly severe shock.

The third step was to put the subject in a situation that demanded participating in the conduct of an abhorrent act. From transcripts recounted in Thomas Blass's biography of Milgram:

Experimenter: Now, if he gets the correct answer, you say "correct" and
  go on to the next line. The correct answer is underlined...
Subject: Oh, I see.
Experimenter: If he gives the wrong answer, you say "wrong" and then
  tell him the number of volts you are going to administer.
Subject: Um-hmm.
Experimenter: Administer the punishment, read him the correct word
  pair once and then go on to the next line. For example, if he indicated
  3 for STRONG ... [The correct answer should have been 2 for ARM]
Subject: Um-hmm.
Experimenter: You would say, "wrong, 15 volts," push the switch, read
  "STRONG arm," and then go on to the next line.
Subject: Okay.
Experimenter: Now, each time he gives a wrong answer, you move up one
  switch on the shock generator.
Subject: Um-hmmm.
Experimenter: It is important that you follow the procedure exactly.

To reinforce the authenticity of the situation, the subject was asked to agree to himself take a 45-volt shock (the only real shock in the experiment). Virtually all subjects indicated that the shock was surprisingly uncomfortable.

As the Learner gave incorrect answers and the subject increased the punishment voltage, the subject heard grunts after some shocks. With even higher voltage, the Learner complained that he had had enough; he begged to be set free; he pleaded for the experiment to end; finally, he stopped answering altogether (these responses were actually recordings timed to certain voltages). As his protests gained urgency, the Learner said, "My heart's starting to bother me now. Get me out of here, please.... Let me out of here. My heart's bothering me. Let me out of here!"

If the subject stopped or hesitated, the experimenter was scripted to calmly but potently recite prompts such as, "Please go on"; "The experiment requires that you go on, Teacher"; "It is absolutely essential that you continue"; "You have no other choice"; "If you don't continue we'll have to discontinue the entire experiment." Notably, the experimenter (authority) never used coercion, never any threat.

Despite the Learner's agonizing pleas, a remarkable 65 percent of participants administered the maximum 450 volts. That is, for two-thirds of all subjects, obedience overrode the prohibition against harming a stranger. The result was a bombshell—including to mental health professionals and even to Milgram. Forty psychiatrists who had not seen the experimental results were asked to predict how far subjects would go. In general, they envisaged that most subjects would not go beyond 150 volts. Their belief was that one-tenth of one percent of subjects would continue to 450 volts.

It was not that the subjects were unfeeling. Milgram's careful *observation* of videotapes of each session revealed that most showed signs of extreme anxiety—sighing, shaking their heads, wiping sweat from their brow, uncontrollably trembling, and laughing inappropriately. At some point in the experiment almost all turned to the experimenter, the authority in the room for reassurance. (Transcript taken directly from Milgram, 1965):

Subject: 150 volts delivered. You want me to keep going?

Subject: 165 volts delivered. That guy is hollering in there. There's a lot of them here. He's liable to have a heart condition. You want me to go on?

Subject: 180 volts delivered: He can't stand it! I'm not going to kill that man in there! You hear him hollering? He's hollering. He can't stand it. What if something happens to him? ...I mean who is going to take responsibility if anything happens to that gentleman?

The experimenter accepts responsibility.

Subject: All right.

Subject: 195 volts delivered. You see he's hollering. Hear that....Gee I don't know.

Experimenter: The experiment requires that you go on...

In this particular case, despite the many, agitated objections, the subject completed the highest voltage level.

At the conclusion of each experiment, the experimenter debriefed each subject, revealing that the Learner was a confederate employed by the laboratory and was never actually shocked. The purpose of the study was not to examine learning or memory, the subjects were now told, but to examine the extent of obedience of authority. Most participants reported feeling a mixture of relief, frustration that they had been duped, and embarrassment that they had not stopped sooner.

Milgram's conclusion in his own words was, " ... I once wondered whether in all of the United States a vicious government could find enough moral imbeciles to meet the personnel requirements of a national system of death camps, of the sort that were maintained in Germany. I am now beginning to think that the full complement could be recruited from New Haven." The finding that authority had trumped morality was almost irrefutable because Milgram's *dissection* of his methods was so meticulous. Subjects were guided to behave "normally" by creating an environment that appeared unquestionably real. Design details included a real-looking shock machine, a believable cover story about memory reinforcement, the application of a real 45-volt shock to the subject, the lack of coercion in the experimenter's prompts, the invariance in recorded learner's protests, and even the color of the experimenter's lab coat.

Another way that Milgram dissected his problem was by isolating contributions to obedience. In a series of four publications (1963–1965), Milgram detailed 18 different versions of the experiment. For instance, did the removal of the Learner to another room make him more abstract and less human? Milgram created physical proximity conditions ranging from (1) the only indication of the Learner's distress was a pounding on the wall at around 300 volts to (2) a "touch-proximity" condition, in which to administer the supposed electric shock the subject had to force the Learner's hand onto a metal plate. Although proximity reduced the likelihood that the subject would complete the experiment, even in the "touch-proximity" condition 30 percent of subjects were completely obedient through 450 volts. Only one variation allowed almost all participants to reject authority. Two additional confederates were added to the subject as Teachers. All three were involved in pulling the switches. First one confederate Teacher and then the other refused to continue (at 150 and 210 volts, respectively). In this scenario, only 10 percent of actual subjects remained fully obedient. Milgram concluded: "The mutual support provided by men for each other is the strongest bulwark we have against the excesses of authority."

Many critics rejected Milgram's results. Some argued that the subjects knew they were in an experiment (unlikely, given their degree of anxiety). Subjects were simply trying to be "good subjects", other skeptics said (but isn't this just another way of being obedient?). Finally, some psychologists objected, suggesting that as society has progressed, situation has become less compelling than independent beliefs.

The last of these criticisms was partially refuted in an experiment conducted over 40 years after the original. Dr. Jerry Burger, publishing in 2009, ran 70 men and women through exactly the same paces as did Milgram, with two major exceptions. Any participant who was knowledgeable about psychology or deemed likely to suffer extreme stress from the experiment was screened out. Moreover, the voltage switches only went up to 150 volts. Seventy percent of participants were ready to continue after pressing the 150 volt switch (79 percent of subjects in Milgram's experiments who went to this point continued to the 450 volt end point). Neither gender nor personality characteristics, including "empathy" and "desire for control," consistently correlated with a tendency to remain obedient. Burger concluded, "Although changes in societal attitudes can affect behavior, my findings indicate that the same situational factors that affected obedience in Milgram's participants still operate today."

Skepticism, however, was the least of the reactions to Milgram's obedience experiments. Critics alleged that the research was grounded in deceit. Subjects, they claimed, were led to act in ways that caused them harm. Institutional review boards with their modern regulations concerning human subjects did not come into effect until a decade later, with the passage of the National Research Act of 1974. Still, intentionally harming research subjects, as scientists had done in Nazi Germany, was scandalous. Milgram himself wrote that deceiving subjects "was not nice," but he felt that there was no other way to obtain results in which subjects would reveal their true behavior. His study, even after a site visit, had been funded, refunded, and considered ethical by the National Science Foundation. Moreover, anticipating the human subjects' concerns raised by the experiment, Milgram went so far as to take the highly unusual step (for the time) of surveying subjects a few months after the completion of the study. Of 856 participants, a full 92 percent returned the surveys. Almost 84 percent said that they were glad to have participated, two thirds reported being no longer bothered by their study-related behavior, and over 80 percent agreed that more studies of the same sort should be carried out.

Nonetheless, after leaving Yale, Milgram was denied a tenure track position at Harvard and ended up settling for an appointment at the little known City University of New York (CUNY). The antagonism towards him, still felt in some psychology circles today, likely arises because Milgram showed us a side of humanity that no one wants to acknowledge. The moral frame that we believe defines humanity was not the frame that subjects chose. In Milgram's 18 experimental versions, he lightened the legitimacy of authority by moving the experiment from Yale University to a lower class storefront. To add heft to the moral side of the balance, Milgram brought the Learner into visual contact and even within arm's reach of the subject. Still fully one-third of subjects delivered shocks to 450 volts. Why?

The answer appears to be the power of situation as a frame. Situation reinforced the heft of authority. Subjects engaged in an experiment that appeared to be legitimate, conducted by responsible individuals, in the name of societal good, and that they were told must be completed. In contrast, the frame of "do no harm" was not actively reinforced by the situation.

Frames, particularly those that are "in our face," are incredibly difficult to break. In a different experiment in which active instructions were pitted against experts' memories, the instructions won out. The subjects were engineers and other high-level professionals who had been given a manual to study. Using an incorrect formula that was printed in the manual, they were told to calculate the volume of a cylinder. They were then given a cylinder of that size and asked to fill it with water, thereby observing the true (different) volume. Despite the work of their own hand, they believed the volume calculated using the erroneous printed formula. Similarly, in Milgram's experiments, the actively operating obedience frame would have been (and was) terribly difficult to overcome. A visceral anxiety reaction is characteristic of frame breaking; it both emerged among research subjects and surfaced in reactions to Milgram's results.

Though Milgram's obedience experiment was groundbreaking, the notoriety that surrounds it cannot be blithely dismissed. Modern-day human rights protections were enacted, in part, to protect subjects against the kind of deception that Milgram's experiments entailed. No matter whether we believe that the ends justified the means or not, we can surely acknowledge that Milgram induced acute anxiety in his subjects. He deceived his participants, thereby pushing research ethics to the limit. The same characteristics that comprise the innovative personality—confidence, autonomy, ambition, and audacity—took this innovator to the edge of convention. Perhaps the adverse consequence of those personality characteristics were the crossing an ethical line; but might the beneficial consequences of Milgram's personality have been the creation of a revolutionary insight?

MILGRAM ANNOTATED: THE USE OF TOOLS OF INNOVATION

Stanley Milgram's *frame shift* not only forever altered science but transfigured our view of civil society. The change was surprising. Harold J. Laski, famed British political theorist, in an article entitled *The Dangers of Obedience,* wrote, " …civilization means, above all, an unwillingness to inflict unnecessary pain. Within the ambit of that definition, those of us who heedlessly accept the commands of authority cannot yet claim to be civilized men." The obedience experiments proved Laski wrong. Milgram's frame shift involved a reversal of our very notion of ourselves as moral beings and as independent agents in society.

What do we learn from Milgram? Perhaps the greatest lesson is how precise and detailed evidence can achieve startling insights. Milgram *dissected* every element of his experimental conditions and laboriously changed one variable after another so as to interpret exactly what he was seeing. Thus his work, while rooted in *observation*, went on to so carefully disaggregate those observations that they gained new meaning.

Milgram used the *power of groups*, building on the work of his mentors. His dissertation, a cross-cultural examination of conformity, came directly from the application of the work of his role model, Soloman Asch, who had designed the classic, initial experiment on conformity. Moreover, it combined the traditions of generations of psychologists who had come before. Milgram's early work also revealed his ability to *change his point of view*, imagining himself as a Norwegian or a Frenchman to interpret those early experimental results.

A powerful *analogy* that influenced Milgram's work was the historical enigma of the Holocaust. Did Germans act inhumanly because there was something aberrant about their culture, or is obedience to authority a universal human trait? Milgram used *expansion* to move from experiments on conformity to the more thorny issue of obedience. But that expansion sprang from his bewilderment, as a Jew and as a person, at man's ability to inflict inhumanity.

Three final tools that completed Milgram's use of the toolbox were: *the right question*; *induction/deduction*; and *recombination*. Milgram's biggest question sprang from the deduction that people, as slaves to conformity, might do almost anything under the influence of authority. The question thus became, Can a situation be powerful enough to overshadow a person's own sense of ethics, indeed of humanity? It was a question that touched on political science (the Holocaust), philosophy (the malleability of moral absolutes), and situational psychology (understanding the power of situation). The question itself required a recombining of disciplinary thinking. Moreover, it was a question informed by both empirical evidence and a heuristic leap from pure psychology into political history.

Finally, Milgram represents a genius whose personality characteristics synergized with his cognitive gymnastics. It is hard to imagine that anyone with less self-sufficiency and tenacity could have accomplished the scope and precision that characterized his Obedience to Authority experiments. It is hard to imagine that anyone with a lesser degree of rebelliousness could have posed and answered one of the most controversial questions ever addressed in science.

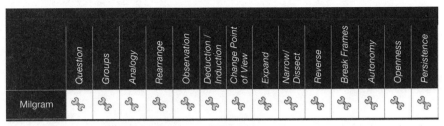

Figure 7.1. Milgram: Tools and Characteristics

8

Inspirations from the Heart

Jerry Morris and Ancel Keys

I t was 1939. A prominent sales executive striding down a Chicago sidewalk to a high-stakes meeting was overtaken by a sudden sensation. Was it unusually hot? Sweat dripping from his brow, he loosened his tie. Why were so many people crowding the sidewalk? They needed to step away—they were suffocating him. Why did he suddenly feel so terrible—so terrified?

Only after his hand had flown up to grip his chest did he notice the growing pain. What could cause something so excruciating? Was it his heart? Surely it must be his heart. In an instant the pain was so vice-like that he could not take another step or say another word. By the time he hit the ground, he was already dead.

In the two decades before World War II, a strange new set of diseases began to sweep the country. On death certificates they were coded as myocardial infarction (heart attack), angina, stroke, and sudden death. Each of these diseases, collectively termed "cardiovascular disease," is caused by a blockage within the arteries that supply the brain and heart. Today, cardiovascular disease is one of the two leading causes of mortality (along with cancer) among men and women in every developed country in the world. Almost one million Americans die from it each year—more than 2,600 fatalities each day. Before the 1920s, heart disease was so unusual as to be a medical curiosity. Residents in training flocked to see a single case. But an epidemic was in the making, and before many experts seemed to notice, cardiovascular deaths had overtaken the long-standing killers: tuberculosis, diarrheal diseases, and cancer. Physicians hoped that the increase was some aberration of coding or counting. It was a false hope. By the 1940s, science belatedly recognized that this twentieth-century scourge, called by many the "executive disease," was all too real and had come to stay.

The bad news is that heart disease has grown to be so common. The good news is that deaths peaked in 1968 in the United States and have been declining at an impressive clip of 26 percent every decade since. Success in lowering the rates of cardiovascular disease is one of the greatest triumphs in modern medicine. How did science slow the blood-letting?

Two epidemiologists, Jerry Morris in London and Ancel Keys in Minnesota, were the first to appreciate a cynical irony of modernity —that when it came to heart disease, social progress was malevolent. The most desired trappings of the twentieth century, a bloody steak and the leisure to spend hours watching TV, both newly available to the middle class, were causing millions of Americans to lose their lives. Our more recently "flipped" twenty-first-century values that carrots are superior to French fries and that the treadmill trumps the couch were the work of these two geniuses.

Morris and Keys both lived lives packed full of achievement; even each man's longevity and end-of-life vibrancy was an achievement. Morris published until six months before he passed away at age 99½. Keys was the guest of honor at a prestigious scientific meeting ten weeks before he died. He succumbed at age 100. The two spent those long and fruitful lives shattering frames.

Jerry Morris, director of the Social Medicine Research Unit of the Medical Research Council in London, was a founder of the new science of social inequities in health. He was studying employment in relation to causes of death in 1948 when he spied something unusual. Curious about "the modern epidemic" of heart disease, as so many were in those days, he noticed that drivers of London's double-decker buses had higher rates of heart disease mortality than conductors on those same buses. How could it be that men from the same social class, working in a shared environment, had such different mortality patterns? It made no sense—surely drivers had it easier, sitting all day, than did conductors, who ran up and down the double-deckers gathering tickets. Morris took a *deductive* leap and made a bold bet. It had nothing to do with stress. Drivers, he guessed, were dying from heart disease as a result of their lack of exercise.

The idea that physically active occupations might improve health was not new. As far back as the eighteenth century, the Italian physician Bernardini Ramazzini, contrasting diseases of various tradesmen, noted that messengers were in better health than tailors and cobblers. "Let tailors be advised to take physical exercise at any rate on holidays," he counseled. In 1863, Edward Smith again stumbled on this truism in assessing the poor health status of London tailors. Indeed, workforce studies using more sophisticated job classifications reported that, in general, physically active workers had lower death rates than sedentary ones. But these simple correlations did not have broad appeal, since no one could tell whether activity led to improved health or whether healthier individuals remained in more physically demanding jobs. The public continued to fear over-exercise and continued to equate leisure with prosperity.

What was new about Morris's work was his application of a tool for *dissecting* problems, a formal set of methods called epidemiology. By taking the question of whether exercise prevented heart disease apart and carefully *observing* its components, Morris would silence previous criticisms. Epidemiology is the study of the patterns, causes, and control of disease in populations. Medicine, too, seeks to understand the causes and treatments for disease, but it focuses on saving one person at a time. Epidemiology, the key science behind public health, focuses on saving thousands. Of the 30 years of life expectancy gained by the average American in the past century, a remarkable 25 of those years are attributable to public health measures (such as ensuring clean water and air, vaccination, food safety, and tobacco policy) each of which was discovered to be beneficial through epidemiology.

John Snow is generally considered to be the father of epidemiology. He was the general practitioner in the London suburb of Soho in 1854 when cholera began to rage. The frame at the time was that disease spread through "miasmas" (bad air) or that it was caused by "humors" (such as blood and bile) specific to individuals. Snow believed otherwise. The well from which the community drew its water, he guessed, was the culprit spreading cholera. However, since the germ theory of disease—that pathogens spread contagion—would not emerge for another half a dozen years, Snow was on shaky ground. Moreover, Snow could not actually see anything unusual about the well water when viewed through his crude microscope. What convinced him was a classic epidemiologic tool: a survey. There is no better summary of Snow's investigative findings than in his own words:

> On proceeding to the spot, I found that nearly all the deaths had taken place within a short distance of the [Broad Street] pump. There were only ten deaths in houses situated decidedly nearer to another street-pump. In five of these cases the families of the deceased persons informed me that they always sent to the pump in Broad Street, as they preferred the water to that of the pumps which were nearer. In three other cases, the deceased were children who went to school near the pump in Broad Street.... (John Snow, letter to the editor of the *Medical Times and Gazette*)

Snow took his data to the Board of Guardians of St. James's parish the next day and the Board removed the handle from the pump. Dramatically, the epidemic ceased.

The removal of the Broad Street pump handle is an episode that epidemiologists continue to celebrate to this day. Yet, as soon as the immediate threat had passed, Soho officials replaced the pump handle and rejected Snow's underlying hypothesis that disease was spread through water via fecal-oral transmission. It was simply too disturbing (disgusting) a frame shift to adopt. Years later, it was realized that the well had been dug only three feet from the site of a cesspit and that fecal bacteria were the source of several pump-related infectious disease outbreaks.

Although germ theory awoke microbiology and infectious disease research, epidemiology remained an embryonic science—that is until Morris helped to refine it.

Morris used the primitive discipline to ask a *sweeping question*: What accounts for the differential patterns of coronary disease among different occupations? The question of what caused the modern epidemic was on many scientists' minds. However, Morris had found a specific clue within a given set of occupations: bus drivers and conductors. He spent five years gathering data to make a case that a cause was exercise. In the end, he noted:

> The suggestion emerged ... that physical activity in work is associated with a lower incidence and severity of coronary heart disease in middle-aged men.... In this type of research, dealing as it often must with material impossible to "control" of less accuracy than might be wished, and from which it is difficult to isolate variables, special precautions need to be taken by the investigator. In the present instance reliance was placed on the power of simultaneous attack on the problem from different directions.

Morris's "attack" of his revelation that cardiovascular deaths among drivers were three times higher than among conductors involved data dissection. The disparity in death rates was not a function of social class, Morris reasoned, since busmen all came from the same social class. Moreover, Morris cleverly showed that the wives of drivers had no higher heart disease rates than the wives of conductors. What was dramatically different between drivers and conductors, Morris discovered, was that drivers sat for 90 percent of their shifts, whereas conductors climbed 600 stairs each day. In a clever piece of additional detective work, Morris also established that body size did not fully account for the association. He obtained waistband sizes of uniforms for each bus driver and conductor from Transport for London, the city's bus agency, and discovered that the activity and heart disease relationship held up among men with small, medium, and large waist sizes.

To further support his hypothesis that what distinguished drivers and conductors was physical activity, Morris brought together the disciplines of epidemiology and pathology using the tool of *recombination and rearrangement.* At autopsy, he compared the coronaries of men engaged in more or less active occupations. Men holding more physically demanding jobs had fewer coronary artery blockages.

Intrigued but still not convinced, Morris went on to use *analogy.* He turned to an occupation that he saw walking all around London—letter carriers. Mailmen, he found, had lower heart disease mortality rates than sedentary government office staff. Indeed, when he arrayed physical work activities from "heavy" to "light," coronary disease death rates correlated perfectly.

Since little could be done to counter the trend toward more sedentary occupations, Morris *reversed* and *expanded* the question. Now, rather than asking whether lack of exercise caused atherosclerosis, he asked, Does exercise both at work and during leisure time have general advantages for health? His wide-ranging research over the next 30 years would create an explosion of evidence favoring advice to get up from the couch. He would create the field of physical activity epidemiology and initiate the worldwide promotion of aerobics.

Like his initial work, Morris's studies on leisure time activity built on previous research and thus the *power of groups.* A prior long-term follow-up study of oarsmen at Oxford and Cambridge Universities had countered a long-standing concern about the dangers of vigorous exercise. Instead, the study found that life expectancies of college athletes exceeded those of insured or general populations. This provided an early basis for Morris's proposal that not only was sedentariness potentially harmful, but activity—even strenuous activity—was potentially good.

Finally, in conducting the precise science needed to prove his theory, Morris *changed his point of view.* He wondered, What do people do all day? What activities do they engage in at work and at play that might affect their health? He created laundry lists of activities from sitting at a desk to lifting boxes, from playing squash to gardening. Then he surveyed groups of men, asking them to recall how much time they spent in each activity, and with this information, he showed that longer duration and more vigorousness activities most strongly protect against heart disease.

Morris *overturned the frame* that labor saving is all good and that over-exercise is dangerous. His paradigm-shifting thinking involved every tool in the toolbox. A flamboyant contemporary, Ancel Keys, was equally transformational in proving the "yang" to Morris's "ying"—that heart disease was not only a disorder of exercise but also of diet.

"Unconventional" and "independent" are adjectives that do little justice in describing the personality of Ancel Keys. Born in 1904 and raised in the town of Berkeley, California, at a time that the University of California Berkeley was still young, Ancel's adventurousness seemed to arise less from his working-class parents and more from the Wild West. Partway through the school year at age 16, Keys decided that he preferred the outdoors to the classroom and took off with only a change of clothes and a thumb pointed South. Keys found himself a well-paying job, but the conditions were not ones that most people would aspire to. Working alone inside a small cave in the desert some miles outside Oatman, Arizona, he spent his days shoveling bat guano. His only connection to other humans was the truck that arrived every morning to pick up his gunnysacks full of excrement in exchange for sandwiches and water. Not until three months into the job did he decide that he had had enough at which point he hitched back to Berkeley and finished high school.

Despite frequent absences and modest grades, Keys's algebra teacher wrote him a glowing letter of recommendation that gained him admission to the University of California. This conversion to convention did little to modify his exploits. After a freshman year piling up on chemistry and calculus classes, at which Keys excelled, he signed onto a merchant vessel bound for Asia. His goal was to try out his German and Chinese skills. In the port of Hong Kong, he tried and failed to make himself understood in Mandarin. But in written Chinese he could bargain with the best of them. Thus, with an astonished crowd looking on, the Westerner purchased a small wooden table, which forever remained one of his most prized possessions.

Over the next dozen years, Keys flitted between prestigious institutions and amassed academic accomplishments. He completed his bachelors of sciences degree at UC Berkeley in three years and a master's degree in zoology in six months. A doctorate in evolutionary biology from the Scripps Institute in La Jolla came next, followed by postdoctoral work on the blood salinity of eels with August Krogh, Nobel laureate, in Coppenhagen. Finally came the study of high altitude effects on human physiology with Joseph Barcroft at Cambridge, where Keys earned a second doctoral degree. When Harvard offered him an opportunity to continue the high altitude research as a junior faculty member, he took it. An expedition to the village of Quilcha, Chile, allowed Keys to measure oxygen saturation at the highest altitude ever tested. He did it by offering himself up to give a blood sample at 20,140 feet. But it was almost at the expense of his colleague and later editor of the *Journal of the American Medical Association*, John Talbot, who after taking the sample had a near-death collapse from high altitude sickness.

Keys's next conquest, although brief, was the hallowed Mayo Institute in Rochester, Minnesota. There he met his lifelong wife and partner, Margaret. Only in 1938 did Keys land for good—at the University of Minnesota. The research shop he would build there, the Laboratory of Physiological Hygiene, would become both famous and infamous.

Keys's vision for the Laboratory was to create an expansive new brand of science. In his own words, "These are not questions of medicine or physiology or biochemistry or psychology or physical education, but invade and partake of all." His *big question* was, How does what we eat affect every aspect of our physiology? Ultimately, the Laboratory grew to reflect the size of Key's aspirations—so large that it could only be housed on the ground floor beneath the University's Memorial Football Stadium—at the legendary Gate 27.

Learning of Key's studies assessing heart sizes among athletes, the military called on him to engage in discoveries of national importance. The first was the development of "K" rations. This dense, pocket-sized packet of foodstuff, including things like a pemmican biscuit, peanut bar, raisins, and bouillon paste, would allow American troops to successfully "march on their bellies" during World War II. It became so ubiquitous (105 million were dispensed in 1944) that, while critical to military success, it came to be reviled by servicemen.

Keys's second military adventure occurred near the end of World War II, when he conducted a unique and uniquely questionable experiment on starvation. A starving Europe would need to be re-fed after the War. In a study in which 36 volunteer conscientious objectors were systematically starved down to three-quarters of their original body weight, Keys hoped to establish an evidence-based approach to treating the ravenous hordes. Producing the most definitive work ever published on the effects of starvation and re-feeding entitled *Biology of Human Starvation,* the study involved one of the most painstaking assessments of physiological function conducted up until that time. Nonetheless, the magnitude of weight loss was shocking. Keys reduced athletic 150-pound men to 112.5 pounds, their skin stretched taunt over their cheekbones and their scapula protruding above their chests.

Despite any useful information it reaped, the study's ethics remain questionable; real acute harm to subjects was done. Moreover, the work never had the intended impact. By the time the massive tome was published, World War II was over and Europe had been re-fed. The starvation study's greatest impact has been in the treatment of women with anorexia nervosa since it demonstrated that the depression, irritability, and obsession with food exhibited by anorexic women is not only attributable to psychopathology but to the classic effects of starvation that had been experienced by Keys's subjects. We are left to wonder whether Keys's curiosity took him a step beyond where any scientist should go.

If any criticism was launched against Keys's starvation experiments, it did not stick. By the end of the war, Keys had acquired the status of one of the country's foremost experts in nutrition. When his reading of the Minneapolis obituary pages stimulated an interest in the rising rates of heart disease, he decided to make that his peacetime pursuit. Perhaps it was his awareness of informal Dutch reports from the nineteenth century showing lower rates of heart disease among non-meat eaters in the Far East; perhaps it was the results from his starvation experiments, which had shown that reducing caloric consumption dramatically lowered serum cholesterol. Either way, Keys *deduced* that the modern epidemic was a function of American dietary excess.

Red meat and egg consumption were on a postwar ascendency. With the opening of the first McDonald's fast food restaurant in 1948, the country would embark on a ravenous love affair with beef. A decade later, one hundred million McDonald's hamburgers had been sold; by the mid-1970s, American beef consumption had doubled. Keys would become a counter-revolutionary, guessing, proving, and promoting a diet full of fresh fruits and vegetables and laden with bread and pasta. He called it the Mediterranean diet.

To prove his dietary theory, Keys turned away from studies of a few to studies of thousands—to the discipline that Morris had used—epidemiology. Such methods launched him on a lifelong quest to establish the link between dietary fat, serum cholesterol, and heart disease. It was a saga that would establish two new subfields: cardiovascular epidemiology and nutritional epidemiology.

The *power of groups* and *recombination* played a major role in Keys's work. His large and complex studies required a multidisciplinary team of statisticians, nutritionists, physiologists, and physicians, each contributing knowledge from their discipline to a larger whole. His Laboratory of Physiological Hygiene would become one of the world's finest centers for conducting cardiovascular epidemiology. Moreover, Keys established research collaborations with institutions around the world. These efforts would yield over 300 peer-reviewed publications, many classics, and a global proliferation of epidemiologic studies.

Keys's work built on the *power of groups*—on knowledge compiled by others. It had been known for decades, if not longer, that being born into the wrong family greatly increased cardiovascular risk. Some clans experienced clusters of hypertension and high blood cholesterol that killed early and often. Moreover, a series of ingenious pathologic studies conducted at the Russian Imperial Medical Institute in the early twentieth century demonstrated that the perpetrator of arterial blockages was fat globules. The pathologist Nikolai Anitschkow went on to feed rabbits diets rich in dietary lipids and cholesterol, and he produced fatty arterial lesions resembling those found in the coronaries of heart attack victims. These were tantalizing clues, but they were far from definitive. As Henry

Blackburn, a modern-day expert in cardiovascular risk recalls, "The state of medical ignorance and cautious attitudes about the possible environmental influences on cardiovascular disease *circa* 1948 can hardly be appreciated today.... Smoking and obesity were merely distasteful; physical activity was dangerous and unfashionable...."

The first study that Keys launched to formally test his diet/cholesterol hypothesis was the Minnesota Business and Professional Men Study. Initiated in 1947, it is credited with primacy for applying a newly developed design to the study of cardiovascular disease: the cohort study. A cohort study measures possible causes at one point in time and effects later. Let's say that victims of heart attack report that they are less likely to drink coffee, suggesting that coffee protects against heart disease. But what if it turns out that the lower intake of coffee occurred because heart attack patients were trying to change to healthier habits? That is, coffee did not cause heart attacks; heart disease caused patients to cut down their coffee consumption. In a cohort study, the epidemiologist would start with interviews about coffee consumption and then would follow subjects over time to establish later disease events. This would clearly establish which, coffee or heart problems, came first.

Like so many great innovators, Keys was able to *dissect* the problem into measurable questions. Rather than simply asking what people ate, he measured serum cholesterol (as well as blood pressure, electrocardiogram, chest X-ray, and skin folds). Moreover, he incorporated the newest techniques for separating cholesterol into alpha and beta lipoprotein sub-fractions, the forerunners of "good cholesterol" (HDL) and "bad cholesterol" (LDL).

Keys selected a narrowly defined set of subjects, further enhancing the validity of his results. The 286 men who enrolled in the Minnesota study were middle-aged businessmen, a group who appeared most susceptible to the new plague. Recommended by local corporations as particularly stable employees, his chosen group would prove to be loyal study subjects for 40 years. He also selected subjects to reflect a range of baseline cardiovascular risk as he notes in publications: " ...first selection was made of 50 most overweight, the 50 most underweight, and another 50 men who were reported by the athletic directors of the local YCMAs and athletic clubs to be especially active in their programs." This tactic increased the likelihood of identifying any effect from diet independent of other factors, almost as one would improve the success of separating sticks in the game "pick-up sticks" by scattering the pieces broadly, rather than by dumping them out in a heap. Finally, with an eye for salesmanship, Keys recruited Edward John Thye, the state's Republican governor, and Bernie Bierman, the beloved coach of the University of Minnesota football team. Such endorsements led a remarkable 92 percent of men recommended to the study to volunteer and 93 percent to remain in the study through 15 years. After 40 years of follow-up, 54 men were still under surveillance; most others had died from heart disease.

The Minnesota Business and Professional Men Study demonstrated what Keys suspected: that cholesterol was one of the strongest predictors of heart disease. It *reversed* public assumptions about good living. Mothers had been plying their children with liver, eggs, and butter. Families had considered heaping platefuls of meat to be a sign of affluence and well-being. Yet, here was Keys demonstrating that men with a cholesterol of >260 were more than five times more likely to develop heart disease than those with cholesterol values of <200. Keys had shattered the frame that the road to good health was through a hearty appetite.

In 1958, Keys *broadened the question*. The query he posed in his Minnesota Business and Professional Men Study had been: Does elevated cholesterol increase heart disease in Minnesota? Now Keys asked, Do differences in diet across cultures correlate to international patterns of heart disease? Invited to a multitude of countries to spread his belief about consuming a diet low in fat, he was impressed with the diversity of regional foods. As each country generated its own data on heart disease and drew its own conclusions, Keys realized that scientists from different countries working together would generate a robust and valid set of global generalizations. This remarkable idea gained support from Dudley White, President Eisenhower's personal physician, whose celebrity status had arisen when he cared for the President after his heart attack. White's endorsement of Keys's work opened doors around the world.

The Seven Country Study was Keys's scientific triumph, validating the insights that would bring him popular fame. Among disparate populations of 40–59-year-old men in the United States, Finland, Greece, Italy, Japan, the Netherlands, and Yugoslavia, he and international colleagues enrolled 12,770 men, mostly from rural communities and consuming traditional diets.

New methods needed to be developed for assessing diet. These employed meticulous *observation*. They also required delving into the lives of people from divergent cultures—thus *changing point of view*. Teams in the various countries catalogued all possible dietary options. Subjects completed dietary surveys that involved weighing all items consumed during a seven-day period, and these surveys were repeated in different seasons. Yet other methods developed by the team involved painstaking assessments of nutritional content. The level of detailed observation is evident from this description in one of Keys's publications: "Nutrients were estimated from chemical analyses of composites of replicate meals and menus...." These methods, a combination of chemistry and epidemiology—a rearrangement of previous survey approaches—have been the basis of nutritional epidemiology ever since.

In explaining the spectacular differences in the rates of cardiovascular disease between middle-aged men in Japan and the Greek islands versus the United States and Finland, Keys *deduced* that diets low (less than 10 percent of daily calories) in saturated fats lowered heart disease risk. This not only explained the low rates in Japanese men, who consumed mainly rice, fish, and vegetables, it also explained the low rates in Greece, where the diet derived 35 percent of calories from fat but where the fat was unsaturated, derived from fruits and vegetables, including nuts and olive oil. In contrast, in Finland, a country where loggers spread butter on their cheese, men consumed particularly large quantities of saturated fat and had particularly high rates of heart attack.

Keys established the counterintuitive fact that it is not dietary cholesterol but dietary fat that mostly determines serum cholesterol. His "Keys formula" remains a tool used to accurately predict serum cholesterol on the basis of diet. A dramatic and widely circulated graph that Keys drew

plotted the logarithm of heart disease deaths in a country versus its average dietary fat consumption. The relationship was a virtual straight line.
We now acknowledge that international comparisons can be misleading;
there are many things beyond diet that produce differential rates of heart
disease. Nonetheless, Keys's main insights have proven valid.

Keys's team, later led by the physician-epidemiologist Harry Blackburn,
would go on to direct many of the most famous multicenter studies in the
field of heart disease. Keys himself would retire in 1972, but before he
did, he would *break yet another frame* and thereby gain prominence well
beyond the world of science.

In 1959, Keys and his wife Margaret jumped beyond the normal confines
of science to publish a popular cookbook espousing the health benefits from
diets eaten in Greece and Italy. Called *Eat Well and Stay Well*, the book combined recipes and research. It sold over 100,000 copies, was translated into
five languages, and introduced to America the famed Mediterranean diet.
The foods featured were those that Keys had come to value for their health
benefits but also for their taste. The January 13, 1961, cover of *Time* magazine
featured a picture of the iconic scientist—the only member of the University
of Minnesota faculty to ever gain such repute. A sequel Mediterranean diet
cookbook, *The Benevolent Bean* (1967), in which Margaret got first billing,
further cemented Keys's celebrity status. With his new wealth, Keys built
Minnelea, a large villa in the Italian village of Pioppi, nestled amidst citrus
gardens. It had a terrace overlooking the Mediterranean.

The Mediterranean diet and regular leisure exercise remain corner-
stones of modern-day advice about maintaining a healthy lifestyle. Keys,
like Morris, used every tool of innovation in the toolbox to break the
existing frame about the healthfulness of comfort foods. As recently as
2010, a Cochrane Review systematically evaluated the world's literature on
whether replacing dietary saturated (animal) fat with unsaturated (plant)
fat reduces risk of heart disease and stroke. According to the review, it does.
U.S. Department of Agriculture dietary guidelines recommend restricting
total daily fat intake to 20 to 35 percent of daily calories. Saturated fats, the
guidelines suggest, should constitute no more than 7–10 percent of daily
calories, or about 140–200 calories (16–22 grams) per day.

Similarly, a 2010 systematic review in the high-impact journal *Circulation* concluded that "[t]here is substantial evidence to indicate that physically active individuals have lower rates of …cardiovascular disease." Exercise among men and women of all ages (with limited data for > 80 year olds) and within all racial/ethnic groups lowers the risk for heart disease, just as Jeremy Morris predicted. The Centers for Disease Control currently recommend a minimum of 150 minutes per week of moderate or 75 minutes per week of vigorous aerobic physical activity. More is even better.

MORRIS AND KEYS ANNOTATED: THE USE OF TOOLS OF INNOVATION

Perhaps the most salient tools that Morris and Keys used to transform global beliefs about what we should eat and how we should move were *dissection* and *observation*. Just as their predecessors gained insight about heart disease through opening up the body cavity and visualizing coronary pathology, Morris and Keys isolated risk factors within populations by using epidemiology. Each of these geniuses pondered over the complexity of the epidemic of cardiovascular disease and meticulously picked out the patterns of lifestyle that caused one person's heart to seize while another's remained healthy. It was like finding some vital thread that, when pulled, would unravel the whole.

The *frame shift* that sprang from the work of Morris and Keys was a *reversal* and it came from asking *the right questions*. Gluttony and inactivity were societal ambitions before the work of these two geniuses. Rather than concurring that these were noble aspirations, the two asked whether there might be unintended consequences. Morris's big question was, What accounts for the differential patterns of coronary disease among different occupations? Keys asked, How does what we eat impact every aspect of our physiology? These were not questions that arose only from initial observations but instead from a combination of *induction and deduction*. Activity and diet as hypothetical contributors to heart disease were initially pure leaps of faith.

Morris and Keys were not only askers of big questions, they were *expanders* of the scientific technique. They used the newly created tools of epidemiology to engage not just a few but hundreds of human subjects. They used *combination* and the *power of groups* to build collaborations with colleagues in different disciplines and around the world. Insights came from building on the work of others but also from building a rich consortium of experts from different cultures and with different perspectives and expertise.

Their success in bringing together so many disparate perspectives may have made it easier for each of them to *alter point of view*. Morris and Keys got into the mind-sets of their subjects. Morris asked, What do people do all day? Keys asked, How do you change the culture of eating if not by enticing people to cook differently? It was not only *broadening perspective* but also *expansion, reversal, the power of groups*, and the orchestration of so many other tools that allowed Morris and Keys to think in ways that, at the time, seemed radical. Their influence created whole new fields of science. Former assumptions were disrupted. What was considered good became bad. Never again would the world embrace progress with quite so much blissful naïveté.

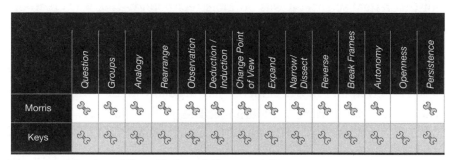

Figure 8.1. Morris and Keys: Tools and Characteristics

9

It's Electric

Thomas Edison

The eighteenth and nineteenth centuries brought invention into the kitchens and living rooms of American families. Engineering innovation, as applied to machines and manufacturing, created a practical mechanism for translating science into prosperity. It was a revolution, one that we call the Industrial Revolution. The mass production of textiles, improvements in steam engines and machine tools, speeding of railroads, and application of coke to iron making were nodal advancements that generated unprecedented, mass improvements in wealth and the quality of life. The revolutionary fuel was not theoretical science; it was tangible technology. This was creativity with a use that people could see and feel.

Thomas Edison, man of 1,093 patents and father of such modern miracles as the phonograph, light bulb, electricity distribution system, telephone receiver, and movie camera, may arguably be the single inventor who most visibly enriched modern life. The question for us is, as an engineer and inventor, did he wander the same mental path as did genius scientists? Edison's personality characteristics were surely those of any eminent innovator. Through superhuman curiosity, self-reliance, and tenacity, this partially deaf man, raised in poverty and lacking formal education, became the celebrity founder of General Electric. Like an oyster encountering a grain of sand, Edison seemed utterly incapable of giving up on an idea until he had turned it into a pearl. Surely, too Edison had intelligence and ingenuity. But did this exemplar of the Industrial

Revolution use the same mental map as did theoreticians and experimentalists—the same tools of innovation?

From birth, Thomas Alva Edison's hopes and dreams rose and fell with the Industrial Revolution. Ironically, however, technological progress and Edison did not start off in sink. When he was six years old, Edison's hometown of Milan, Ohio, was decimated when it refused to give free right-of-way to the Lake Shore Railroad and so was bypassed by the main rail line, losing 80 percent of its economy. It was 1853, and Thomas's father, Sam, was forced to move his wife and seven children to Port Huron, Michigan, where, having been separated from a fortune in real estate, the father took to dabbling in lumber and grain. But after the Milan debacle, Sam was, as Matthew Josephson notes in his biography of Edison, "no steady provider."

Thomas Edison's progress in school followed a similarly abortive course. He later recalled in a *New York Herald Tribune* interview, "I was always at the foot of the class. I used to feel . . . that my father thought I was stupid." When, according to legend, he overheard a teacher calling him "addled," he ran from the schoolroom and refused to return. Henceforth, his mother, from whom he felt unwavering encouragement, schooled him at home.

At age nine, Edison's accommodation with technological advancement took a dramatic turn. Indeed, somewhat surprisingly, it grew into unbridled passion. His mother happened to introduce him to the illustrated R. G. Parker's *School of Natural Philosophy*, a compilation of simple experiments in the natural sciences. Guided also by a used *Dictionary of Science*, the boy created a laboratory in his bedroom, which, after sulfuric acid spilled on the furniture, was relocated to the cellar. There he isolated himself for days, working on electricity and the telegraph.

Samuel Morse, Joseph Henry, and Alfred Vail had developed the electrical telegraph system in 1844. As the first device that could send instantaneous, long-distance messages, the telegraph created a communications revolution. The machine worked by sending electrical impulses across a wire. On the receiving end, a device that pushed an armature connected to an inked wheel on a moving tape. This created a series of dashes and dots that represented the alphabet. Telegraph operators soon learned that the paper recording was extraneous; the audible clicks created by the machine could be readily understood by a trained ear. Skilled operators transcribed up to 30 words per minute. To become a telegraph operator was the aspiration of many science-minded boys as it was for Edison.

Unlike other boys who were satisfied building crude telegraphs in their cellars, however, Edison was not content with a play model. He intended to build a proper Morse code telegraph—but to construct such a sophisticated apparatus required capital. When the railroad came through Port Huron in 1859, Edison, at the age of 12 and against his parents' wishes, insisted on taking a job as the "candy butcher," selling snacks to passengers. Young as he was, he set off on an adventure that took him into the sanctums of rail line engineers and Detroit machine shops. He had to find his way to unfamiliar places, mix with unsavory older men, and work 14-hour days. It was not all excitement—there were seemingly endless hours of downtime. But not for Edison, who built himself a train-board laboratory.

Despite his early progress toward invention, events conspired against the budding prodigy. The worst was the onset of deafness. As Edison later recalled, "I haven't heard a bird sing since I was twelve years old." Feeling utterly isolated, the boy could have taken on the mantle of an invalid and receded into the pages of history, but instead the tragedy only served to arouse him. He vowed to become self-reliant. His refuge became the Detroit Public Library. There he systematically read everything from the bottom shelf to the top, from Burton's *Anatomy of Melancholy* to Newton's *Principles*.

By age 15, Edison's ever enlarging self-reliance and self-confidence assumed an entrepreneurial flavor. Having taken on news sales for his rail line, he convinced the telegraph operators to post the top news stories before the train got to the station, thereby hyping the headlines. When the train arrived, Edison was able to sell huge lots of newspapers at scalper's prices. Edison's development as both an inventor and a businessman was well under way. .

That year, Edison achieved his early life's ambition. When he saved the three-year-old son of the station agent from being crushed by an oncoming rail car, the agent, MacKenzie, offered Edison whatever he wanted in the way of reward; the adolescent requested to be trained as a telegraph operator. Over the next several months, MacKenzie did just that. Edison readily learned the profession and found work, but it was not to last. Job after telegraph job fired the young man for monkeying with the equipment or for letting messages pile up while he stopped to think through an idea. Colleagues from New Jersey to Kentucky lent Edison money to avert destitution. But with his wages forever squandered buying instruments and electrical wire and his thoughts forever elsewhere, it soon became apparent that being a telegraph operator was not to be Edison's destiny.

During this time, Edison was besieged, even in his dreams, by all sorts of schemes and inventions about electricity. Edison's hero was the scientist Michael Faraday. Like Edison, Faraday was poor and lacked formal education. Yet the great British scientific experimentalist had discovered one of the most fundamental concepts in all of physics—electromagnetic induction. Electromagnetism, the force caused by interactions between charged particles, both electric and magnetic, was first discovered by Hans Ørsted, a Danish physicist, in 1820. What Faraday realized a decade later is that electricity and magnetism are two sides of the same coin. In particular, a changing magnetic field induces a current in a nearby circuit. Faraday's insights into electromagnetism (James Maxwell would later formalize them in mathematical terms) could not be more central to physics. Electromagnetism is one of the fundamental forces within the visible world. In addition to governing the physics of electricity and magnetism, electromagnetic forces hold atoms together, account for chemical interactions, and explain classical mechanics.

Faraday's discovery had equally important practical implications. It became the basis for many types of motors and for his own invention of the electric dynamo, the ancestor of the modern power generator. Faraday's dynamo took the production of electricity beyond the scale of what could be created by a simple battery. It created the kind of industrial scale energy that would make many of Edison's inventions possible.

After years of dreaming, Edison decided to throw in his lot as a full-time inventor. In Boston, his first patent (filed October 1868, granted No. 90,646), for a telegraphic vote-recording machine, was a commercial bust. His second patent (filed January 1869), for a stock ticker, was more successful, but arguments with his backers led them to sell the rights, and Edison was left with nothing. Finally, Edison completed work on a dream he had had for a decade—a duplex telegraph that could send more than one message across a line. Having secured an $800 loan, he tested it between Rochester, New York, and New York City. It didn't work. With the unpaid loan still outstanding, the penniless vagabond borrowed yet another few dollars from some luckless friend and took the boat to New York City. Ever the optimist, Edison was sure that in this new city his prospects would change.

Market speculation in gold saved Thomas Edison, but not because someone gave him a lucky investment tip. Edison's savior was a telegraphic device, the Law's indicator, a machine that continuously transmitted the price of gold to brokers' offices around Wall Street. In a historic twist of fate, Edison happened to be inspecting the complex device out of personal curiosity when it broke down. Chaos ensued as frantic messenger boys flooded the office with escalating demands for gold quotes. While its inventor, Samuel Laws, stood by dumbfounded, Edison found the problem (a spring that had fallen off and dropped behind two gear wheels) and fixed it. He was immediately employed, and by using his salary as seed capital, he finally succeeded in patenting several useful telegraphic inventions. One, an improved stock ticker, by 1871 had generated half a million dollars in orders from Western Union.

Edison's early telegraphic patents (150 of them) used *analogy* to elaborate on earlier designs but departed little from convention. However, as his creations became bolder, his use of the tools of innovation became more evident and more diverse. The "quadruplex" telegraph, for instance, was Edison's boldest brainchild up until that time. It allowed currents moving in opposite directions (previously patented by Stearns) as well as currents moving in the same direction (Edison's Holy Grail) to all flow over a single line. What allowed the invention of the quadruplex was *changing point of view.* Almost always, Edison drew a picture in order to "see" an idea. In this case, the design still eluded him, so he built a pump in which water could be forced to flow back and forth between valves, and he used this to imagine how electricity would flow between circuits. The quadruplex was a major advance in the efficiency of telegraphic function; it generated plenty of capital for Edison's new endeavors.

What came next was not a stride toward more ingenious patents, but a catapult. And it was accomplished with a *frame shift* but not one that produced a single invention; instead one that produced an entirely novel approach to invention. In 1876 in a New Jersey pasture overlooking the railway line between Philadelphia and New York, the ever ambitious designer built a barn-like structure that would became the first-ever factory for industrial creativity. He called it Menlo Park. All of the latest and best equipment, a set of tools and instruments like none that had ever been accumulated into a single private laboratory, stocked it. Expert technicians made up the most accomplished of staff. Menlo Park broke all customary assumptions that inventors worked alone and on the edge of privation. Today, a century later, industrial research and development (R & D) laboratories are a requisite part of organizations from IBM to General Electric to Microsoft. Menlo Park, the first industrial laboratory, was an idea that jumped beyond any of Edison's contemporary's imaginings.

The structure of Menlo Park, 100 feet long and 30 feet wide, was daring not only for its equipment and size. It was also an impudent expression of Edison's expectations. Edison famously told the physicist George Beard that Menlo Park would turn out "a minor invention every ten days and a big thing every six months or so." As ridiculously boastful as that sounded, Edison surpassed his prediction. Over a period of six years, Menlo Park produced about 400 inventions, or about an invention every six days. At Menlo Park, Edison *expanded the question* of invention from, How does one design a new device? to, What is the maximum quantity and pace of useful inventions that a crack team can produce?

The level of productivity at Menlo Park was not one that anyone, even Edison, could have achieved alone. It required the *power of a group.*

Edison's acolytes, many of whom stayed with him for decades, brought a wide variety of technical skills. Moreover, Edison had an eye for finding the best talent. He brought them from all over the world: Charles Batchelor, chief mechanical assistant, from England; Ludwig Boehm, master glass-blower, from Germany; John Kruesi, clockmaker, from Switzerland. Mathematician Francis Upton, consulting engineer William Hammer, and draftsman Samuel Mott came from America. Their contractual work schedule was six days a week, ten hours a day, but because Menlo Park was in the middle of nowhere, the workday generally extended well beyond that. To motivate his team, Edison allowed his expert technicians to drive the day-to-day progress, and he organized financial incentives so that the men often shared in profits.

Edison had a gift for concurrently juggling *induction and deduction*. On the one hand, his ability to manage the particulars of multiple experiments at once is legend. It was said that at one point he had 44 simultaneous ventures going on in Menlo Park. Edison himself oversaw every facet of the simultaneous projects, getting updates and bringing suggestions. He could divide up tasks into discrete pieces and distribute these to his stable of able technicians while never allowing his vision to waiver. At the same time, he lived by deduction. He once remarked to an associate, "It has been just so in all of my inventions. The first step [in invention] is always intuition and comes with a burst." That is, Edison's driving vision derived from an internal progression of logic, or even dreams. The execution, on the other hand, was a long climb up a ladder consisting of empiric, objective rungs.

Perhaps the central essence of Edison's genius was his practicality —his *recombination* of not only induction with deduction but of invention with business. This was not only a rearrangement but a *reversal* of then-current views that science and technology were altruistic. Edison, as would any good businessman, prioritized the work of Menlo Park not to meet society's needs but to meet society's wants—that is to respond to critical market demand. It was a capitalist brand of science. Just as the market set prices and thereby values, so Edison valued commercial considerations in deciding what he and his team would invent. Ultimately, this anti-romantic practicality reversed the basic philosophy of invention. And it made industrialization on the scale of Menlo Park a financial success.

Edison's first triumph at Menlo Park—indeed the invention that earned him the name "the Wizard of Menlo Park"—was the phonograph. Without question, the phonograph was a transformative innovation. It changed the world into a place wherein machines talked. When set to "play," the device would shock an audience by greeting them with a recorded message inquiring about their health, asking what they thought of this new gadget, and bidding them a cordial good night.

The innovative methodology behind the phonograph derived from Edison's ability to *rearrange and combine* things that already existed. A first input built on the work of Alexander Graham Bell, who had patented the first practical telephone in February 1876. Originally, it worked like this: a thin soft-iron disk, or diaphragm, was placed near a magnet wrapped in copper wire. The sound waves from a voice striking the diaphragm made it vibrate. This produced impulses in the copper magnetic coil attached to the diaphragm, which induced a current over a line. At the other end, a receiving diaphragm was set to vibrate in accord with these electrical impulses, thereby reproducing the original sounds. Bell's contraption, although a media hit, was far from perfect. It produced sounds that were soft and indistinct, and it could only send or receive, not both. An improvement that Bell patented in January 1877 marginally improved the voice quality and allowed both the sender and receiver to talk over the same line. Nonetheless, the telephone was not ready for long-distance communication.

Edison fixed that. His patent application in February 1878 both improved the telephone's range and its fidelity. The problem of range was resolved by replacing the line with an induction coil, through which a battery's flow would produce much stronger electrical impulses. The problem of sound quality was tackled by the invention of the carbon grain microphone. Carbon grains, Edison had previously discovered, changed their resistance in response to changes in pressure. By *deduction*, he now guessed that carbon's elasticity could prove beneficial in transmitting voice vibrations. Indeed, the changing resistance of carbon in response to the movement of the telephone's diaphragm dramatically improved the transmitted volume and voice quality and became the standard used in the manufacture of telephones for a century.

The second input that Edison would rearrange to invent the phonograph was the telegraph repeater. Only months before his patent application for the carbon microphone, Edison applied for a patent to improve telegraphy, a device designed for "indenting upon a sheet of paper [actually, embossing upon a disk revolving in spiral pattern on a platter] the characters received from a distant station, and using such sheet to transmit the same message, thus providing an automatic device for transmitting the same message more than once from one station to different stations." In other words, the telegraphic repeater could record, store, and later play messages. It was a direct prelude to the phonograph; what the telegraph repeater did for Morse code, the phonograph did for the human voice.

One final input influenced Edison's thinking about the phonograph. In 1837, Leon Scott had produced a machine called a "phonautograph." The apparatus involved a sheet of paper coated with lampblack and fixed to a rotating cylinder. Onto this, a pig's bristle fixed to a diaphragm traced a pleasant visual pattern, representing the sound vibrations from a voice. Although it was only a parlor toy that created a pleasant image, it represented a critical step in translating between sound and a tangible representation thereof.

Interestingly, the rearrangement of these building blocks happened almost spontaneously for someone paying close enough attention. The voice became an instrument of telegraphy when, during experiments on the carbon microphone, Edison attached a short needle to a diaphragm so that when the diaphragm vibrated (though its sound could not pierce his deafness), the needle pricked his finger. Meanwhile, the telegraph repeater became an instrument of the voice. Edison noticed that while the stylus was zipping along recording dots and dashes, a spring that was a part of the apparatus began to hum. Edison commented at the time that its almost musical quality sounded like an indistinct human voice.

After several months of trial and error, the components and materials that Edison was putting together, pulling apart, and putting back together again started to create a meaningful whole. Just after Thanksgiving in 1877, Edison recorded in his notebook a sketch of what would become the first phonograph. It consisted of two parts: (1) a spiral grooved, brass cylinder mounted on a feed screw and covered with a thin, pressed sheet of tin foil; (2) a stylus connected to the center of a diaphragm, which was in turn attached to a telephone mouthpiece. Shouting into the mouthpiece while winding the crank caused the vibrating diaphragm to move the stylus along the tin foil, creating an imprint. Then the foil was rewound and a corresponding playback stylus was applied while re-cranking the machine at the same pace of the original recording.

Remarkably, John Kruesi, Edison's ingenious craftsman, upon receiving the drawing and being famously told, "The machine must talk," produced a viable prototype. When Edison shouted into the mouthpiece, "Mary had a little lamb," the ditty replayed audibly. Edison declared that he "was never so taken aback in all my life." Edison was not the only one. The phonograph was a sensation. Hordes descended on Menlo Park, and the news was carried around the world. Oddly, over the next ten years, Edison did little to commercialize the phonograph. He left much of the job of perfecting it to Alexander Graham Bell and others.

In the meantime, Edison completed the invention for which he is best known, which earned him his greatest number of patents (389), and which became his first mammoth commercial success—the light bulb. Most commentators say that perfecting the incandescent light was more plodding than perceptive, since they maintain that the invention was a simple elaboration of previous designs. Work by other inventors had, in fact, by the 1830s and 1840s established many of the attributes of the modern light bulb. James Lindsay, Warren De la Rue, John Starr, Alexander Lodygin, Jean Robert-Houdin, Joseph Swan, and Heinrich Göbel had designed electrical source lamps in which light emanated from a glowing filament. Some had even created a vacuum within a glass bulb to avoid oxidation of the wire. These attempts produced lamps that worked crudely. However, the devices' shortcomings, including being short-lasting, expensive to produce, and drawing too much current, made them impractical for commercial use.

Skeptics suggested that anyone could have eventually overcome these limitations. That is unlikely. The technical problems that had foiled previous attempts in the hands of others were not minor. They were embedded within the existing frame. The design in the hands of Edison only succeeded because he *frame shifted*.

First, for Edison a light bulb was not just a light bulb. It was one component of a system. Edison imagined the question not in terms of a single device, but in terms of an expansive system of lighting. Second, the long-held assumption that incandescent lamps needed to be of low resistance, Edison realized, was wrong. Low resistance filaments exacerbated several of the shortcomings that hindered commercialization; even worse, within a system of lighting, such problems would be amplified. These frame shifts caused Edison to take a completely different scientific approach to distributed illumination.

Edison's first frame shift involved *expansion* beyond a bulb to a whole. Neil Baldwin's biography, *Einstein: Inventing the Century,* describes Edison calling in the media and announcing to journalists his vision that what was needed was to build an entire electric power system. "All parts of the system must be constructed with reference to all other parts, since in one sense, all parts form one machine," he said. The inventor then allowed backers to set up the Edison Electric Light Company "to own, manufacture, operate, and license the use of various apparatus used in producing light, heat or power by electricity." Notably, both events occurred more than a year prior to his successful refinement of the light bulb and even before he had embarked on any serious research. Although one of Edison's most famous aphorisms was "Invention is one percent inspiration and 99 percent perspiration," the man was always ahead of himself with bold visions and driving aspirations. In this particular case, he got too far ahead, since he had raised expectations so publicly and so prematurely. Nonetheless, he was correct in envisioning and ultimately building all components of a distributed system of lighting, in which the bulb was only a part.

The second frame shift was to reimagine the laws of electricity. The electrical axioms that underpinned Edison's conception of a system of incandescent lamps came from Ohm's law. The problem was that Ohm's law had been consistently misunderstood by university-educated physicists. Ohm's law, proposed by the German physicist Georg Ohm in 1827, is the guiding mathematical principle that links various components of electricity. Expressed as $I = V/R$, the law states that the electrical current (I) flowing between two points varies directly with the potential difference (V) across the points. Thus, amps of current are greater with higher voltage. At the same time, amps of current are higher with reduced resistance (R).

Imagine two buckets of water connected by a hose. When one bucket is lifted, gravity forces water through the hose to the other bucket. Voltage can be thought of as the potential difference in pressure or the difference in height between the two buckets. Electric charge is the quantity of electrons in the system, analogous to the quantity of water. Current, measured in amperage, is the flow rate, or the amount of water leaving one bucket for the other. Resistance can be produced by partially blocking the hose. More water flows (more current) when the lifted bucket is suspended higher (higher voltage) and when the hoses are opened wide (lower resistance). Again, Ohm's law says that current is greater with larger voltage and with lower resistance.

Edison believed that a lighting system had to function using fixed voltage. In the case of buckets, this would equate to all being at the same height. Edison came to the conclusion of consistent voltage through his own *analogy*: to gas lamps, the only system of domestic lighting that existed at Edison's time. Gas was transported through a vestigial system of pipes. While hazardous (gas leaked into water sources, readily exploded, and caused dizziness and headaches), gas served as an example of a distributed system of lighting. Edison realized that gas pipes created consistent lighting when gas flowed at a constant pressure. Similarly, current would create a consistent electrical system if connected by wires carrying a single voltage.

Edison's understanding of Ohm's law came from his gut. It was the job of Menlo Park's first mathematician, the Princeton-trained Francis

Upton, to provide the careful calculations that confirmed the boss's famed intuition. In an oft-repeated story, Edison tested the newly hired Upton by handing him a pear-shaped glass bulb. "What is its cubic content in centimeters?" Edison asked. An hour later, as Upton had just drawn the shape on a piece of paper to calculate the geometry, Edison reappeared, demanding his answer. Upton requested more time, to which Edison replied that the answer should have been obvious by now. Simply fill the bulb with water and then spill the water into a graduated cylinder and measure the volume, Edison told the chagrined mathematician.

Upton's task was to prove another of Edison's beliefs about an electrical system—that lamps within a system of lighting needed to have high resistance. All previous attempts at developing light fixtures had used carbon or platinum filaments of low resistance. Based on Ohm's law, Edison knew that low resistance at a given voltage means increased current flow. But he *deduced* that increased current would be infeasible. First, more current requires conduction through larger lines. When Upton calculated the amount of high-cost copper wire needed to conduct enough electricity through a low resistance parallel circuit, he found that the copper requirement was unacceptably great. Moreover, more current would produce more heat and would thus more quickly burn out filaments.

In fact, because the filaments would exist in a distributed system, Edison realized they would need to be of particularly high resistance. A single power line distributing electricity to a number of fixtures, as Edison envisioned it, is called a parallel circuit. In a parallel circuit, the total resistance $(1/R_{total})$ becomes $1/R + 1/R + 1/R$. The more lamps connected, the larger becomes $1/R$ but the smaller becomes R. For example, two resistors in parallel, each having 10 ohms of resistance $1/10 + 1/10$, produce a total resistance of $2/10$ or $1/5$: 5 ohms. Although it seems counterintuitive, the more resistance in each component of a parallel circuit, the lower the total resistance. A smaller resistance once again equated to greater current flow and a return to the problem of needing more copper wiring. A parallel system, then, needed even higher resistance within each bulb to maintain sufficiently low current flow. Once again, Upton did the math and calculated a maximum efficiency. As Edison had guessed, the magical formula was high resistance, high fixed voltage, and low current. Such a system would use only one-hundredth the amount of copper conductor that had been used previously. With this remarkable piece of frame-shattering intelligence, Edison set out to light New York!

But finding a filament of sufficiently high resistance was no small task. Edison knew that high resistance could be achieved by reducing the cross-section of the bulb's fibers (similar to using small bore hoses). Thinner filaments would also have the advantage of better dispersing heat and thus being less likely to melt. But the thinner the filament, when subjected to the large amount of heat produced by a high voltage system, would more often it would fuse or liquify. At this point, Edison noticed that the gas emitted by heated metals lowered their melting points. To attain the highest possible melting point required removing all surrounding gas, that is, creating an almost perfect vacuum. Fortunately, his timing with respect to vacuum technology was perfect. Edison ordered the newest model Sprengel mercury pump from Europe, and when its arrival tried his patience, he dispatched Upton to Princeton to borrow the only one that resided in America. With this, he would ultimately create a vacuum to one millionth of an atmosphere.

By now, Edison's laboratory and the cadre of craftsmen and technicians who inhabited it had grown substantially—and none too soon. Teams were dispatched, each taking a *dissected* component of the larger project of developing the new light bulb. One perfected the pumping methods to maximize the vacuum. A second sought the perfect material to light within a sealed vacuum globe. Finally, a third group worked on designing a dynamo that could power a multiple circuit at a high, constant voltage.

To find the perfect filament, Edison's use of the *power of groups* allowed rapid-fire, serial testing of about 1,600 different fibers. Platinum seemed to have promise, but it was expensive and rare. Finally, Edison returned to his old friend, carbon. Lampblack was a common by-product of coal-burning chimneys. Edison was in the habit of kneading the carbon cakes to give his fingers something to do as he thought. Legend has it that one day, while kneading lampblack into a thinner and thinner cord, he had a "Eureka" moment. The true story is likely less serendipitous in

that Upton's calculations had shown that a remarkably thin carbon filament (no thicker than 16/1000 of an inch) was needed in order to achieve
the required resistance. At one-tenth the diameter that anyone had previously achieved, Edison and his team took many attempts to reach the
specifications via a carbonized sturdy thread.

On October 22, 1879, a bulb with this filament construction burned
for 13.5 hours before the glass cracked. Immediately thereafter, a slightly
improved version burned 40 hours. The men had not slept for two days, yet
the second test's success set up a great cheer. Edison, in contrast, appeared
contemplative and then reportedly said, "If it can burn that number of
hours I know I can make it burn a hundred."

The following month, the light bulb patent that Edison submitted
included a variety of recipes for creating the filament and within several
months the team had developed carbonized bamboo, lasting over 1,200
hours. The idea for bamboo came from Edison's recollection of examining
a few threads from a fishing pole he had used during a trip to Wyoming a
year earlier. Bamboo, Edison recalled, was a more steadfast material than
cotton thread. It was a testament to his remarkable powers of *observation*
and his memory for detail. Moreover, it made for a beautiful analogy: the
tenacity of a bamboo lamp filament matched the tenacity of its inventor.

In 1880, Edison patented an electrical distribution system and founded
the Edison Illuminating Company, the first inventor-owned electric utility. In 1882, he switched on his Pearl Street generating station's power
and provided 110 volts of direct current (DC) to 59 customers in lower
Manhattan. Meanwhile, Edison Lamp Works, the bulb manufacturing
company, in its first year of operation produced 50,000 lamps. The generation of DC current, which Edison had worked to perfect, ultimately
lost out to Nikola Tesla's invention of alternating current (AC). Tesla's AC
current, promoted by Edison's archrival George Westinghouse, traveled
over far longer distances than did DC without loss of power. AC could be
stepped up to high voltages for long-distance carriage and then stepped
down for distribution to customers. Edison mounted a "war" to try to convince the American public that AC was dangerous, but even the Wizard
could not win that one.

EDISON ANNOTATED: THE USE OF TOOLS OF INNOVATION

Thomas Edison, iconic inventor of things with a use, is widely recognized as one of America's greatest creative geniuses. His mental processes show us that genius inventors have everything in common with genius scientists. His curiosity, autonomy, and determination drove him to ceaselessly question previous assumptions. Despite his focus on practicality, ideas were what interested him. Edison used virtually every imaginable tool of innovation.

Edison's greatest mastery was for the tool of *rearrangement and recombination*. The consummate *observer*, Edison could recognize things that might turn out to be useful, discard things that were not, and distinguish between the two. He was an *analogy* detective, a pack rat for objects that might be put to a different use.

Even *groups* were put to a different use by Edison. One of his greatest *frame shifts* was not a device but a place—Menlo Park. At Menlo Park, technicians in multidisciplinary teams, wielding state-of-the-art equipment, created the first industrial laboratory. Such teams had a unique opportunity to concentrate on sub-components of a *dissected* problem. Teams that worked in parallel on the invention of the light bulb included those that perfected internal vacuum and those that designed a dynamo that could power a multiple circuit at a high, constant voltage.

Menlo Park not only epitomized the tools of *groups* and *dissection*, but also that of *reversal*. The then-current view was that science and technology were altruistic. Edison believed that technology needed to meet the demands of the market. Rather than inventing what people (in his view) needed, he invented what people wanted. Of course, in doing so, he needed to imagine the wants of consumers, that is, to *change his point of view*. He could imagine the usefulness of improving telegraph technology because he had been a telegraph operator, but he had to envisage broader priorities in seeking to invent the phonograph and the film projector.

Every aspect of Edison's thinking was larger than life. He was able to solve the problem of the invention of electric light by *expanding* beyond the question of how to create a bulb to the question of how to construct a whole system of lighting. He was not satisfied with remaining a back-room inventor but instead became the entrepreneur creator of Western Electric. His was a mind that perhaps will never be replicated, but it was also a mind that is not inexplicable. The idea leaper (*deductionist*), the obsessive detail person, the introvert, the group leader—Edison was nothing if not complex. But the process by which he invented can be understood, at least in part, through the lens of the tools of innovation.

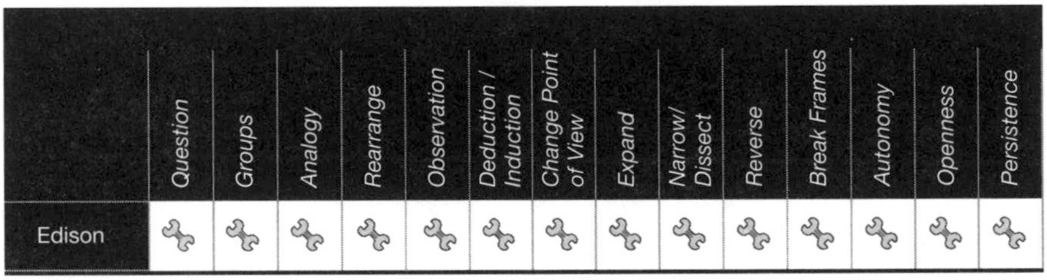

	Question	Groups	Analogy	Rearrange	Observation	Deduction / Induction	Change Point of View	Expand	Narrow/ Dissect	Reverse	Break Frames	Autonomy	Openness	Persistence
Edison	✀	✀	✀	✀	✀	✀	✀	✀	✀	✀	✀	✀	✀	✀

Figure 9.1. Edison: Tools and Characteristics

10

Two Luminous Lives

Marie Curie and Ernest Rutherford

At the turn of the twentieth century, two scientists in countries on opposite sides of the English Channel revealed the mysteries of radiation: Marie Sklodowsky Curie, in France, and Ernest Rutherford, in England. Both were forces of nature—individuals who are revered as being among the most elite in the history of science. Both were immigrants: Curie from Poland, Rutherford from New Zealand. Both were awarded the Nobel Prize for fundamental discoveries (Curie won two). The final resting place for both established them as national heroes: the Paris Panthèon for Curie and Westminster Abbey for Rutherford. Finally, both left scientific dynasties: Marie Curie's daughter Irene won the Nobel Prize in Chemistry, and a dozen of Ernest Rutherford's protégés won Nobel Prizes in science.

Nonetheless, Curie and Rutherford were very different kinds of innovators. Marie Sklodowsky Curie's goals were achieved through the tenacity of observation after observation. She shunned flashy guesswork. Her work was hugely influential in that she discovered the radioactive elements polonium and radium, but it did not involve revealing new truths about the atom—it did not employ frame shifting. In contrast, Ernest Rutherford used experimentation not so much as an end but as a means. Although considered to be one of the greatest experimentalists of his era, observations for him were a way to pry open flawed assumptions and to create seismic deductions. Rutherford changed the topography of science. He transformed fundamental beliefs about the nature of atoms and created the field of nuclear physics.

The dawn of the era of radiation, which launched the careers of Curie and Rutherford, is universally attributed to Wilhelm Roentgen, who in 1895 discovered X-rays. He was the lucky beneficiary of serendipity. Roentgen was experimenting with cathode tubes, popular at the time because they produced a mysterious light. An eerie green glow was produced by a battery hooked up to metal plates at the ends of a glass vacuum tube, which started a flash at the cathode (negatively charged) end and disappeared into the metal plate at the anode (positively charged) end. Many scientists wondered if this phenomenon had something to do with fluorescence, in which certain substances glow after absorbing energy, such as from sunlight. But no one really knew. Roentgen was tinkering with these "cathode rays" to see what he could discern. After wrapping one of the glass tubes in black paper so that the rays would not escape, he plunged the room into darkness to check the light seal. Suddenly, he noticed that a screen covered with barium-platinum cyanide, stored for another purpose several feet away, began to fluoresce. How had the rays escaped from the tube? The effect was jolting.

What came next was even more disconcerting. The reclusive Roentgen shut himself up for weeks trying to understand how the tube could transmit rays through a covering. He changed one parameter and then another. At one point, he tried putting his hand between the source and the screen. On the screen was transmitted his eerie skeleton.

In December 1895, Roentgen's paper on X-rays, delivered to the Physical-Medical Society of Würzburg, electrified the world of science. Roentgen's report included photographic plates of X-rays, one of which was the hand and bulging ring of his wife Anna. Her comment was, "I have seen my death"—words that reflected the cataclysm the photographs caused in the scientific establishment. What could this absolutely weird phenomenon mean? The following year, the topic of X-rays generated over 1,000 scientific papers and 49 books or pamphlets. The first Nobel Prize in Physics in 1901 was awarded to Roentgen.

Henri Becquerel, heir to a scientific dynasty of fluorescence and phosphorescence experts, made the next great discovery. Being a phosphorescence man, he wondered if that phenomenon, the storing and emitting of light after sun exposure, might explain X-rays. From his library of phosphorescing materials, he tested for X-rays in one after another. Finally, placing a salt of the element uranium (potassium uranyl disulfate) on a photographic plate that had been wrapped in black paper and then exposing the crystals and plate to light, he hit the jackpot. Where the uranium had laid there was a shadow. The uranium appeared to be emitting rays, like X-rays, that could penetrate what should have been light-impervious paper. If the uranium was fluorescing, as he guessed, then the effect was driven by sunlight.

He had jumped to just the wrong conclusion but as luck would have it, serendipity revealed his error and brought him fame. Paris was cloudy for the next several days. So his next experiment never got direct sunlight. He put it in a drawer and some days later, in a pique of frustration he decided to process the photographic plate, thinking he would find a faint impression. What he saw was an image that was surprisingly intense. He had discovered that the uranium itself (not stored sunlight) emitted the rays. It was not fluorescence—it was something entirely unknown. Becquerel took the opportunity to call the effect Becquerel rays, and for his discovery he received the Nobel Prize in Physics two years after Roentgen.

Few scientists could figure out what the Becquerel rays emitted from uranium might be good for so, unlike X-rays from cathode tubes, they gained little research popularity. Lord Kelvin, the brilliant English physicist, however, discovered that Becquerel rays could be measured since they produced electrical activity in the air around them, also called ionization. Marie Curie, who at that moment happened to be searching for a topic for her doctoral dissertation was attracted by the ability to measure the rays and also by the obscurity (and thus lack of competition) in the field. She decided to make uranium rays the topic of her work.

Marie Sklodowsky Curie was a woman of firsts, as her second daughter, Eve, points out in an adoring biography. She was the first woman to receive a doctorate in France, the first woman anywhere to receive a doctorate in physics, the first female professor at the prestigious Sorbonne in Paris, and the first person to receive two science Nobel Prizes. Born in 1867 in Warsaw, Marie descended from a maternal and a paternal line of educators. Both sides of the family had lost their fortunes through disastrous involvements with Polish national movements. This left the children penniless—so much so that Marie had to first support her sister, Bronislawa, in her medical studies in Paris before embarking on her own higher education. Not until 1891, at the advanced age of 24, did Marie follow Bronislawa to Paris to pursue degrees in physics and chemistry and subsequently in mathematics at the Sorbonne. Her meager finances forced her to live in a tiny garret and to tutor at night. Even at that, she barely made ends meet. In rigidly hierarchical French society, she had two major strikes against her: she was an immigrant and a woman. She spent the rest of her life burdened by a sense of isolation and resentment about being an outsider, struggling to gain acceptance.

Her husband, Pierre, would be her perfect complement both temperamentally and professionally. Home-schooled and slow to seek a Ph.D., which would have garnered him a mainstream university teaching position, Pierre took a position at the second-rate industrial school, the École Municipal de Physique et Chimie Industrielle. There, his growing reputation in the field of magnetism went relatively unheeded. He was afforded only the most rudimentary laboratory and this he shared with his new wife. Nonetheless, two years after their marriage, Marie and Pierre had produced a daughter, Irene, and fashioned an intense, collaborative professional life.

Pierre's brilliance at invention would open the door to Marie's first major discovery. Together with his brother, Jacques, he had invented a sensitive device to measure electrical charge, called an electrometer. With this device at its core, he and Marie erected out of leftover grocery crates a wild contraption called an "ionizing chamber" to support her doctoral thesis experiments on uranium. At the bottom of the device was a metal disc on which a test substance was placed. This disc was charged, and if the substance placed upon it could ionize the air, a second disc suspended above would become electrified. The time it took for the upper charge to become saturated (reach a maximum charge), as measured by the electrometer, depicted the intensity of the substance's radiation. Marie Curie spent hours, days, weeks, stopwatch in hand, precisely calibrating the electrometer and resolutely clicking off careful *observations*. These were to prove decisive.

After confirming the work of Becquerel and Kelvin about uranium's ionizing current, Marie Curie pressed on with signature determination to test every known element she could get her hands on. At first, this led to nothing. Thus she moved on to further *dissect the question* by trying minerals that represented mixtures of elements. Again, nothing.

In February 1898 her laboratory notebook recorded that the mineral pitchblende, a common source of mined uranium, produced ionization on the electrometer about fourfold greater than expected. This must have been a complete shock, but Marie's notebook simply recorded the value and then outlined a careful retracing of her steps. She retested pure uranium and methodically evaluated a variety of uranium-containing compounds, including pitchblende. Once again, the pitchblende was far more radioactive than uranium. In exertions that now became relentless, she tested a host of other minerals and came across another, aeschynite, also emitting more ionization than pure uranium, although it contained no uranium at all. These observations were so unexpected and so intriguing that Pierre abandoned his own experiments on magnetism to work beside Marie. Pierre had already shown Marie the *power of groups* and their synergy would now become decisive.

The findings of high activity in pitchblende and aeschynite triggered two *deductive* epiphanies for which the Curies were awarded the 1903 Nobel in Physics, along with Becquerel: (1) that the minerals contained a new element; and (2) that radiation revealed some fundamental, unknown property of atoms. In a paper on "Rays Emitted by Uranium and Thorium Compounds," presented to the French Academy of Sciences by her mentor Gabriel Lippmann (because neither she nor Pierre was a member authorized to present for themselves) in April 1898, Marie wrote that her findings "... [lead] us to believe that these minerals may contain a much more active element than uranium." How did she draw this prescient conclusion? Likely it was by means of *analogy* to another recent elemental discovery.

The periodic table of the elements was first proposed by the Russian chemist Dmitri Mendeleyev in 1871. By arranging elements in rows by ascending atomic weight relative to hydrogen (with an assigned atomic weight of one), he discovered a subtle magic. The columns revealed remarkable chemical similarities. He gave the table the name "periodic" because the chemical properties of the elements are mystically cyclic. Mendeleyev was clever not only in uncovering this reality but in realizing that of the 73 elements known at the time, a continuous array put some in the wrong columns. So, he left spaces in several cells on the assumption that there existed as yet undiscovered elements. He was right. Brilliant minds took little time filling in the blanks with new elemental finds.

Inert gases such as argon and helium joined the table in 1894–1895 and became the analogy from which Curie probably drew insight. Lord Rayleigh, Cavendish professor at Cambridge (as we will see, the first in an eminent line of endowed Cavendish professors who shaped the story of radiation), observed that nitrogen captured from the air had a slightly higher atomic weight than nitrogen attained from the earth. Although the finding was subtle, Rayleigh focused his subsequent work on what might be the cause. Possible explanations were that the air contained an impurity which was heavier than nitrogen. Alternatively, it could be that dirt contained an impurity lighter than nitrogen. Rayleigh pursued the latter explanation, which proved to be wrong. William Ramsay, at the University of London, pursued the former. In an experiment involving the removal of all of the oxygen, carbon dioxide, water, and nitrogen from a sample of clean air, he isolated a previously unknown gas heavier than nitrogen with the unusual property that it refused to combine with any other gas. He called it "argon" (Greek for "inert" or "lazy"). This, along with his further discovery of an entire family of related, inert atmospheric gases including neon, krypton, xenon, and helium, won him the 1904 Nobel Prize in Chemistry and a knighthood. Marie, who was a prolific reader of scientific writings in German, French, Polish, and English, almost surely knew this story. Her assumption that pitchblende contained some unknown impurity, a new element was thus a reasonable guess, based on similar logic.

Marie's report on the emissions from uranium and thorium compounds included another striking interpretation. When measuring pure elements, the amount of radioactivity was directly correlated to the quantity of uranium or the quantity of thorium present. She suggested that if one unit of an element gave one unit of radiation, then radiation must somehow be directly linked to some unitary elemental structure. Not through direct observation but by *deduction* did she suggest that radiation had to represent some innate quality—some "signature" of the atom.

However, none of the next five years of Marie's life (or thereafter) would be spent pursuing this clue about the fundamental nature of elements, one that would ultimately lead to a massive frame shift. Instead, she continued her pursuit of the elusive new element. Working in a makeshift shed that provided little protection from the Parisian winters, she chemically stirred through huge vats containing tons of worthless uranium mining residue. Her hands became burned and deformed by radiation. Yet, slowly and methodically, she drew out not one new element, but two. One was initially admixed with bismuth, and she called it "polonium," in honor of her native land. The other was in the fraction containing barium and turned out to be an element with a level of radioactivity 100,000 times that of uranium—radium. These won her the 1911 Nobel Prize in Chemistry.

Marie had surely made major discoveries that helped to evolve science. To do so, she used the tools of innovation—*observation, analogy, dissecting the question, deduction/induction,* and *working in groups.* But she never challenged the constraints of accepted theory. The revolutionary job of smashing the conventional frame—and ultimately smashing the atom by revealing its innermost secrets—she left to scientists in a rival nation: J. J. Thomson and his outrageously creative protégé, Ernest Rutherford.

Like Marie Curie, Rutherford was the ultimate outsider. When he arrived on scholarship to Cambridge in 1895, there could have been almost no greater contrast between the usual students from manicured, private schools and this big, boisterous fellow with a glass-rattling laugh. Had it not been for two powerful characteristics that propelled Rutherford out of his family farm in New Zealand—brains and ambition—he might have never surpassed his uneducated father. But when the telegram arrived announcing that he had won the "Exhibition of 1851 scholarship" issued from the proceeds of the London World's Fair and given subsequently on a rotating basis to a single student from the colonies of Australia or New Zealand, he threw down his spade and famously cried, "That is the last potato I'll dig." Rutherford had already revealed a prodigious academic potential. He had won scholarships to a New Zealand high school (Nelson College) and university (University College, Canterbury), where he excelled in all subjects, particularly mathematics, physics, and astronomy. Friends later claimed that it was not so much that he was brilliant but that he had a unique combination of concentration, passion, and scientific instinct.

By the time he boarded the ship to London, Rutherford had demonstrated a capability in common with Pierre Curie: talent as an inventor. Like Pierre, Rutherford's inventions would serve him admirably in designing experiments. In his luggage, Rutherford carried an apparatus for receiving radio waves that he imagined would shape his future. Radio waves, discovered less than a decade earlier by Heinrich Hertz and soon to make a multimillionaire out of Guglielmo Marconi, were becoming all the popular rage. Once settled as a fellow in England's most prestigious physics laboratory, Cavendish at Cambridge, Rutherford began to perfect his radio equipment. Soon he could send signals through stone walls and over a range of up to 60 feet. But building a radiotelegraph system was not in Rutherford's future.

J. J. Thomson, the Cavendish professor and director of the Cambridge laboratory, became Rutherford's role model and drew the young man into the exploration of radiation. Using an apparatus that was a *rearrangement* of prior devices but that bore Rutherford's distinctive imaginative genius, the young trainee verified the ionization of air from Becquerel rays and X-rays. But he went further. These rays, he showed, were of two distinct types. One type had a sizable electrical charge and thus was strongly ionizing, but could not penetrate even a few sheets of aluminum foil. The other made less ionization but was more piercing. He called his two new categories of rays alpha and beta. These insights presaged the first glimpses inside the atom.

In 1897, two years after Roentgen's discovery, J. J. Thomson made a discovery that figuratively blew the atom apart. As with all rays, such as light, a debate raged between the Germans, who believed that cathode rays were waves, and the English, who believed that they were particles. Anyone who could show that the rays were altered by electromagnetic forces strengthened the case for particles, since such influences were not thought to alter waves. The trick was to alter the magnetic forces within a cathode tube so as to clarify whether cathode rays had a particulate mass and the electric forces to determine whether they had a charge. To go beyond previous failed attempts, Thomson *changed his point of view*. He imagined himself sitting in a cathode ray tube and dodging the "jolly little beggars," as Rutherford called them. Using this new viewpoint, he was able to devise a series of modified cathode tubes, which, by altering the placement of electric and magnetic forces, *dissected* their impact on the cathode rays. Thomson concluded from these experiments: "As the cathode rays . . . are deflected by an electrostatic force as if they were nega- tively electrified, and are acted on by a magnetic force in just the way in which this force would act on a negatively electrified body moving along the path of these rays, I can see no escape from the conclusion that they are charges of negative electricity carried by particles of matter."

Balancing the electric and magnetic forces within the apparatus, Thomson was able to discern the electric to mass ratio. These *observa- tions* and some shrewd *deductive* calculations led Thomson to deduce that the charged mass within cathode rays was a thousand times smaller than hydrogen, translating to a billionth of a billionth of a billionth of a gram. Thomson had made one of the great discoveries of the age—that the atoms within cathode rays carried within them "corpuscles," a name that was later changed to "electrons."

Atoms, prior to Thomson's startling discovery (for which he received the Nobel Prize in Physics in 1906 and was knighted in 1908), had been unquestioned as indivisible. For a century, scientific progress, including the periodic table, assumed that atoms were the smallest unit of matter, with each element represented by a fixed number and mass of atoms. According to this view, if elements could not be subdivided, then neither could atoms. Thomson's idea that atoms were composed of *sub*atomic structures shook the foundations of science.

But the mayhem had only just begun. The young Rutherford watched as Thomson used tools including *observation, changing point of view, deduction/induction,* and *dissecting the question.* Thompson's *frame shift* proposing subatomic particles made a formidable impression on the young protégé. No one could have hoped to be more dynamically propelled toward igniting a transformation in understanding the atom. Rutherford started by posing the *biggest, hairiest imaginable question.* Instead of Curie's question (How do substances give off radiation?), Rutherford asked, What is an overarching theory for the nature of matter?

Rutherford's first discernment about the nature of matter was that it is far more unstable than anyone had ever imagined. Taking his first faculty position at McGill University in Montreal after leaving Cambridge in 1898, Rutherford would spend nine years observing something incredible—that elements "transmute." Transmutation? The claim was even more disruptive than Thomson's theory of subatomic particles. It was alchemy—the changing of one "immutable" element into another—a process that, centuries before, had been refuted as impossible.

An anomaly, an unexpected *observation,* triggered Rutherford's transmutation discovery. It was an observation that Marie Curie had decided to ignore. Rutherford, in contrast, was obsessed by it. When he entered the room where his colleague R. B. Owens was measuring ionizations given off by the radioactive element thorium, the measurements in the air changed. It appeared that something as seemingly inconsequential as opening a door altered ionizing emanations. Further experiments showed that the gaseous substance emanating from thorium had, in Rutherford's words, "the power of producing radioactivity in all substances on which it falls." The Curies (a year earlier) had published that their entire lab was becoming radioactive. But they attributed this phenomenon to the laboratory storing and emitting energy—like good old-fashioned phosphorescence. Rutherford, in contrast, imagined radioactive contamination as just the *reverse*: not a gain of energy but its loss. Moreover, to Rutherford, emanation was something utterly radical—a property never before seen and fundamental to certain atoms. The Curies were continuing to work within the constraints of their circumscribed question, How do substances give off radiation? whereas Rutherford was thinking within the far more *expansive framework* of, What is an overarching theory for the nature of matter?

At this critical juncture, Rutherford benefitted from the *power of groups*. Frederick Soddy, a chemist trained at Oxford, was drawn across the Atlantic by an advertisement for a university position in Toronto. As he had not bothered to first submit an application, Soddy's arrival was met with the disappointing news that the position had been filled. Fortunately, Soddy then proceeded to McGill, where he quickly became the other half of Rutherford's much-needed chemist-physicist team.

In a series of 19 papers written together at McGill, Rutherford and Soddy *dissected the question* of emanation into pieces such as: the nature of the emanating gas; the impact of emanation on its product and its parent; and an atomic description of these events.

First, Rutherford and Soddy identified the radioactive emanation from thorium as some kind of inert gas. By *analogy* to an experiment reported by William Crookes, they were able to discern its properties and its impact on its parent. Crookes had been able to chemically extract a gas from uranium (he called it uranium X) that had chemically distinct properties from its parent element and now contained all of the parent's radiation. Over the course of 1902, Rutherford and Soddy used a similar chemical process to produce thorium X. As they reported in several historic papers, thorium X was a gas, chemically distinct from thorium, yet it removed all of thorium's radioactivity. Moreover, the radioactivity in thorium X decayed, losing half its radioactivity in four days, then half that again in another four days, and so on, down to an undetectable limit. That is, thorium X's radioactivity was lost exponentially over time; this systematic and predictable loss, Rutherford realized, was a geologic clock.

What did all of this mean? The alteration from thorium into thorium X and from uranium into uranium X, Rutherford and Soddy argued, was not only due to the loss of radiation and electric charge but also due to the loss of atomic mass. At first, this was pure *deduction*—a logic that said that if an element changes chemical properties, it must be because it is changing atomic mass. Mixing *induction and deduction*, the physicist and chemist demonstrated that conversion of thorium to thorium X was not simply the loss of beta rays, which by then had been discovered to be Thomson's electrons, but instead a loss of alpha rays. Alpha particles, Rutherford later demonstrated, were the inert gas helium. Helium, which has two electrons but also two protons and thus an atomic mass of two, when lost from thorium explained why thorium changed not just its charge but its chemical properties. Thorium, minus helium, no longer had the same atomic mass; elements with new atomic masses are, by definition, dissimilar elements. Indeed, Rutherford discovered that, given enough time, all radioactive elements eventually emanate into other elements until they reach the element lead. That is, elements capable of radiation transmute or change from one elemental mass to another elemental mass—from one element to another.

Like Thomson's demonstration of electrons, Rutherford and Soddy's work on the transmutation of radioactive elements shattered a *frame;* indeed, it created a scientific shift that was nothing other than tectonic. It was a frame shift borne of persistent work and the use of many tools: *broadening the question, reversal, observation, analogy, dissecting the problem, the power of groups*, and *induction/deduction*.

The Curies found Rutherford's suggestion of transmutation to be absurd. Within two weeks of Rutherford and Soddy's 1902 paper, "The Cause and Nature of Radioactivity," the Curies shot back a paper in which they accused Rutherford and Soddy of making a premature rush to judgment. Again, in 1903, Pierre Curie and Rutherford crossed swords, with Curie questioning the "material nature of the emanation" and Rutherford responding that he was not claiming "ordinary chemical change" but instead "subatomic change." But the die was cast. While the Curies' thinking remained resolute, Rutherford had dragged science into the nuclear age.

Rutherford was not a sprinter but a marathoner. He won the 1908 Nobel Prize in Chemistry "for his investigations into the disintegration of the elements, and the chemistry of radioactive substances." In his acceptance speech, he quipped that he had seen many a transmutation in the laboratory, but none as impressive as the "instantaneous transmutation" of transfiguring him from a physicist into a chemist. Nonetheless, it was a coveted distinction, one that for most scientists is achieved at the end of a career. But Rutherford was not "most scientists." His biggest discoveries were still before him.

How did this man, whose dominating yet fun-loving personality and volatile temper could induce both love and fear, accomplish so much so quickly? First, by all accounts, he was gifted at constructing equipment and experiments that facilitated access to the evidence needed to answer a question. Second, he was a man of powerful ambition. In a letter to his mother in 1902, he wrote, "I have to keep going as there are always people on my track. I have to publish my present work as rapidly as possible in order to keep in the race." Finally, the boldness of his imagination knew no bounds. More than once, colleagues suggested that he pause before leaping to some new deduction. But the big man from the backwoods was simply not capable of caution. As Rutherford developed a framework for subatomic alchemy, he seemed to also have developed a professional alchemy—an unerring ability to turn his temperament into gold.

The year following his Nobel, Rutherford conceived one of his most profound and legendary ideas. The process he used once again reveals his use of tools of innovation. By now Rutherford had returned to Europe, where the center of the world's scientific action was, to become professor and director of the physics institute at the University of Manchester. Marie Curie generously supplied the new lab its essential experimental ingredient—radium. Rutherford once again surrounded himself with the brightest young scientists of the age. One of these was an amiable German technician named Hans Geiger; another was a 19-year-old undergraduate student named Ernest Marsden.

Rutherford's newest insight grew out of appreciating an *observed* oddity. Years earlier, he had observed that the line of alpha particles shot out of a microscopic "gun" was not quite a clean straight line but was instead a bit hazy. Marsden was tasked with improving a piece of equipment that Rutherford and Geiger had invented to measure the speeds and trajectories of alpha particles. The device shot alpha particles ejected from radium through a tiny slit in a lead chamber. These travelled down a long vacuum tube and hit a target. Through a microscope, the hits appeared as "scintillations," or brief sparks of light. Rutherford and Geiger had noticed that alpha particles, when shot onto various types of foil (made up of elements like lithium or aluminum or gold), sometimes departed from a straight path.

Marsden's modification allowed the team (*a powerful group*) to see microscopic deflections through a broader angle, and this change made it apparent that the denser the element coating the foil, the greater the scatter. Indeed, a few alpha particles seemed to be so greatly deflected by the density of gold that they ricocheted back toward the marksmen. Rutherford's astonishment at this oddity he later explained this way: "It was almost as incredible as if you had fired a 15 inch shell at a piece of tissue paper and it came back and hit you." Geiger, Marsden, and Rutherford had no idea what it meant. After trying to *dissect the problem* through designing other permutations of the experiment, they all drifted off to other things—except Rutherford, who characteristically did not by any means give up.

At Christmas of 1911, Rutherford described to Geiger a radical, new "nuclear theory." For a year, he had contemplated the scattering of alpha particles; from those musings, he had slowly formulated a novel (still accepted today) atomic model. The empiric behavior of alpha particles hitting various targets was the basis for his reflection, but the theoretical construction of the atom was a logical leap of deduction. Thus, Rutherford's first tool in devising his new nuclear theory was *induction/ deduction*.

Rutherford's second tool was *changing point of view*. Figuring that the alpha deflections must represent an interaction with another atom, Rutherford tried to imagine what each subatomic particle was encountering. That is, he put himself in the place of an alpha particle. Over and over, he imagined the collisions, calculating the forces based on how he imagined the alphas and target-atoms each looked.

The use of yet a third tool of innovation was inherent as he engaged in this thought experiment: *dissecting the problem*. Rutherford had isolated a single aspect of his question of what an atom looks like. He focused on the atom's leading edge and within that simulated various possibilities.

A fourth innovation tool, *reversal*, helped Rutherford flip a key assumption underlying all previous atomic models. Previous models had assumed that the atom was mostly "something," such as electrons embedded in a kind of plum pudding (the J. J. Thomson model). Rutherford suggested that the atom was mostly nothing. Its central charge was positive and dense, accounting for 3,000/4,000ths of its mass. But the core, according to Rutherford, took up only one-billionth of the atom's volume. As Richard Reeves notes in his biography of Rutherford, the size of the nucleus as compared to the volume of the proposed atom was equivalent to a pin placed inside St. Paul's Cathedral.

Finally, Rutherford used *analogy*. Around this super-dense core (he coined the term "nucleus" two years later) orbited lightweight negative bits, as the planets orbit the sun. This completely bizarre and earth-shattering model, which Rutherford intuited from the behavior of the electrons in his scatter experiment, turned out to be utterly correct. Subsequent work by Niels Bohr, a theoretical physicist from Copenhagen who became one of Rutherford's coworkers, resolved the question of why electrons do not fall into the atom's core. Bohr calculated that this seemingly unwieldy arrangement would be perfectly stable assuming a combination of centrifugal force and Plank's quantum theory, which said that electrons jump into new orbits when they absorb energy. This contribution won Bohr the 1922 Nobel Prize in Physics. But it was Rutherford, through the use of *observation, working in groups, deduction/induction, dissecting the question, changing point of view, reversal,* and *analogy,* who had conceptualized the famous frame break that we now accept as the contemporary atomic model.

Rutherford's audacious theories had now made him the unequivocal father of nuclear physics. The rest of his life was punctuated with accolades: a knighthood in 1914; president of the Royal Academy of Sciences 1925–1930; elevation to the First Baron of Nelson, New Zealand; and the Cavendish professorship at Cambridge. He inherited the Cavendish professorship from Thomson in 1920 and revived that great laboratory from its Great War nadir. As his coworkers returned from their wartime experiences, they reenergized by each working on a project that they imagined might lead to a Nobel Prize. Indeed, a dozen of them would go on to win that honor. Rutherford himself would go on to be the first to artificially change one element into another (nitrogen into oxygen) and to predict the existence of the proton (his protégé Chadwick later discovered it); under his direction, John Cockcroft and E. T. S. Walton would smash the first atom.

Rutherford and Marie Curie, the two radiation scientists that were so alike and yet so different, had one final historic interaction. In 1910, Rutherford suggested the creation of a single international radium standard. Marie's life had by now had been arrested by tragedy. Pierre had been killed while crossing a busy Paris street in April 1906. She had been tainted by a subsequent scandal with a married man that had almost robbed her of her second Nobel Prize. Finally, her beloved radioactivity had ruined her health. Symptoms that included burns on her hands, chronic anemia, debilitating pains, cataracts, and ringing in her ears had almost entirely halted the prodigious pace of her early research.

By the time Rutherford discussed with her the possibility of appointing a committee to develop an international radiation standard, Marie's contemporaries widely considered her outdated and "obstinate." Nonetheless, she had the largest collection of purified radium in the world, and her name was synonymous with the element. She agreed to make the standard, but then insisted that it reside in her laboratory. Rutherford gently reminded her that such an important international measure must be held at some neutral location, such as the Bureau of Weights and Measures at Sèvres. Ultimately, Marie conceded. By February 1913, she was on a train carrying a glass vial that she had sealed herself, containing 21 milligrams of pure radium chloride, the basis for comparison for future radium measures on five continents.

Somehow this final partnership between the two greats seems particularly fitting. Together they changed the world. Curie had discovered radium; with that new element, Rutherford had opened a subatomic world.

CURIE AND RUTHERFORD ANNOTATED: THE USE
OF TOOLS OF INNOVATION

Both Curie and Rutherford were eminent innovators, yet while Rutherford produced a surprising series of transformative revelations, Curie's range of tools of innovation was more circumscribed. Their most powerful commonality was the use of *observation*. Curie's discovery that pitchblende produced ionization well in excess of what she expected incited her to engage in an inexorable search for radioactive minerals, precisely measuring and recording as she went. Rutherford was the consummate experimentalist, known for plucking unique glimpses of nature from the clarity of his senses. Similarly, both *dissected* problems—Marie spending years sifting through a series of approximations of plutonium and radium until she had isolated these elements. Meanwhile, Rutherford (along with Soddy) *dissected the question* of emanation into questions that allowed for the characterization of subquestions—for example, concerning its natural history—that ultimately led to the conclusion that elements are not immutable.

Analogy was also a shared tool that led both geniuses to *deduce* fundamental truths. Curie drew her deduction that pitchblende's unusual level of ionization reflected the presence of another, more powerful element from the logic that had led predecessors to the discovery of inert gases. Rutherford used analogy to deduce the structure of the atom: he posited that around a super-dense core orbited lightweight negative bits, just as the planets orbit the sun.

Finally, the work of both Curie and Rutherford was facilitated by close collaborators (the *power of groups*): Pierre in the case of Marie; Soddy, Bohr, and others in the case of Rutherford. The utility of these professional pairings was to create skill synergies—Pierre invented the equipment on which Marie made discoveries. Soddy as a chemist and Bohr as a theoretician complemented Rutherford's excellence in experimentation.

Beyond those tools, Rutherford used all of the others, such as *rearrangement, changing point-of-view, reversal,* and *expansion* to *break frames*. In hypothesizing the structure of the atom, Rutherford *changed his point of view*, figuratively placing himself inside an alpha particle. Moreover, he *flipped* the key assumption that the atom was mostly "something" (the plum pudding model) to an assertion that most of the volume of the atom contained nothing—electrons floating in space. His use of *rearrangement* commonly allowed Rutherford to create novel apparatuses that could reveal the unexpected. Finally, Rutherford was forever *expanding* into new questions and theories, not only concerning the disintegration of radioactive elements and the structure of the atom, but also the theory of subatomic particles, the demonstration of transmuting one element into another, and his prediction of the existence of the proton.

From all of this, Rutherford became the uncontested father of nuclear physics, breaking *frames* that elements are immutable and that one cannot change into another. The world was never the same after Rutherford had been in it. Yet, even his extreme breed of genius can be, with the use of tools of innovation, to some degree, understood.

	Question	Groups	Analogy	Rearrange	Observation	Deduction / Induction	Change Point of View	Expand	Narrow/ Dissect	Reverse	Break Frames	Autonomy	Openness	Persistence
Curie	🔧	🔧	🔧		🔧	🔧			🔧			🔧		🔧
Rutherford	🔧	🔧	🔧	🔧	🔧	🔧	🔧	🔧	🔧	🔧	🔧	🔧	🔧	🔧

Figure 10.1. Curie and Rutherford: Tools and Characteristics

11

Immunology and the Uncommon Man

Paul Ehrlich and Elie Metchnikoff

---

n 1895, Albert Nobel, the childless, multimillionaire industrialist who made his fortune perfecting dynamite and other instruments of societal destruction, left in his will a surprisingly constructive gift. The majority of Nobel's considerable fortune was directed to an annual awarding of prizes to selected individuals who had achieved the "greatest benefit to mankind." Although the giving of the first prize was postponed by the legal wrangling of Nobel's disappointed relatives, the behest ultimately created the world's most coveted recognitions in the fields of physics, chemistry, literature, physiology or medicine, and peace. Each Nobel Prize has a single purpose: to acknowledge exemplary contributions to a distinct area of endeavor. Arguably, then, the 1908 Nobel Prize in Physiology and Medicine, was unusual in that it had a duality of intent—to recognize the founders of the nascent field of immunology and to bring peace to its warring factions.

The two 1908 recipients were immunology's prime combatants. Paul Ehrlich was a disciplined German whose contributions were based on a methodical and industrious character, overlaid with skill as an experimental chemist. Ehrlich's work in the area of acquired immunity included his discovery of a variety of antitoxins and antibiotics and a proposed structure for antibodies. Ilyas Mechnikov (Westernized to Elie Metchnikoff) was a fiery Russian who envisioned a grand theory of innate immunity.

He twice seriously attempted suicide. Then, in an almost spiritual moment of insight, he crystallized a theory that immune cells constitute a vigorous warrior class involved in defense and self-regulation. It was not so much a simple discovery as it was a revolutionary doctrine.

Of the two innovators, science immediately recognized Ehrlich as a messiah. The work of Metchnikoff was forgotten for 40 years, and even when his theory was dusted off, most scientists failed to fully appreciate his genius. As described by Alfred Tauber in his retrospective on the scientist, "Metchnikoff has been assigned to the wine cellar of history, to be pulled out on occasion and celebrated as an old hero." Yet, while Ehrlich elaborated on a concept already accepted (antibodies and acquired immunity), Metchnikoff recognized an entirely new arm of the immune system—innate immunity.

Acquired and innate immunity are now considered inseparable in defining every organism's defense against infection. Understanding them led to the development of a wide array of prevention and treatment strategies that liberated millions from the vicissitudes of deadly contagion. Infectious disease was the leading cause of death throughout the world in the nineteenth century. Today, among developed countries, it is not even in the top seven. Sanitation, vaccination, and antibiotic use have tamed the scourges of our ancestors. Plagues that once emptied cities, lost wars, and toppled governments are now mostly limited to history books. No longer do we wait to name our babies, not knowing if they will live to see their first birthday. Immunology gave modern society the security of survival.

Immunologic theory, in brief, states that humans, along with almost all other animal and plant species, have developed an array of host defenses in the battle against viruses, bacteria, and other invaders that would otherwise kill us. There are two general arms of the immune system, each composed of cells and proteins. One is a non-specific first line of defense, called innate immunity. The other is specific to each particular pathogen, ensuring that with every new encounter, we are primed to respond ever more vigorously; this is called acquired immunity.

Innate immunity employs a cast of cells such as basophils, eosinophils, and phagocytes. This last category, phagocytes, discovered by Metchnikoff,

in turn includes what are now known as macrophages, monocytes, neu-
trophils, and dendritic cells. All of these cell types function in an ever
ready search-and-destroy capacity to remove infections and other invaders. Phagocytes are the backbone of the innate system (their name literally
means "eating cells"). They are non-specific in their aggression against
pathogens or foreign particles, wrapping them in cytoplasmic extensions,
then spraying them with deadly acidic enzymes. We now know that, in
addition to eating pathogens, phagocytes call into action the other, more
specific arm of the immune system—the adaptive response. Phagocytes
serve up foreign antigens to the cells of the adaptive system and they trigger signals, such as cytokines and complement that initiate blood vessel
dilation, trigger pain, and tell the adaptive cells to ramp up their recognition and destruction capabilities. Phagocytes also have a function
independent of defense against foreign invasion. They serve to clear cells
that die from old age or injury (called programmed cell death, or apopto-
sis). Thus "eating cells" not only protect against outsiders but, when war-
ranted, also protect us against ourselves.

The acquired arm of our system of immune defense, in contrast,
enlarges the fight against particular infections. Evolutionarily, the adaptive response is more modern than innate immunity, and it is thus found
in vertebrate animals but not in lower species. The adaptive response
brings in immune reinforcements so that pathogens encountered more
than once are each time attacked more forcefully. The main cellular sol-
diers in the adaptive response are lymphocytes (T and B). B lymphocytes
manufacture antibodies, which are like little protein bombs released
into the circulation to blow up antigens. T cells do hand-to-hand combat with infected cells, ripping into and destroying them. Either way,
upon encounter with a specific antigen, T and B cells produce clones and
thus can expand multifold. When an attack is over, the ranks of adaptive immune cells shrink back to about their original size, but they retain
memory cells, which can rapidly remobilize.

Immunology, the study of this array of defenses against pathogens,
grew out of the discovery of infectious agents and their ability to spread
contagion. Louis Pasteur and Robert Koch in the 1860s and 1870s

proposed and proved the germ theory of disease. Their discoveries that single "germs" caused single diseases and that instead of spontaneous generation, germs produced both spoilage and disease by spreading their spores through the air, created a kind of scientific gold rush. The gold was new pathogens and the payoff was vaccines and anti-toxins. Within a generation came the development of microbiology techniques to culture bacteria, the Gram's stain to detect bacteria in tissues, and the petri dish to grow bacteria.

Pasteur is credited with the manufacture of the first vaccine. It was a lovely case of serendipity. Upon leaving for vacation, Pasteur asked his assistant to infect chickens with cultures of chicken cholera. Instead, the assistant went on his own vacation and only later performed the experiment. When the leftover cultures that the assistant gave the hens did not sicken them, Pasteur decided to reuse the birds. But what happened next was just the opposite of what the scientist expected. Even when exposed to virulent bacteria, the previously injected chickens refused to die. The failed experiment was immediately recognized by Pasteur as one containing a priceless insight. Pasteur deduced that the chickens had been initially infected with sub-potent bacteria and that this had made them immune. Similar immunity from smallpox using a vaccine consisting of a close but less virulent relative (cowpox) had been achieved by Jenner a century earlier. Jenner achieved this breakthrough by noticing that milkmaids who contracted cowpox were almost never sickened during smallpox epidemics. In the case of smallpox, a related but weaker infection had produced a kind of natural vaccination and thereby created immunity. Analogously, Pasteur reasoned that a weakened cholera bacteria had serendipitously become a man-made vaccination and thereby generated immunity.

Working with his colleague Emil Roux, Pasteur guessed that the same logic might work for other diseases. In 1895, he vaccinated a boy named Joseph Meister, who had been mauled by a rabid dog, with rabies anti-toxin that had been grown in rabbit nerve tissue and then left out to dry. Had it not worked, Pasteur, who was not a physician, could have been ostracized or even indicted. Fortunately for the scientist and for history, the boy did not contract rabies, and Pasteur was hailed as a hero. Both the building of the famed Pasteur Institute (which would play a central role in Metchnikoff's later life) and the rush to create new vaccines and anti-toxins originated from this feat.

Paul Ehrlich was a protégé of Koch, who, with Pasteur, pioneered germ theory. Like Pasteur and Koch, Ehrlich drew on the *power of the group* that had created the "find-an-infection/create-a-vaccine" paradigm. Trained as a chemist, Ehrlich proposed one of the founding principles in immu-nology. It was that antibodies and antitoxins grow out of immune cells that are involved in pathogen attack. His idea was *analogous* to a contem-porary idea that the action of enzymes occurs when they bind to recep-tors "like a key in a lock." Ehrlich similarly envisioned antibodies to be keys capable of locking up pathogens. According to his theory, antibody side chains grew on B lymphocytes when induced by pathogens; these antibodies then broke off from their parent cells to circulate as "magic bullets," specifically killing the pathogen that induced them.

Similarly, while working on stains that would differentiate cell types under a microscope, Ehrlich *deduced* that if a dye binds to one cell but not another, then maybe a poison could kill a pathogen but spare normal cells. This idea, a variant on the lock-and-key idea, led him to *dissect the prob-lem* of creating a cure for syphilis with carefully *observed* experiments on hundreds of compounds, looking for the "magic bullet." Ultimately he found the first effective remedy for syphilis—an arsenic compound called Salvarsan. Salvarsan was the first antibacterial and thus broad-ened the armamentarium against infection beyond vaccines and antitox-ins. Ehrlich's work involved an empiric search for treatment "keys". His goal was not to overturn the theoretical underpinning of germ theory but instead to cleverly elaborate on the existing frame. Although Ehrlich made enormous strides in moving immunology forward, he did not take science down a previously uncharted path.

Elie Metchnikoff yearned to tackle a much *larger question*: What is a unifying, guiding principle in physiology? The question's audacious-ness allowed him to leap beyond the existing frame and land upon an entirely new theory of immunity. Metchnikoff, raised in a village near Kharkov, was a wunderkind from a family of Jewish intellectuals.

His maternal grandfather was the first acknowledged secular Jewish writer in Russia, and his older brother, Lev, became a prominent sociologist and geographer. From an early age, Metchnikoff had grandiose ideas about solving the mysteries of biology and he had the driving ambition to match. He completed a four-year degree in natural sciences at Kharkov University in two years and published his first peer reviewed paper in 1861 at age 16. His early years as a scientist were spent wandering between Germany, Italy, and universities in Russia (he popped in and out of the newly formed Odessa University three separate times). Volatility punctuated Metchnikoff's early academic life; he engaged in, sometimes violent, protests and published attacks on a colleague for purportedly plagiarizing his work. During this period, when his passionate marriage to Ludmila Feodorovitch ended with her death to tuberculosis, Metchnikoff attempted to take his own life by ingesting a large dose of opium. Several years later, when his second wife, Olga, was stricken by typhoid, he again attempted suicide, this time by injecting himself with enough relapsing fever bacteria to cause a near-fatal illness.

It was not until Metchnikoff's self-imposed exile from academia in 1882 to a private laboratory in Messina that his life settled down and his work crystalized. In Messina, Metchnikoff made the sentinel discovery that led him to his theory of active host defense. By the time he joined the Pasteur Institute in Paris a half a dozen years later, his academic home for the remainder of his life, he had found his vision.

Metchnikoff's thinking in devising his theory of active host defense involved *breaking a preexisting frame*. His radical theory proposed that immune cells are not passive, as Ehrlich and all others had imagined. Instead, Metchnikoff proposed the *reverse*—that phagocytes actively battle disease. Moreover, they do this because immune cells are "disharmonious." Rather than internally collaborating for the good of the whole organism, Metchnikoff imagined that each cell keeps all others in check so as to maximize its own self-interest. Metchnikoff's bizarre (for its time) idea of disharmony grew as an *analogy* from Darwin's theory that species engage in a struggle for survival of the fittest. Metchnikoff argued that if survival of the fittest exists between organisms, it should also exist within a given organism.

Metchnikoff, like Darwin, used a fresh *point of view* to apply this analogy. Just as Darwin had imagined himself as a plant, Metchnikoff changed his perspective to imagine himself as a cell engaged in battle.

Metchnikoff's philosophy of disharmony represented a radical *reversal*. To appreciate just how radical, consider that, since the time of the Greek philosopher-physician Hippocrates, the health of human beings was believed to reflect a primary state of intrinsic harmony. Four basic humors—blood, phlegm, yellow bile, and black bile—interacted to maintain vigor. Disharmony between these humors brought disease, which could be regained through interventions such as blood-letting. Metchnikoff's reversal—his view of active conflict in the body's inner sanctum, flew in the face of the accepted view that a placid accord defined the condition of health. From the notion of disharmony between cells, it was a small step to imagine an organism with specific, active modes of defense against external agents. Said another way, Metchnikoff asked not, How does disharmony cause disease to come about? but the reverse: How is disharmony essential for the normal process of health?

The clue that ignited Metchnikoff's theory of host defense came from animals on the lowest rungs of the evolutionary tree: embryonic sponges and starfish. Embryos start out somewhat like sandwiches. Their cells arrange themselves into layers, like the ham or cheese or lettuce between slices of bread. Each layer goes on to become one or more organs. Metchnikoff, along with his colleague Koveleski, demonstrated that in the early development of sponges, migrating cells came to form a layer that differentiated into the gut. He called these cells "phagocytes," or "eating cells." In animals without a gut, he realized that these cells had two qualities: (1) they served the function of digestion; and (2) they retained their wandering nature. From this *induction, he made a deductive* leap. He wondered, Could these wanderers that develop into eating cells be the same cells that, in organisms higher up on the evolutionary tree, create cellular disharmony? Could their function go well beyond the digestion of nutrients? Phagocytes became Metchnikoff's obsession.

After some years of *dissecting the question* by meticulously *observing* phagocyte function in one animal species after another, from the simplest mollusks to mammals, Metchnikoff embarked on a single experiment that unified his vision. He needed to challenge phagocytes with an external invader to investigate how they responded. Taking a needle from a Christmas tree he had bought for his relatives' children (he never had children of his own), he embedded it in the transparent body of a starfish larva. That night, he reported, he could barely sleep from anticipation. The next morning, as he had hoped, the splinter was surrounded by phagocytes. In one fell swoop he had demonstrated that phagocytes eat not only nutrients but also pathogens—they create a first line of defense against invaders. Within months, he had moved from induction to deduction, articulating his life's ambition—his grand theory of host defense, which he called "phagocytosis theory."

Metchnikoff envisioned phagocytes as freely moving about the body, policing against infections, injury, and unwanted cellular growth. In later years, he *expanded* this large role even further to assert that just as phagocytes devour the tadpole's tail to create a frog, phagocytes play a general "identity" function in defining the structure of cells within embryos. That is, they sculpt the shape and size of developing organs. Later, he also claimed that in the aging process, phagocytes clear the body of normal cells slated for elimination. All of these assertions proved to be true, although it took up to a century for science to catch up. In 1964, for example, Metchnikoff's theory of senescent (aging) cell clearance was "discovered" and termed programmed cell death. Giving credit where credit is due, Metchnikoff's grand theory was grand indeed. It might accurately afford Metchnikoff the title of "father" of fields as wide-reaching as inflammation, immunity, autoimmunity, and aging research.

Just as he imagined his phagocytes defended the body, Metchnikoff relentlessly, fanatically defended his theory. He had little choice. His phagocytosis theory came under immediate attack to which he responded with his magnum opus, *Immunity in Infectious Diseases* (1901). Although Metchnikoff's theory was far-reaching and metaphysical, his scientific approach to defending it was precise and filled with detailed evidence. As his wife Olga's biography describes him, "His was a wrestler's temperament: obstacles exasperated his energy and he went straight for them, pursuing his object with invincible tenacity…"

But Metchnikoff's defense of phagocytosis and disharmony did not prevent him from inventing new, grand theories. In subsequent work, Metchnikoff posited that, with aging, toxins emanating from intestinal microbes spread through the body to weaken normal cells. Phagocytes, Metchnikoff claimed, in attempting to suppress these toxins, only cause more damage. That is, phagocytes can be not only heroes but self-defeating villains. Fortunately, Metchnikoff believed that he knew an anti-aging remedy: eating curdled milk or yogurt slowed man's natural deterioration. Probiotics, which we may consider a New Age fad, turn out to be another of Metchnikoff's inventions.

By character as well as cognition, Metchnikoff was a master innovator. The man knew no moderation. He was a font of romantic ambition and relentless determination. While these traits made him at times combative and unbalanced, they also powered his contributions. In many men, doggedness causes a prejudice against others' ideas; later in his career, that may have become the case for Metchnikoff. But early on, he was suffused with curiosity. His work was influenced, perhaps even directed, by using the *power of the group* as he incorporated ideas of Darwin and Koveleski. Indeed, Metchnikoff's whole sense of spirituality centered on a belief in ideas. By his own report, science—if appropriately used to understand nature—could lift man from his misery and despair.

EHRLICH AND METCHNIKOFF ANNOTATED: THE USE OF TOOLS OF INNOVATION

Co-winners of the 1908 Nobel Prize, Ehrlich and Metchnikoff represented two sides of a coin. Each contributed one aspect to the currency that we now know maintains immunity. Ehrlich was the obsessive, Metchnikoff the hysteric. Ehrlich remained within the paradigm of his scientific fore-bearers; Metchnikoff disrupted.

Ehrlich's contributions were nothing to scoff at—discovering how antibodies are formed and identifying the first antibacterial against the great scourge, syphilis. But while his contributions were sentinel, they remained just one floor above the constructions of his *mentors,* within the "find-an-infection/create-a-vaccine" paradigm. *Analogies* such as the lock-and-key metaphor behind the action of enzymes informed his theory of the function of antibodies. Similarly, the differential staining of cells led him to argue that a poison might kill a pathogen but spare normal cells. From this *deduction,* he applied pain-staking *dissection* and *observation,* for example, trying hundreds of compounds until he happened upon the syphilis remedy, Salvarsan. Salvarsan, the first anti-bacterial, became the grandmother of penicillin and other antibacterial agents. Ehrlich stands as an example of how evolutionary genius saved millions of lives.

Metchnikoff, in contrast, was in all ways disruptive. His guiding *question* was so bold as to be almost impudent: What is a unifying, guiding principle in physiology? He used the same tools as did Ehrlich (anal-ogy, building on historical group contributions, observation, induction/deduction, and dissection). But he also *reversed* notions that had been held since the time of the Greeks, in particular theorizing that health was not an intrinsic state of harmony but indeed an ongoing battle-ground. This implied a *frame shift* in which certain cells were not pas-sive bystanders to infection but instead active combatants. To envision such a shift, Metchnikoff *changed his point of view,* imagining himself as a cell. Once he placed phagocytes into this warrior role, he went on to imagine *expanded* capabilities, including freely moving about the body policing against infections and injury, shaping cell growth in embryos, clearing the body of senescent cells during aging, and even being self-destructive.

In a profound way, Metchnikoff created a metaphor that has since fueled science: "the war on disease." The hope of eradicating, eliminat-ing, and triumphing over disease has fired contemporary aggressiveness in pursuing cures. In 2011, the National Institutes of Health spent $31 billion and supported 3,000 institutions in battling illness. The war metaphor has led us to glorify scientists as we do warriors, to invest in medicine as we do in defense, and to imagine that science and technology have almost mythical potential for averting peril.

	Question	Groups	Analogy	Rearrange	Observation	Deduction / Induction	Change Point of View	Expand	Narrow/ Dissect	Reverse	Break Frames	Autonomy	Openness	Persistence
Ehrlich	✦	✦	✦		✦	✦			✦			✦		✦
Metchnikoff	✦	✦	✦		✦	✦	✦	✦	✦	✦	✦	✦	✦	✦

Figure 11.1. Ehrlich and Metchnikoff: Tools and Characteristics

12

Connectivity

Paul Baran and Other Web Creators

The *New York Times* headline read, "Jobs Steps Down, Saying He Cannot Meet His Duties." It was August 25, 2011. Steven Jobs, who died just weeks thereafter from pancreatic cancer, announced that he would be resigning as chief executive of the computer giant Apple, Inc. Within hours, hundreds of glowing tributes about him were posted to the World Wide Web. A prominent technology blogger wrote: "Through the mist of my eyes, I am having a tough time focusing on the screen of this computer. I want to wake up and find it was all a nightmare." Subsequent *Times* coverage equating Jobs to the revered Thomas Edison, who brought society the modern-day equivalent of light and sound, likely constituted over exuberance. But Jobs was beloved by millions for the artistry with which he connected people to the Internet. The accolades, while respecting the man, also revealed our love affair with the Web.

Today's "connected" world is entirely different from that of Edison —indeed, from the world just a generation ago. Young men and women going out on dates compete for attention with their partner's smartphone. Libraries are empty while students surf Wikipedia. Newspaper sales plummet as Americans adopt opinions from online political blogs and take direction on sources from Google. The Web has utterly and completely changed our lives. But the path by which we got to this place was not simple and not obvious. It started and ended with revolutionary innovations: (1) the groundbreaking technologically that initiated it; and (2) the social frame shift that empowered it. Between these bookends, the

Web's creation was the work of a large group of evolutionary hackers. Thus, the Web was not created by any one person or even any single group, but instead by both revolutionary and evolutionary innovators.

Born in the early twentieth century, Paul Baran invented the paradigm that powers the Internet. A Polish Jew, raised by a small business owner, Baran was encouraged to do something practical. After completing a master's degree in engineering, he found himself attracted to the usefulness of computers. Baran, however, would turn out to be no ordinary programmer.

While working at the military subcontracting agency RAND, Baran became consumed with the concern that a Cold War nuclear attack would disable the integrity of military communications. Starting in 1959, Baran focused intently on finding a mechanism to avoid, in his words, "...a most dangerous situation created by the lack of a survivable communication system." He *deduced* that a fail-safe system needed the ability to avoid the usual hub-and-spoke communications pattern in which a strike to the central node would be disabling. After three years of intensive thinking, Baran came up with a futuristic concept that he called "packet switching."

Telephones had for a century set popular expectations about how instantaneous communication systems should be organized. Baran's bold *frame-shift* assaulted a variety of those assumptions. The shift from the telephone frame proposed a rewiring, or *rearrangement*, of the normally hierarchical phone line composition. When connecting phone calls, each user is routed to a local office and, if the call goes beyond the local calling area, the local office routes it to a regional or national switching office. Taking out a central hub disconnects a large number of users. What Baran envisioned to replace this was a web containing myriad switching nodes, each with up to eight links to other nodes.

According to a *Wired* magazine interview he gave years later, Baran's insight in creating his distributed network came from neurology. Neurologists were writing about how the brain could compensate for damage by relying on a network of connections such that intact functions overcame disabilities. *Analogously*, in Baran's decentralized and redundant design, a single point of damage could be readily overcome by routing through alternative nodes.

Baran's second shift away from the telephone frame proposed a repro-gramming. Over telephone wires, calls are transmitted via circuit switch-ing, in which one party at one end talks to another party at another end through a dedicated circuit. The emphasis is on the route, rather than the recipient (since a phone line can be attached to any phone). In packet switching, the situation is *reversed*. The recipient is emphasized, the route is not. Each message has a "to" and "from" label, but its route is not set. Like a letter placed in a mailbox, it gets passed from node to node inside a web of connected computers until it reaches its labeled destination. A similar arrangement had developed within the telegraph system—mes-sages were passed between and held within stations to smooth out traffic jams over lines. The computer nodes in Baran's scheme could "talk" to each other, providing instant updates on bottlenecks so as to calculate the shortest and quickest route. But routes would handle many messages almost simultaneously, and as long as a message got to the intended end computer, its pathway was flexible.

A final aspect of Baran's counterintuitive scheme was to envision messages being sent in pieces rather than transmitted whole. Digitized into a series of zeros and ones (binary bits), each communication would be chopped into a standard size of 1,024 bits. A small message might go off in one chunk, but a larger one would have its various packets sent by different routes, stored within different nodes, and then reassembled upon arrival.

To make this strange concept work effectively, Barran *dissected* the switching node characteristics and realized that they would need to be high speed, low storage, and inexpensive—characteristics that did not exist within computer technology at the time. Baran drew pictoral rep-resentations as he combined his eccentric concepts into a systematic and complex whole. This way of *changing point of view* helped him to arrive at the deduction that the machines running the system would need to be small, simple mini-computers. The logic behind the *deduction* was that, despite the multiple transfers and storages of messages, the nimbleness of small, fast computers would make it appear to the user that the interaction was happening in real time.

Baran's conception had a number of inherent downsides. Packets had to be disassembled and reassembled. Messages needed to contain address and control information. Pieces of packets could arrive out of order. However, the design achieved Baran's major goals: to make communications efficient, robust, and safe. Moreover, it attained a goal that Baran noted at the time and that would turn out to be prophetic: "Most importantly, standardized data blocks permit many simultaneous users, each with widely different bandwidth requirements to economically share a broad-band network made up of varied data rate links." That is, the system would be agnostic to computer specifications, like supporting conversations between people speaking different languages.

By the time Baran had completed his 11-volume thesis and related memoranda describing packet switching, he had expanded well beyond his original question. The question had been, How could one construct a communications system that was immune to nuclear attack? The *question had now expanded* to become, How could universal connectivity be maximized? It was question of massive scope. As Baran noted, "It is now time to start thinking about a new and possibly non-existent public utility…for the transmission of digital data among a large set of subscribers." Moreover, the system was, in Barans words, "User-to-user rather than center-to-center." That is, it eliminated centralized control; it was pluralistic. Packet switching tilled the ground for web-based social egalitarianism.

The similarity between Edison's invention of the light bulb within a system of lighting and Baran's invention of packet switching within a public computing utility is hard to ignore. Edison had to work out each of the many details needed to make not a single light bulb but a whole system of lighting; Baran had to support not a single conversation but a whole system of communication. Both men were challenged to *deduce* how one thing leads to another, while working *inductively* on the basis of known *observations*.

How radical was this concept of nimble little networked computers working in real time? Very. The first electronic computer was constructed only about a dozen years before Baran began his work. ENIAC was described as a general purpose electronic digital calculator. Initiated in 1943 by John Mauchly and J. Preper Eckert at the University of Pennsylvania and not completed until 1945, ENIAC was built on an army contact for use in World War II. It comprised over 18,000 vacuum tubes, weighed 30 tons, and filled a 20 by 40 foot specially air-conditioned room with its heat-producing tubes and wires. Its first task was to compute whether it was feasible to build a hydrogen bomb (the answer was "Yes").

Not until 1959, the year Baran started working on packet switching, did IBM commercialize computers built with transistors rather than vacuum tubes. In the meantime, crude systems for computing storage and random access memory (RAM) were introduced. However, computers in the 1950s were costly and cumbersome. To harness their possibilities required lots of money (hiring a programming expert) and loads of time. An operator fed pre-typed punch cards into the machine for batch processing. Depending on the length and complexity of the programs in the queue, turnaround times could be hours or more. If the computer found a programming error, the user had to start over from scratch. Many a college student spent late nights frantically submitting, waiting, and resubmitting code to meet a class deadline.

Microcomputers hit the market in the late 1950s when an entrepreneur named Ken Olsen left the Massachusetts Institute of Technology (MIT) to create the Digital Equipment Corporation (DEC). Really no more than terminals, microcomputers interfaced with the computer but also interacted directly with the user. Rather than using batch processing, these worked by a concept called time sharing. Time sharing allowed perhaps 100 users to log on and be serviced in turn through teletype machines that printed the computer's response. Although this represented an improvement, especially for high-volume users, the downside of time sharing was that the machine now had to use precious operating time to coordinate tasks. The more users logged on and the more intensive the calculations, the slower the computer's response. Baran's idea, although built loosely on batch processing, was miles ahead of that idea. It might have been considered science fiction were it not for the fact that another group of visionaries almost simultaneously conceptualized it and went on to try it.

Those visionaries were not at AT&T, the company Baran and his sponsor the Air Force approached to test the system. AT&T soundly rejected Baran's system. The visionaries who first operationalized packet switching were a group of British computer scientists led by Donald Davies. The motivation behind the British system was not survival but connectivity: the greatest access to scarce computing resources. That meant maximizing efficiency, which was another wonderful attribute of packet switching. In 1967, Davies and his team built Mark I, a packet-switching prototype that served about 60 lines and connected users to two mainframe computers. Although it "worked," Davies hit up against his own sponsorship blockade and thereby failed to develop a hoped-for national expansion.

The next phase of this trans-oceanic game of ping-pong reverted back to the United States, where fortunately the ball landed in what is arguably America's most unconventional funding agency. ARPA (now named DARPA) was founded in 1958 in response to Sputnik and was tasked with "creating or preventing strategic surprise." Although housed within the Department of Defense, DARPA mostly contracts out to universities, its projects focused on the development of high risk/high gain technology. At the time one of its main initiatives was to develop computer-based technology through its Information Processing Techniques Office (IPTO).

At IPTO, Bob Taylor and Lawrence Roberts believed that they could build the first digitally connected community—they called it ARPANET. In good part, the motivation was pedestrian; IPTO's university contractors were bleeding the agency dry for more and more individual computers. ARPANET would allow them to share computing resources. However, innovation as disruptive as ARPANET would predictably not be easy to accomplish. Taylor thus decided to ask a *team* of investigators who already had IPTO contracts and a high level of interest to communally contribute to developing a model system. Thus a group at UCLA, Stanford, UC Santa Barbara, and Utah become the collaborative trailblazers who evolved the prototype for the Internet.

It didn't take long for the university group to hit a roadblock. How could they connect computers, each with its own idiosyncratic operating system? Wesley Clark of Washington University in St. Louis drew on an *analogy* to propose a solution. Just as computers serve humans, little computers could serve big computers. The packet switching software could be programmed to work on a mini-computer sub-network. It would mean programming only a single type of machine (subsequently called interface message processors, or IMPs). IMPs would form a connected inner ring, with each host computer linking to its respective mini-computer.

The idea turned out to be brilliant, not only in overcoming the technical hurdle but in clarifying how to *dissect* into sensible parts the complex problem of creating a network. "A layered system is organized as a set of discrete functions that interact according to specified rules," according to Janet Abbate in *Inventing the Internet.* "The functions are called 'layers' because they are arranged in a conceptual hierarchy that proceeds from the most concrete and physical functions (such as handling electrical signals) to the most abstract functions (e.g. interpreting human language commands from users)." Layers were the way to divide up the networking problem. Each layer functioned independently; just as a plumber does not have to understand the entire sewage system to fix a toilet, layers did not need to understand how the others worked to ensure their own performance.

The layer of programming packet switching within the IMPs was something that no one had ever done before. Roberts put it out for competitive bid. He selected a small, elite operation comprising ex-faculty from Harvard and MIT called Bolt, Beranek, and Newman (BBN). BBN was brilliant at dissecting and averting the possible future problems that ARPANET would encounter. For example, to guarantee that message packets were transmitted reliably, BBN created a checking algorithm in which, after each delivery, the sending IMP waited for an acknowledgement from the receiving IMP, indicating that the message had arrived intact. If, after waiting a specified time, the acknowledgement did not come, the package was resent. Similarly, IMPs were programmed to signal neighbors to send them replacement programming should they go down. If the IMP was still damaged, it would shut itself off so as not to corrupt the rest of the system. These clever strategies provided the degree of message quality and efficiency that the AT&T engineers had thought impossible.

A Network Working Group was charged with the all-important tasks of developing host computer protocols and finding ways to improve the system. The people who ended up taking a lead were graduate students. Vinton Cerf and Bob Kahn, who would later morph ARPANET into the Internet, described their newfound autonomy: "We were just rank amateurs, and we expected that some authority would finally come along and say, 'Here's how we are going to do it,' and nobody ever came along." The conventions that the *group* developed were a manifesto to the power of inclusiveness. "First, there is a tendency to view a written statement as *ipso facto* authoritative and we hope to promote the exchange and discussion of considerably less authoritative ideas. Second, there is a natural hesitancy to publish something unpolished, and we hope to ease this inhibition." Such rules removed all constraints on the free-wheeling exchange of ideas.

By the end of 1969, the first four sites had been linked, and by 1971, all 15 of ARPA's contract sites were connected to ARPANET. But it looked better than it was. Many sites were not really using the network, and the addition of new sites was slow. For a new site to get onto ARPANET meant having to buy an IMP (at a cost of over $100,000). Next, the site had to do the programming to hook their host to the IMP and to prepare their host for multi-use tasks that were estimated to take one person-year to program. Once on-board, the aggregate of host resources was Christmas and New Year's wrapped into one, but accessing the software on other hosts was daunting. There were few published protocols to provide help. There was not even an up-to-date directory of what other hosts had available. It was all pretty frustrating. Robert's vision for ARPANET to form a digital community sharing resources was a general flop.

Yet, ARPANET itself was a partial success because it hatched unexpected benefits. One was e-mail. Ray Tomlinson, a programmer at BBN, adapting an earlier program, created the first working version. It transferred mail between machines and included the familiar host and user address names. Before long, e-mail was ARPANET's most popular service. ARPANET's initial purpose had been to provide access to the rich computing resources residing on host machines. But the unanticipated popularity of e-mail was a flag that a major value of the Internet would be to provide access between one user and another.

The path between ARPANET and modern connectivity had many more twists and turns. The conceptual leap that turned ARPANET into the Internet was a process for overcoming the incompatibility between computers and networks. Vinton Cerf and Robert Kahn, who had teethed on ARPANET as students, worked with users worldwide through the mid-1970s to build a set of common standards that would overcome the problem of incompatible computers. To do so, Cerf and Kahn rearranged and modified many of the concepts already developed within ARPANET. They did away with IMPs and instead created a single protocol that would be used by all machines, called Transmission Control Protocol (TCP). TCP would take over the responsibility of the former IMPs for ensuring reliability and validity such as verifying safe message arrival, overseeing data flow and providing a physical connection between networks using gateway computers. All of this made it easy to add new networks. Since gateways connected entire networks, each having many hosts (whereas IMPs had had a single host attached), Cerf and Kahn added a unique feature, an IP address. IP would be a simple universal protocol that would run on gateways and pass individual packets between machines, whereas TCP would run within individual networks and order messages between pairs of hosts. Together, this pairing of common protocols became known as TCP/IP and is still in use today.

In late 1977, the creators of the Internet attempted a daunting experiment. From a van on a California freeway, they sent packets of data through three different networks via gateways on two continents. The message was received error-free. It was rousing proof: the Internet existed!

Yet, while the world revolved around bulky, mainframe computers, the Internet would remain a light under a bushel. In 1975, then, when *Popular Electronics* proclaimed on its cover the arrival of Altair 8800, the first personal computer, it unknowingly lifted the cover from the Internet and allowed its illumination to shine forth. Altair 8800 was small enough to fit on a desk and cost $397. Its creator, Ed Roberts, declared that it would "eliminate the Computer Priesthood." Two years later, Apple, Inc., released Apple II. Unlike Altair, which required assembly by the knowledgeable aficionado, Apple II was sold ready for use by the novice.

By now the military (who still ran ARPANET) had had more than enough of caretaking a large and diverse computer network. They had tried to off-load ARPANET to a commercial parent without success. But the plasticity of personal computers made a network more desirable. To speed the process of transfer, the military cleaved from ARPANET its own fire-walled military network (MILNET). Moreover, a fund of $20 million was set up to finance computer manufacturers to implement TCP/IP on all machines. By 1990, almost all computers in the United States had incorporated these protocols. This created the ultimate pluralism and eliminated the need for any single company to own the Internet. Instead, the Internet would be available to any network that wanted to play.

By 1990, academics were beginning to consider the Internet a real boon. For consumers, it remained a bust. There was no easy way to find things, most applications remained technical, and what was available was generally in plain text—that is, until Tim Berners-Lee, working at CERN, the European Organization for Nuclear Research, launched the World Wide Web. Building upon a remarkably futuristic program called hypertext that had been written by a Harvard graduate student 30 years earlier, Berners-Lee built a language that allowed data, independent of format, to be accessed by a server. He called it HTML, and by the end of the year, he had created a server for HTML Web pages and a browser and editor to view and manipulate documents. HTML could pull up graphics, music, and images, as well as text. Now we were talking! Appealing Web pages, photo swapping, and music sharing all became possible. Berners-Lee's superiors at CERN had no understanding of what he had done and no interest in supporting his work. It was shelved twice, yet Berners-Lee plowed on. Then, in 1992 and 1993, a series of hackers (enthusiasts improving on systems and software) released browsers for the UNIX, Macintosh, Next, and Windows systems.

It didn't take long (a year) for Marc Andreessen and Jim Clark to found Netscape, the first commercial Web browser. That same year, the cover of *Time* magazine featured a cover story on "The Strange New World of the Internet." Sixteen months after its founding, Netscape became the largest initial public offering in Wall Street history. Between 1988 and 1994, the number of networks connected to the Internet rose from 240 to 32,400. In 1994, 3.8 million computers were connected. In the next several years, the number doubled about every 12 months. According to Wikipedia, the number of global internet users in 2010 was estimated to be 1.86 billion, connecting about 22 percent of the world's population. After three decades of development, networking had come to fruition by means of a user-friendly human-computer interface.

Packet switching was the first frame break: a technological revolution that invented the Internet and produced the Web. Connected users initiated the second frame break: a social revolution created by the Web. Connectivity has transformed the world into a democratic, egalitarian collective. Pluralism is the watchword of the twenty-first century. In matters technological, economic, social, and political, users of the Web control content in a way that is (historically) surprising. Marketing over the Web is "pull" rather than "push," meaning that businesses try to lure shoppers rather than condition them. The political revolutions of 2011 in Tunisia, Egypt, and Libya used the Web to organize from bottom up rather than top down. Genetics breakthroughs come from Open Source collaborations more often than from the lab of a solo researcher. Artist wannabes use YouTube to find their way to the limelight.

Users of the Internet every day undertake creativity with a purpose. This is a new form of innovation, yet innovation it is. *Time* magazine recognized the transformation in 2006 when it chose as its Person of the Year—"You." Commerce, of course, has been a major feature of the Internet, as demonstrated by the millions of businesses currently operating through the Web, but consider all of the non-capitalist connectivity that is none other than self-expression and social connection: from FaceBook and

Linkedin to Zooppa (a site for creative talent) and the almost $2 billion industry of multiplayer online role-playing games (MMORPGs).

Mass collaboration has created valuable goods outside classical commerce. Linux is a particularly powerful example. Hackers, such as Richard Stallman from MIT, objected to manufacturers limiting user autonomy. With the help of volunteers recruited from Usenet groups, Stallman built a partial suite of free software to be compatible with the widely used UNIX operating system and called it GNU. The major thing missing from GNU—the "kernel" or programming that connects hardware and software—was provided by a Finnish graduate student named Linus Torvalds, who wrote the operating system Linux. Torvalds posted an offer to a Usenet group to download the system and make improvements. Collaborators showed immediate enthusiasm and started providing free-ware GNU applications so that the whole suite could be developed without licensing constraints. By 1993, Linux had 100,000 lines of code. A 2001 study showed that the Red Hat Linux 7.1 version had grown to 30 million source lines of code, representing over $1 billion in free labor. Rigorously debugged by thousands of developers and adapted to every conceivable type of machine, it has overtaken the Windows Server as the operating system of choice for Web servers and for desktop animation. Linux has become the poster child for a growing library of computer resources called Open Source.

Mass collaboration and self-expression have also contributed to providing open access to one of the world's most precious resources: information. Just as Benjamin Franklin's free library informed Thomas Edison, so the Internet enlarges the vision for spreading understanding. It is the aspiration of Jimmy Wales, founder or Wikipedia: "Imagine a world in which every single person on the planet is given free access to the sum of all human knowledge." But to achieve this audacious goal, Wales had to confront his own discomfort with equality. His first attempt to build an online encyclopedia, called Nupedia, involved a rigid, multilevel system of expert review. It went nowhere. In 2001, Wikipedia's editor came across WikiWikiWeb, a site in which users discussed and collaboratively edited documents. Eight days later, in January 2001, Wikipedia went online.

By the end of the month, Wikipedia had 617 articles. In 2011 there were nearly 4 million English version articles, and Wikipedia was published in over 240 languages.

The organizational structures of Wikipedia and Linux are volunteer-based, nonprofit, and democratic. Yet the truism that has emerged is that many eyes maintain truth and accuracy. (That, however, assumes there is a "truth.") Pages on Wikipedia are edited and re-edited, as volunteers sometimes disagree over veracity. The most edited content page on the site is the article on George W. Bush. As of July 2011, it had been edited 44,435 times. According to the Wikipedia archive, controversy has arisen around his National Guard service and whether it is appropriate to categorize him under the heading "alcoholic." However, by external comparison to the "gold standard" *Encyclopaedia Britannica*, a 32-volume set formerly printed once every several years, Wikipedia was found by experts reviewing comparable articles from both sources to have no more factual errors. The conclusion: the two sources are equally valid. In 2012, *Britannica* announced that it would no longer publish a paper version of its encyclopedia.

The Internet has dramatically changed our world. The transformation was unpredictable. It involved using every innovation tool and breaking not one frame but two: (1) how communications are transmitted; and (2) who controls social experience. Between these frame shifts was a long and complicated evolution. When Baran conceptualized packet switching in the 1960s, it is unlikely that he envisioned the modern World Wide Web. Today, few of us can imagine the impact of connectivity on the world of tomorrow. It took a generation of Web development to get here. Who knows what will happen next?

BARAN AND OTHER WEB-BUILDERS ANNOTATED: THE USE OF TOOLS OF INNOVATION

The building of the Internet and the World Wide Web represented evolutionary progress achieved by a *group* whose achievements were step-wise and technical, between two *frame-shifting* innovations. Various evolutionary group members certainly used subsets of the tools of innovation, such as Wesley Clark's *analogy* that, just as computers serve humans, little computers could serve big computers. In the end, however, there was a revolution produced by Internet hackers whose egalitarian zealotry created a frame shift in our expectations about social communication.

The first *frame shift* was cleaner and clearer—it was packet switching. Paul Baran's revolutionary conception involved a rewiring or *rearrangement* of existing hardware, but it was more—a switch from the centralized topology of the telephone system to decentralization; from the transfer of complete conversations to a process of cutting messages into snippets only to be understood after end-user reassembly; from massive mainframes to an impetus for nimble mini-computers.

Packet switching was a *reversal* from an emphasis on a route to an emphasis on the recipient. He called this "user-to-user rather than center-to-center." The *analogy* is one of a letter placed in a mailbox, passed from node to node until it reaches its labeled destination. The act of getting to the recipient is what counts, not the cities through which the letter passes.

Baran's overarching *question* was how to achieve universal connectivity: communication without bounds. In imagining his massively connected system, he had *expanded* beyond the original intent of ensuring communications security and beyond the realm of the military to the realm of everyman. His intention was to create a "non-existent public utility."

Like Einstein, Baran was a constructor of mental models, which he often conveyed through pictures. From these, he was able to make surprising *deductions,* such as that the machines running his packet switching system would have to be small, nimble, and fast—that is, simple mini-computers—a hardware form that (similar to Edison's public utility) did not exist at the time.

The boldness of his conception was not just based on a leap of faith. It was based on *breaking down* the problem into pieces, each of which he had *observed* or could imagine on the horizon: digitized (binary) messages, nodal telegraph communications, and the emergence of small, mini-computers.

In the end, it was all unexpected. Baran was not just a technical wizard, he was a genius. His work involved the use of the tools of innovation, but these formed a blueprint for something that had emergent properties that were utterly unimagined. Baran, the ARPANET group, including Cerf and Kahn, Berners-Lee, and many others created a hardware/software infrastructure that generated a social revolution. The Internet and Web today allow for a previously unknown brand of global democratic pluralism.

	Question	Groups	Analogy	Rearrange	Observation	Deduction / Induction	Change Point of View	Expand	Narrow/ Dissect	Reverse	Break Frames	Autonomy	Openness	Persistence
Baran	✃	✃	✃	✃	✃	✃	✃	✃	✃	✃	✃	✃	✃	✃

Figure 12.1. Baran: Tools and Characteristics

13

A Modest Proposal for Saving Mankind

Norman Borlaug and the Green Revolutionaries

f one were to catalogue the absolute essentials needed to sustain humans as a species, the list would have relatively few entries, topped by food and sexual reproduction.

In 1798, Thomas Malthus, the famed British economist and demographer, argued that exactly these two requisites for survival, sustenance and sex, were on a collision course. His booklet, *An Essay on the Principle of Population,* was an apocalyptic counterpoint to the Romantic philosophy of the eighteenth century, which had envisioned a world of almost limitless improvement. Malthus's premise was simply that population increases geometrically: 2, 4, 8, 16, 32..., whereas food production increases arithmetically: 2, 3, 4, 5, 6. If this arithmetic is correct, then eventually demand will necessarily outstrip supply. As Malthus put it, "I think I may fairly make two postulata. First, that food is necessary to the existence of man. Secondly, that the passion between the sexes is necessary and will remain nearly in its present state.... Assuming then my postulata as granted, I say, that the power of population is indefinitely greater than the power in the earth to produce subsistence for man."

The natural consequences of overpopulation as Malthus saw it were war, pestilence, and famine. To avoid the apocalypse, Malthus suggested limiting population growth; he was more sanguine about increasing food production: "We may be quite sure that among plants, as well as among animals, there is a limit to improvement, though we do not exactly know where it is.... No man can say that he has seen the largest ear of wheat, or the largest oak that could ever grow."

By the end of the 1960s, that limit to food production appeared to have been reached. An estimated 900 million people, almost a quarter of the entire world's population, were malnourished. Five million children, skin stretched taunt over swollen bellies, were dying every year from diseases such as diarrhea, pneumonia, and measles that rarely slay better fed children. The only thing preventing large swaths of Latin America, Africa, and Southeast Asia from slipping into famine were food shipments from more fortunate nations. Paul R. Ehrlich's 1968 book, *The Population Bomb*, predicted a coming Malthusian catastrophe. Indeed, Ehrlich claimed it had already arrived. Like Malthus, Ehrlich dismissed an agricultural solution and focused instead on immediate and decisive population control in the form of contraception. "I have yet to meet anyone familiar with the situation who thinks that India will be self-sufficient in food by 1971," he said.

But the predictions of both Malthus and Ehrlich proved to be wrong. In the second edition of *The Population Bomb*, published only three years after the first, the statement that India was incapable of agricultural self-sufficiency had been removed. India was well on its way to food security through a societal transformation termed the "Green Revolution." The Green Revolution had not only averted the immediate worldwide calamity, it looked to be a sustainable panacea for feeding humanity.

On its face, the Green Revolution—an astonishing, manifold increase in crop productivity throughout Latin America and Southeast Asia—did not overturn any scientific theories. Wider distribution of fertilizers and pesticides, investments in irrigation, and modernization of agricultural management were not novelties. Scientific breakthroughs from the prior century allowed the fabrication of the new crop varieties that fueled the Green Revolution. Somehow then an outcome both surprising and transformational emerged out of nothing terribly out of the ordinary. How did it happen?

The Green Revolution has been described as an exemplar of evolutionary innovation. It involved the tools of innovation, perhaps the most important being the power of groups, but it stopped short of frame shifting. No basic assumptions were breached. Despite its name, no revolutionary overturning of paradigms took place. Yet, evolutionary or revolutionary, transformational innovation it was—and its triumph continues to feed the modern world.

The emergence of agriculture dates back to the Paleolithic period. By 9500 B.C.E., archaeological evidence from the Levant region of the Fertile Crescent shows the presence of the eight so-called founder crops, including wheat, barley, peas, lentils, and flax. Wheat was the first of these to be farmed on a wide scale. Nonetheless, farming was no guarantee of food security. History reminds us that many of the peoples of the world experienced cyclical famine when freezing, floods, and droughts destroyed crops. Farmers launched sporadic skirmishes against Mother Nature by growing the best adapted plant varieties they could find. But to win the hearts and stomachs of humanity required advances in science. Darwin's evolutionary theory suggested that plant species could be actively manipulated so as to achieve adaption to given environments. Gregor Mendel's breakthroughs in genetics demonstrated how.

Gregor Johann Mendel, an Augustan friar at the Abbey of St. Thomas in Brno, modern-day Czechoslovakia, is considered the father of classical genetics. A renaissance man, Mendel spent much of his time in his study teaching and writing about meteorology. His legacy, however, was fashioned outside of his study indeed behind the monastery in a two-hectare experimental garden. Between 1856 and 1863, Mendel's intensive study of the patterns of heredity among thousands of pea plants, led him to posit two utterly surprising "laws," or principles, of genetics. Today, these laws are the backbone of classical genetics. At the time, however, Mendel's two-part paper, *Experiments on Plant Hybridization,* delivered to the Natural History Society of Brünn in Moravia in 1865, had virtually no impact. Indeed, Mendel's work was cited only three times in the next 35 years andas far as historians can tell, it was unknown to Charles Darwin. Yet Mendel's "laws" explain a fundamental assertion in Darwin's theory—how genetics allows for species diversity—and the application of Mendel's laws enabled the Green Revolution.

Mendel's brilliance was to wade through a sea of complexity in order to grasp the essence of clarity. Consider trying to discern the grand plan that produces one flower that is purple and another white and yet another that is purple outlined in white. To detect the essence within this ocean of variety, Mendel set up scientific conditions aimed at creating purity. He *dissected the problem* by selecting only pea plants that were true-breeding (consistently produced a single set of characteristics). He chose character-istics that he could record as yes/no, such as color and shape. He bred for more than one generation—a decision that turned out to be the only way he could have uncovered some patterns of inheritance. Finally, he con-tinued to collect data until he had a large enough sample size to provide statistical certainty.

From this elegant design, Mendel meticulously *observed* every aspect of fully 29,000 pea plant hybrid crosses. His laboratory notebooks over-flow with painstaking details. But he was not simply a great inductive observer. He was a deeply capable *deductive* logician, and as such he even-tually coaxed out patterns from this mass of information that crystallized into his laws of genetics.

Here is what Mendel's experiments showed. Mate two pea plants: one that breeds pure white flowers and one that breeds pure purple flowers. All their offspring have purple flowers. We call this a first generation cross. Then take each of the offspring pea plants and cross it with itself. In this second generation, there will be, on average, 3 purple flowers to every 1 white flower. Mendel discerned from this apparent oddity his first law, the *Law of Segregation*. It said: (1) traits are inherited in discrete "units"; (2) offspring inherit one unit from each parent; and (3) traits may not show up in a given generation, even though they can still be passed on.

Today, having powerful laboratory techniques through which we can see chromosomes and track their behavior, we can translate these princi-ples and apply them to human genetics: (1) traits are inherited via genes; (2) every individual has two alleles, or copies, of each gene, one carried in the father's sperm and the other in the mother's egg; and (3) one of these alleles dominates over the other so that usually only dominant traits become apparent as offspring characteristics.

In the above example, purple (P) is dominant and white (w) is recessive. For the parent pea plants to breed true, the parental alleles must be PP and ww. In the first generation, since all offspring get one allele from the mother and one from the father, the four possible crosses are: Pw, Pw, Pw, and Pw. All the plants are Pw. Then in the second generation when Pw is crossed with Pw, the combinatorial possibilities among offspring become: PP, Pw, Pw, and ww. Recalling that P is dominant and so any plant with a P is purple, in the first generation, all are purple (all Pw). In the next generation three are purple (PP, Pw, Pw) and only one is white (ww).

To come to the *Law of Segregation*, Mendel juggled *induction with deduction*, but that juggling did not stop at the first law. Because Mendel also observed crosses in which two traits were being transmitted at the same time, he realized that traits are inherited independently of each other. His *Law of Independent Assortment* said that the ratio of flower color remains 3:1 purple:white, even as another trait is being inherited. So as color is inherited 3:1, so pea shape is also inherited in a ratio of 3:1 wrinkled:smooth.

Mendel's Laws of Inheritance were simply too far ahead of their time to be understood. Even in 1900, when they were "rediscovered" by three scientists who validated them, they remained highly controversial. Mendel's laws stated that traits are inherited in discrete units. On the face of it, though, inheritance appears to occur by a blending of parental traits, such as the occurrence of purple flowers outlined in white. R. A. Fisher, the father of statistical genetics, showed that discrete factors contributing to an individual trait can appear to be blended if several factors or genes contribute all at once. That is, blending can appear when a number of inherited genes are combined. Moreover, when Thomas Hunt Morgan proposed his theory that chromosomes are the messenger of heredity, Mendel's model of discrete traits fit Morgan's theory perfectly.

Mendel's laws have far-reaching consequences. Darwin's theory of evolution found its biological basis in the fact that genes combine to produce variability and that genes compete for survival. Were Mendel alive today, he would be awed by individually tailored chemotherapy based on tumor genetics, regeneration of tissues via genetic engineering, and stem cells manipulated genetically to treat heart failure. Clearly, Mendel took his place in history as the originator of ideas that changed science and humanity. Sadly, the Augustinian monk did not live to see any of the impact of his genius.

Nonetheless, with Mendel's laws in hand, agronomists had a set of principles by which they could artificially improve the breeding of plants. The deliberative breeding of hardier varieties allowed for enhanced agricultural productivity, and by the early 1900s, scientists had developed techniques for refining and selecting crop characteristics.

One of the first experts in the field was Nikolai Vavilov, director of the All Union Institute for Plant Industry in Petrograd (now St. Petersburg). His task was to feed the newly formed Soviet Union's masses, a goal that became an obsession for the Soviet leadership. Guided by Mendel's laws, he tirelessly expanded the Institute into 400 research centers around the Soviet Union. With some real success, these centers began to enlarge agricultural output. Between 1916 and 1933, Vavilov traveled to the corners of the globe to collect and catalog the largest international seed bank ever assembled, consisting of 250,000 varieties. However, the purity of Vavilov's faith in Mendel was, sadly, to become his undoing. Trofim Lysenko, a powerful Soviet functionary who distrusted foreign beliefs including an adherence to Mendelian genetics, labeled Vavilov as a reactionary. In 1940, Vavilov was ousted from the Institute, arrested, and transferred to a Siberian forced labor camp. He died there, never knowing that the winds of political change would restore his good name. Today his beloved Institute is called the V. I. Vavilov Institute for Plant Industry.

Agricultural abundance was no less important in the U.S. Henry Wallace, Franklin Delano Roosevelt's secretary of agriculture and subsequently vice president, was the mastermind behind the profusion of farming productivity in the Midwest. Having developed the first commercialized strain of hybrid corn in 1923, he founded the Hi Bred Corn Company, which perfected and marketed new scientifically bred varieties. In less than a generation, hybrids had almost completely saturated the Midwest corn market. As a result of this initiative, along with progress in fertilizer and irrigation, the number of bushels of corn produced per acre in the United States quadrupled from 24 in 1931 to 110 in 1981.

In 1941, just before his vice presidential inauguration, Wallace visited Mexico, where, as an agronomist, he spent many hours touring farms. Eighty percent of Mexicans lived on the land, most of them subsistence farmers. Wallace saw that their corn yields were often less than 20 bushels per acre—often only 10—and the people were starving. Henry Wallace became committed to doing something about food scarcity in America's neighbor to the South. Upon his return to the United States, he enlisted the help of Raymond Fosdick, president of the Rockefeller Foundation. A high-powered scientific mission was sent to Mexico, led by an internationally renowned plant pathologist from the University of Minnesota, E. C. Stakman. Stakman's team recommended that the Rockefeller Foundation do something that it had never done before—collaborate with the Mexican government to set up a permanent station in Mexico, stocked with a handful of U.S. experts. Their mission would be no less far-reaching than to end hunger in Mexico.

Getting the right personnel, of course, would be critical to the success of the project. To head what Rockefeller called the Office of Special Studies, they asked George "Dutch" Harrar, one of Stakman's former students, who was fluent in Spanish and possessed the forceful vigor necessary for such a challenge. For the plant pathologist, they asked another of Stakman's former students, Norman Borlaug.

Norman Borlaug was not someone who, in his early years, many would have pegged as the man who would come to be called the "father of the Green Revolution." He grew up on his grandparents' 120-acre farm and later on his parents' adjacent farm near the town of Saude, Iowa, in a corner of the state known as little Norway. His was a typical farm boy childhood, slogging through mud, milking cows, and forking hay. A rudimentary education, initiated in a one-room schoolhouse, afforded him such ill preparation that he failed the entrance examination to the University of Minnesota. But the experience served as a catalyst. Instead of going back to his little corner of the state, he enrolled in the University of Minnesota College of General Studies (designed for students who couldn't make it into mainstream programs) and demonstrated a relentless competence that, two quarters later, earned him entry into his chosen school—the College of Agriculture.

Near the end of Borlaug's undergraduate program, Professor Stakman (who later led the Mexico mission) saw the young man at a wrestling tournament and was impressed with his grit. Borlaug was simultaneously taking his team to the Big Ten semifinals, acing his courses, and courting his future wife. When the professor quizzed Borlaug, he found in the young man a surprisingly deep pool of knowledge and a bottomless well of curiosity. Borlaug, in turn, attended the professor's lectures, including one he found particularly compelling entitled "The Shifty Little Enemies (Rusts) That Destroy Our Cereal Crops." Rust was a plant disease that regularly wiped out half of a seasonal wheat crop. Stakman's call to overpower this ubiquitous foe was so persuasive that Borlaug vowed to ask the professor for an apprenticeship if he ever got the chance. Indeed, when a job with the National Forest Service fell through, Borlaug did just that, and Professor Stakman responded with the offer of an assistantship toward completion of a Ph.D.

In 1943, when Rockefeller came calling about the Office of Special Studies agronomy program in Mexico, Borlaug was doing a World War II stint as head of the biochemical laboratory at E. I. DuPont de Nemours. The offer meant going to a country where he did not speak the language and temporarily leaving his pregnant wife and one-year-old child for the several months that it would take him to get established. Stakman described the project as "tough, demanding... grinding." Borlaug accepted.

Over the next several years, Borlaug took over the wheat-breeding program and developed a series of rust-resistant, broadly climate-adapted wheat strains. These hardy breeds produced enormously high crop yields; they would become the heart of the Green Revolution. As described by his official biographer, Leon Hesser, Borlaug's success involved several innovations. The ones that Hesser describes, along with still others that are evident from Borlaug's own words, involved the use of *dissecting the question, observation, working in groups, induction/deduction, rearrangement,* and *changing point of view.*

Borlaug became a relentless experimentalist whose chief methods were *breaking the problem* into composite parts and applying keen and persistent *observation*. To crossbreed requires exhaustively manipulating one characteristic at a time (à la Mendel) with only the vaguest hope that trial and error will result in the desired characteristics, like sorting through a ton of garbage looking for a lost diamond ring. Borlaug's comment about this was, "Crossbreeding is a hit-or-miss process. It's time consuming and mind-warpingly tedious. There's only one chance in thousands of ever finding what you want, and actually no guarantee of success at all."

Tiny tweezers are used to surgically remove the male stamen. This ensures that the plant's own pollen (sperm) will not pollinate itself. The emasculated plant is then covered with a glassine bag to avoid external pollination. Two days later, the pistil (ovary) is hand-fertilized from the pollen of another, selected plant to obtain a cross, or hybrid. After a growing season has elapsed, the scientist carefully examines and records the characteristics that are produced. Then the entire process is repeated, season after season.

Borlaug was uniquely hands-on; if anyone was going to get their nails dirty, he was. When, soon after initiating his studies,, a Mexican scientist told him, "We don't do these things in Mexico. That's why we have peons," Borlaug responded, "That's why the farmers have no respect for you. If you don't know how to do something properly yourself how can you possibly advise them?" Indeed, during the cross-breeding season, Borlaug often took a sleeping bag and his food into the fields and spent days cooking over a campfire and sleeping on the ground. Despite the long odds, Borlaug's team had enormous success. Whereas most plant geneticists made a few dozen crosses in a season, within a decade, Borlaug's team had painstakingly crossed 6,000 plants. The nugget that he was searching for, ever so carefully inspecting each plant, was just one or two in these thousands. After working at it for over two decades, Borlaug's team would develop just 75 novel strains, only four of which would become the backbone of Mexican wheat production.

Work on this scope could not be done without the labor of a *group*. His team was not a hierarchy, it was a collaborative. Their brute force had already brought wheat yields up by 40 percent when, in 1952, Borlaug hit on a single collaboration that in one fell swoop doubled yields yet again. Dr. Orville Vogel, an eminent U.S. Department of Agriculture wheat breeder, had successfully crossed a drawf strain of Japanese winter wheat named Norin 10 with a normally tall U.S. wheat plant. When Borlaug heard of this, he realized that the new strain had the potential to overcome a chronic problem in Mexican strains. The tall Mexican wheat plants, when their growth was accelerated by fertilizer, became so gangly that the weight of their grain-laden heads caused them to fall over. This presented an absolute limit to the usefulness of fertilizer. At Borlaug's request, Vogel sent some of his most promising Norin 10 hybrids. Crossed with his best adapted Mexican varieties, the result was magic—plants with short stiff stems, sporting many heads full of grain. When grown with ample fertilizer, Borlaug's Mexican hybrids had, by 1956, achieved the holy grail of Mexican wheat production: self-sufficiency.

The victory of Borlaug's dwarf Mexican wheat varieties was only one of the legacies that came from teamwork. The other was the development of intellectual capital. Training scientists from many countries provided the leadership for what became the International Spring Wheat Yield Nursery, consisting of stations around the world that shared novel wheat varieties. Through this vehicle, dwarf varieties of high-yield, rust-resistant wheat were disseminated throughout Latin America and Southeast Asia. Borlaug believed in sharing early and often. Rather than waiting to discover the perfect strain, he released new hybrids to the marketplace anytime that adequate testing showed them to be useful. Closer to home, Borlaug hired Mexican boys who typically could not read or write and developed the most capable of them into future technicians. One of these technicians, Reyes Vega, ultimately became the superintendent of the Mexican research center, developing a technique that massively increased the efficiency for pollinating wheat plants.

Forever reaching for desired characteristics led Borlaug in 1946 to his most novel innovation. Roberto Maurer, who owned a moderate-sized farm near Ciudad Obregon in northwestern Mexico, had planted a crop with some signs of rust resistance, although the variety had other problems.

Borlaug wanted to go and see it.He also had learned that nearby was an experimental agricultural station that, when it had been built a decade earlier to take advantage of the fertile soil in the region, was considered state of the art. The problem was that from Borlaug's office in Toluca, just outside Mexico City, Ciudad Obregon was 2,000 kilometers away, over undeveloped roads. Borlaug hitched a ride on a privately owned trimotor Fokker, a lumbering propeller plane that took two days to get there. He arrived to find the agricultural station overrun by weeds and neglect. But nearby farms were thriving, and after several days of visiting them and collecting specimens, he returned to Toluca—with an idea.

Borlaug *deduced t*hat he could *rearrange* plants to adapt to the climate and geography of both his own region and that around Ciudad Obregon. He called this logical leap of faith "shuttle breeding." It went against the then-standard belief that plants must be bred for a particular climate and locale. But, interestingly enough, history repeats itself and Borlag's inspiration turns out to have been the rebirth of an old idea. The Incan Empire, widely distributed between coastal and highland regions of Peru, had similarly experimented with growing and adapting plants to different altitudes. Borlaug hoped to produce two experimental crops each year by growing wheat during the summer season in his own high-altitude, rain-fed region of Toluca and then breeding the most interesting seeds during the winter in the low elevation and amply irrigated region near Ciudad Obregon. That was just what the Incans had done, thereby doubling their crop yields and sustaining an ever-expanding empire. For Borlaug, two research stations would double his speed in growing novel varieties and expand his scientific progress. It was an idea so foreign that George Harrar, director of the Office of Special Studies, was convinced it was impossible. Twice he denied the request to move equipment across the country. Only when Borlaug tendered his resignation did Professor Stakman, then chairman of the Rockefeller Foundation's Agricultural Advisory Committee, step in to mediate.

The shuttle breeding program not only accelerated the pace of breeding, it had an added benefit. By growing crops in two different and distinct environments, the crops became broadly adapted—so much so that when later transplanted to India, Pakistan, and China, they would flourish. This characteristic, in addition to the plants' rust resistance and fertilizer-responsive high yields, made them perfect varieties to trigger a worldwide transformation in agricultural productivity.

Borlaug used one last tool of innovation: *changing point of view.* To Borlaug, wheat was like a person. He learned, as he said, "to tell the status of a wheat plant from its look, manner of growth, disease reactions, feel, and movement." He could tell the strains apart by their "personalities," such as their characteristic rustle in the wind. He had gotten so close to his crops that he could empathize with them. This may have provided a more personal motivation, along with his more general altruistic goal to feed the masses. He wanted to ensure the health of his wheat plants.

Clearly, then, Borlaug's work—and with it the availability of hybrid wheat varieties—sparked the Green Revolution. But it was kindling without a match. The match was fertilizer. The downside of the new hybrids was that they flourish only when stimulated by huge amounts of chemical nutrients.

Of the key minerals that plants need to grow, the one required in the greatest abundance is nitrogen, a building component of proteins and nucleic acids. Nitrogen makes up 79 percent of air. However, this gas is so highly chemically bonded that it is inert; that is, it does not react with other chemicals. To be used by plants, nitrogen must be combined with hydrogen to form ammonia (NH_4) or oxygen to form nitrate (NO_3); that is, it must be "fixed." The main natural contributors to nitrogen fixation, so essential to the sustenance of all life on earth, are soil and water bacteria. The bacteria species *Rhizobium*, for example, are major players in nitrogen fixation, living in root nodules of legumes such as soybeans and chickpeas. Fixed nitrogen is taken up from the bacteria by plants. But, of course, this cannot be a one-way street. When animals excrete the remains of what they have eaten or when plants die, organic material returns ammonia to the soil, where it feeds the nitrogen-fixing bacteria. This beautifully calibrated cycle of production and use is called the nitrogen cycle.

Unfortunately, modern agriculture has disrupted and strained the nitrogen cycle to the point of breaking. Monoculture, the growing of a single crop, reduces ecosystem diversity and symbioses. Crops grown in one place are carried off to be consumed in distant lands, and with them go valuable nitrogen reserves. Thirsty hybrids need excessive quantities of nitrogen. These patterns have depleted soils since the time of the Industrial Revolution. Modern-day plants do not grow without artificial nitrogen enrichment. Through the end of the nineteenth century, natural deposits of nitrates maintained agricultural production, but these were quickly running out.

The most abundant source of nitrogen is in the air. It appeared that a method called the Birkeland-Eyde process, which used hydroelectric power to produce an electric arc that could oxidize nitrogen, might capture this rich source. A large hydroelectric company in Norway tried to commercialize the Birkeland-Eyde process, but the operation proved to be too energy inefficient. Fortunately, a dozen years later, Fritz Haber and Carl Bosch had an even better idea.

In his acceptance speech upon receiving the 1918 Nobel Prize in chemistry, Fritz Haber, a German chemist, notes that by the time that he and Bosch had discovered a chemical process for manufacturing ammonia, so many had tried and failed that most scientists believed it was impossible. "Such prejudice," he stated, "... deter(s) one from becoming too deeply involved in the subject." Haber was not so much innovative as he was determined. His approach built on a flicker of hope from earlier experiments in which, at high temperature, nitrogen and hydrogen could be directly combined. Using iron as a catalyst and pushing the temperature in his experimental chamber up to 1000°C, Haber discovered that a small but consistent proportion of nitrogen from air decomposed into ammonia. Haber switched to manganese, which worked at lower temperatures, and then tinkered until he had uncovered the optimal temperature, pressure, and mixture of nitrogen and hydrogen to maximize the reaction. Ultimately, the process consisted of passing nitrogen and hydrogen over four beds of catalyst, with cooling between and a recycling of unreacted gases. The conversion rate from gas to ammonia became a whopping 97 percent. Since its efficiency has never been surpassed, the Haber-Bosch process remains the modern standard, and it produces mass quantities of ammonia.

Unfortunately, Haber's story did not have a happy ending. During World War I, the prize-winning chemist, also an arch German nationalist, orchestrated the development of wartime chemical weapons such as chlorine gas. Both his wife, Clara, and their son, Hermann, would commit suicide over Haber's role in directing the development of these heinous agents. Later (in World War II), the chemical weapons which Haber so ardently defended, became the poison of choice against his own people, the Jews. Zyklon B, developed in Haber's institute, became a ubiquitous agent for mass murder in the gas chambers. When the Nobel Laureate found himself reduced to "just another Jew" who was forced to flee from Nazi-occupied Germany, he was a despised man—a man without a country. Chaim Weizmann, later to become the founding president of Israel, generously offered Haber the position of director of Palestine's new research institute (now called the Weizmann Institute), an offer which Haber gratefully accepted, hoping to resurrect his work and reputation. Ironically, however, on his way to Palestine in 1934, a heart attack overtook Haber. He never reached the Holy Land.

Today, according to the United Nations' Food and Agriculture Organization, "the world produces enough food to feed everyone on the planet. World agriculture produces 17 percent more calories per person today than it did for each person 30 years ago, despite a 70 percent population increase. This could provide everyone in the world with at least 2,720 kilocalories per person per day." Yet, in 2010, the UN estimated that a whopping 925 million people (13 percent of the world's population) remain malnourished. Hunger in the modern world is no longer the result of scarcity but of structural inequity—the inability to pay for food and the lack of food distribution.

Moreover, for all that the Green Revolution has achieved, it can only go so far. And it is unclear how much farther that is. Large inputs of energy are needed to produce fertilizer, and fertilizer overuse results in soil degradation. Yet agricultural production must not only continue at its current pace but must accelerate to keep pace with an ever enlarging world population. Whether this can be done using present technology, even with genetic engineering, is unclear. The Malthusian nightmare, then, has not necessarily been eliminated so much as it is delayed.

BORLAUG AND THE GREEN REVOLUTION ANNOTATED: THE USE OF TOOLS OF INNOVATION

The Green Revolution was no revolution at all, but an evolution of innovative approaches. The underlying foundation of knowledge about fertilizers and plant husbandry had been known for at least a half century. The question was obvious: how to make Mexico (and other nations) agriculturally self-sufficient. Saving the world simply did not require a revolution. What was needed was for Norman Borlag, "father of the Green Revolution," and others to attain the step-wise advances of growing hardier species more quickly and equitably.

Borlaug's favorite tools were *dissection* and *observation*. To attain the optimal plant species took years and thousands of cross-breeds, discovered through a painstaking process of individually selecting for and then *combining* each desired characteristic.

Borlaug was not only an empiricist. He *deduced* some big ideas. One of these was his guess that he could coax plants to adapt to various climates and geographies, in particular to his own region of Toluca near Mexico City and to Ciudad Obregon in the Northwest. He called this logical leap of faith "shuttle breeding." It was a belief that *expanded* beyond the pre-existing presumption that plants had to grow in a single climate.

Perhaps the most exotic tool Borlaug used was to *change his point of view*. His sensibility toward plants was so great that he could "tell the status of a wheat plant from its look, manner of growth, disease reactions, feel, and movement." For him, plants had personalities.

The arduous work of manipulating thousands of plant varieties was not a job that could be done alone. Successes such as Borlaug's dwarf Mexican wheat varieties were the work of a *team*. Ultimately, Borlag trained not just Mexican scientists, but agronomists from around the world. Building a trusted network of connections made it possible to share the most up-to-date crop varieties throughout Latin America and Southeast Asia. In the modern age, social networks and connected economies provide a robust platform to achieve the promise of global group innovation. It cannot come too soon. Be it evolutionary or revolutionary, the need for a next great leap in agricultural innovation is upon us. Hopefully, scientific innovation will continue to deliver us from a future apocalypse.

	Question	Groups	Analogy	Rearrange	Observation	Deduction / Induction	Change Point of View	Expand	Narrow/ Dissect	Reverse	Break Frames	Autonomy	Openness	Persistence
Borlaug		✿	✿	✿	✿		✿	✿	✿			✿	✿	✿

Figure 13.1. Borlaug: Tools and Characteristics

14

Medications Everywhere but Only One Pill

Russell Marker, Arthur Hertig, and John Rock

How long can famine, despair, and social upheaval be held off by an enlarging food supply? It likely depends on the rate at which the population is burgeoning. In 1963, the population growth rate, or the proportion increase from one year to the next year, peaked at 2.2 percent (so if theoretical year one has 3 billion people, year two will have 66 million more). By October, 2011, the size of humanity had doubled from its 1963 count to a bloated 7 billion. Many of humanity's most pressing problems—climate change, water scarcity, and the extinction of species, to name a few—are a result of overpopulation. The pressure to curb population growth thus remains one of humankind's greatest priorities. Fortunately since the 1960s there has been tremendous progress with the 2009 population growth rate having declined to 1.1 percent. It has been a true triumph—indeed, a triumph of science.

Science's first and best solution to curbing population growth came in the form of a tiny, round pill. Not just any pill—*the* Pill, a medication that, like the celebrities Oprah, Diana, and Elvis, wears its status in its name recognition. The Pill—oral contraception—was the first form of birth control that broke the indestructible link between sex and procreation. Because women did not need to use it at the time of intercourse, contraceptive choice shifted from being the prerogative among men to becoming a choice made by women. Previous methods, such as condoms and diaphragms left married women whose husbands opposed these as unpleasant, to the whims of nature and to the fate of bearing an over-abundance of children. Unmarried women, before the era of the Pill, engaged in intercourse at their peril. The Pill, according to John G. Searle, chairman of the pharmaceutical giant G. D. Searle which launched the first formulation, Enovid was, "our organization's greatest contribution to mankind . . . . It is a positive answer to a world threatened by overpopulation, and the resulting poor subsistence, poor shelter, and poor education that surplus people are forced to endure."

Like the Green Revolution, the Contraceptive Revolution transformed society in a way that was surprising. Some have suggested that this single medication triggered virtually every social trend among women in the last half of the twentieth century. The rise of women in the workforce? Higher divorce rates? Women's altered interactions with the medical establishment? Increased attainment of equal rights? The true impacts are unclear; what is clear is that the world after the Pill was very different from the world before.

Like the Green Revolution, even though the social disruption that resulted from the Pill was revolutionary, the science was not. Inventing the Pill was evolutionary innovation. The development of the Pill represented the step-by step progress that built upon foundations within three separate disciplines: chemistry, biology, and medicine, and the work of a host of individuals. Still, some of the scientists involved wielded the tools of innovation like true geniuses.

To create the Pill first required the realization that hormones control fertility and that the key fertility hormones are estrogen and progesterone. The famous British physiologist Ernest Starling, along with his brother-in-law William Bayliss, discovered in dogs the hormone secretin in 1902. Hormones are chemicals produced by one tissue and carried by blood to another organ where they have physiological, often reproductive or metabolic, effects. By the 1910s–1920s, hormones had become quite the rage. Insulin had been discovered to treat diabetes and thyroxine to overcome thyroid deficiency. Natural sex hormones were not only hyped to treat menstrual irregularities but to enhance virility. Animal gonadal extracts became a thriving over-the-counter market, despite their questionable efficacy and safety.

Ludwig Haberlandt in Switzerland and George W. Corner in the United States, among others, by the end of the 1930s had described the function of estrogen and progesterone. Within the female reproductive cycle, book-ended by the menstrual cycle and marked at mid-cycle by ovulation, estrogen predominated the first half and progesterone the second half. Ovulation and progesterone were intimately linked. Ovulation triggered the production of progesterone; progesterone, depending on when in the cycle it was given, either stimulated or inhibited ovulation. By 1939, both pure crystalline ovarian estrogen and progesterone had been isolated, the former earning the chemist Adolf Butenandt the Nobel Prize.

Progesterone and estrogen, members of the steroid hormone family, are comprised of four fused rings (three six-sided and one five-sided), each made up of carbons. The various side chains of hydrogen, oxygen, and other elements that hang off these carbons give each steroid hormone its specific character. Steroids are often converted one into another. Within the ovaries, estradiol (estrogen) is synthesized from testosterone, which, in turn, comes from progesterone. In other organs, too, hormones are inter-converted; in the adrenal glands, cortisol (which turned out to play a leading role in the saga of the development of the Pill) also originates from progesterone. Thus, progesterone might be considered the gatekeeper. From its conversion comes testosterone, estrogen, and cortisol.

Indeed, the key to developing the Pill was a requirement for the commercial production of inexpensive, orally potent progesterone. The "inexpensive" requirement was realized by Russell E. Marker, who profited not at all from his discoveries and disappeared into oblivion. The "orally potent" element was provided by Carl Djerassi, who became fabulously wealthy and famously decorated.

Chemical synthesis in the laboratory is a difficult and arduous process. It has been described as building a house without being able to see the building blocks. " …To synthesize something as complicated as a steroid," stated Leonard Engel, "one must find, for each step of the way, a chemical reaction that places the right atom in the right spatial configuration and the steps must be so ordered that later ones don't undo what was accomplished earlier." When the house building is not residential but commercial, that is, accomplished in the hyper-competitive world of pharmaceutical companies, as was done by Marker and Djerassi, the work becomes even more formidable. Such was the challenge that went into formulating the building blocks that made up the Pill.

Russell Marker's synthesis of progesterone is one of the most apocryphal stories in science. The son of a western Maryland sharecropper born in 1902, Marker's early motivation was quite straightforward—as he put it, "To get out of farmwork." This led him to walk three miles plus ride a train four miles a day to attend high school. Against his father's wishes, Marker pursued undergraduate and graduate degrees at the University of Maryland. Organic chemistry attracted him in part because it was considered by his fellow students to be particularly difficult. After completing his doctoral thesis, which was soon published in the prestigious *Journal of the American Chemical Society*, Marker's advisor informed him that he needed one additional course in physical chemistry to graduate. Marker refused to take it, arguing that his lab work had already provided him mastery of the material. While the requirement was not negotiable, his advisor offered an extended fellowship while Marker completed it. In response, Marker simply quit. The great chemist would rise to the stature of full professor and publish 213 articles, many in his field's top journals, without ever attaining a Ph.D.

In his first academic job at the esteemed Rockefeller University in New York City in 1928, steroids immediately attracted Marker's interest. Adolf Butenandt's synthesis of progesterone, which won him the Nobel Prize in 1939, followed nature's blueprint of conversion from cholesterol. But Butenandt's process required massive quantities of bovine and sheep spinal cords and brains to produce miniscule quantities of progesterone at great cost. The only consumers who could afford the scarce resource were the breeders of world-class race horses. In horses (and women), tiny amounts of injected progesterone could "cure" individuals prone to miscarriages, allowing them to achieve successful pregnancies (oddly dependent on how it is taken, progesterone can either assist or avert pregnancy).

Marker felt certain that he could do better if he started from a family of plant sterols called sapogenins. He may have gotten this idea from the *analogy* between sapogenins and cholesterol (from which derives progesterone), both of which have a long side chain hanging off the same end of the steroid backbone. Or he may have been reaching back to the use of plants, such as Queen Anne's Lace, date palm, myrrh, and pomegranate, which had been used by women throughout history to provide medicinal contraception. Marker's mentor reacted to the plant synthesis idea with more than skepticism, indeed with rejection. One of their Rockefeller colleagues, Walter Jacobs, had experimented with sarsaparilla roots containing sapogenins and had shown "beyond any doubt" that the side chain hanging off the steroid backbone and in need to removal to form progesterone was inert. It would simply not react with other chemicals and thus could not be detached. When Marker announced that he would pursue this avenue anyway, he was told that progesterone was off limits. The dispute provoked Marker to repeat his doctoral program behavior—to take a walk. If he couldn't pursue steroid chemistry at Rockefeller, he would find a place where he could. Within the year he was working at Pennsylvania State College (only later to become a University) at less than half the salary and a fraction of the prestige.

Marker's first success at Penn State was producing 35 grams of pure progesterone from the urine of pregnant women. The concept derived from a clever *analogy*: progesterone is produced when, after ovulation, what is left inside the ovary is a corpus luteum, or yellow body. If the egg becomes fertilized, the corpus luteum turns into a progesterone factory, manufacturing sky-high quantities of progesterone to support the growing embryo. Thus, pregnancy is an excellent source of progesterone. Marker's 35 grams of injectable progesterone was the largest batch ever produced and, at $1,000 per gram, he had tapped into a gold mine. Parke-Davis, Marker's sponsor was delighted with the product and saw no reason to push their luck. With a stable of pregnant bovines they planned to corner what had previously been the all-European sex steroid pharmaceutical market.

Marker, in contrast, saw the bovine pregnancy avenue as a side trip on the way to his main destination of producing progesterone from plants.

He no longer saw the problem as others did. The question that science had been asking was, How do we maximize the efficiency of changing cholesterol into progesterone? Marker's question became, What is the best way to make progesterone? No longer was Marker interested in the best way to get to the end. His energies were entirely focused on the best source for the beginning. He had taken the question and both *flipped* and *expanded* it.

After repeating the failed experiments by his former colleague at Rockefeller, Maker became further convinced that the previous approach was mistaken. The sapogenin side chain, he believed, contained reactive oxygen atoms that could be removed under specific acidic conditions. With assistance by a graduate student, Ewald Rohrmann, months of trial and error ensued. Marker *dissected the problem* into a matter of type of acid, timing, and temperature. Using dozens of acids and varying the temperature and timing, he and Rohrmann tried over and over to pry off the unwanted atoms. Finally, the crude spectrometer they were using to indicate how close they were to the wavelength of progesterone showed that they were getting hot. After checking the purity of their product using more sophisticated analyses available from a laboratory in New York, they were sure. Pure victory—they had come within two easy steps of progesterone. Marker had found a novel five-step process for the conversion. As he immediately reported in the *Journal of the American Chemical Society*, the sapogenin "was inert in boiling with acetic anhydride for 24 hours, [but] when heated in a sealed tube overnight at 200 degrees it gave a new product." This subtle change in temperature and time had created the "Marker degradation." It remains today the foundation for a multibillion-dollar steroid manufacturing industry.

For many scientists, this discovery would have been the ticket to kick back and enjoy fame and fortune. For Marker it constituted a new challenge. Marker remained committed to his question of finding the beginning—the perfect source of sapogenin. He was convinced that he had not yet found it. At every conference he attended, he begged botanists to send him plant sources. Partial successes came from a Japanese plant of the *Dioscorea species,* which produced a special form of sapogenin called diosgenin. The ease of producing progesterone from diosgenin narrowed Marker's search. Yet, it also *expanded* his quest. What had now become clear is that he needed quantity—a large plant that grew in abundance. With botanical colleagues in tow, he traveled to Texas, Arizona, and California, in each place discovering, examining, and naming new sapogenin-producing plants. Four hundred species were collected; 40,000 kilograms of plant material examined; eleven new sapogenins isolated; two entirely new steroids identified. Finally, in Texas, Marker's alertness to *observing* local botanicals brought to his notice a photo in a book showing an enormous tuber from the *Dioscorea species*. He was elated. Perhaps this inedible yam called *cabeza de negro,* found in the Veracruz province of Mexico, was the large and abundant sapogenin he had been searching for.

It was in November 1941, a month before Pearl Harbor. The American Embassy was urging all Americans to stay out of Mexico, not knowing on which side that country would enter the war. Nevertheless, Marker ventured to Mexico twice. Unable to get a permit and abandoned by his Spanish-speaking botanist guide, he continued to Veracruz alone, taking the public bus. There, a local store owner was able to produce large amounts of *cabeza de negro*. It turned out that locals cast pieces of the plant into the water to kill fish; *cabeza de negro* closed fish throats and caused suffocation.

Back home with his booty, Marker found that the dried *cabeza de negro* tuber made a fine sapogenin. But neither Parke-Davis nor any other pharmaceutical company would back him to establish a small progesterone production facility in Mexico. They simply considered a non-U.S. facility too risky. Marker could not be deterred. "…I drew out of the bank half of my meager savings and returned to Mexico," the maverick later recounted. That capital funded the collection of 10 tons of *cabeza de negro*, which he then converted (using the laboratory of a friend in exchange for one third of the progesterone produced) into three kilograms of progesterone. At the then current market price, it was worth a whopping $240,000.

The next year, 1943, Marker resigned from Penn State. He would sign a patent application for the Marker degradation process, he informed Parke-Davis, only if they prepared the paperwork before he moved full-time to Mexico. Parke-Davis did not believe him. A year later when they came to find him, he told them their time had passed. The Marker degradation went unpatented.

Upon arriving in Mexico, Marker took the only approach he could think of to find laboratory facilities and trained personnel. He opened the yellow pages. There, under the heading "Laboratorios," he unearthed a company called Hormona, founded by Emerik Somlo and Federico Lehmann. Together, the three drew up the papers for a new company, which they called Syntex. A year and 30 kilograms of progesterone later, the deal had collapsed. Marker and Somlo had had a falling out over profit sharing. When Marker tried to sustain a new company of his own, based on finding a new yam, *barbasco,* which provided an even higher yield of sapogenin, his staff came under threat of physical harassment. (Marker claimed it was the hand of Somlo.) Even though Marker was producing progesterone at a rapid clip, he was forced to abandon ownership and sell his assets to a European firm, which ultimately merged it into the pharmaceutical giant Organon. Organon remains one of the major producers of hormones in Mexico today.

Marker said later that he was happy he had not patented the Marker degradation because he preferred to "leave the field open to anyone who wished to produce in competition, to force the price of the various hormones down to a point where they would be available for medical purposes at a reasonable price." Indeed, by 1949, the price of injectable progesterone had plummeted to $5 per gram; within a decade, a gram would cost only cents.

By then, however, Marker's passion for chemistry had grown cold. He destroyed all of his laboratory notes and letters and walked out, not on just another employer but on his entire profession. His last publication was a review of possible plant sources for cortisol. Once again, Marker would be prescient.

Cortisol turned out to be the spark that ignited the discovery of the ingestible progesterone needed to make the Pill. When demonstrated to be a miracle treatment for rheumatoid arthritis, demand for cortisol soared. The obvious source was synthesis from progesterone. Syntex was poised to be a major player in the race for the cortisone patent, but Marker and his methods were gone. Somlo, frantic to find a new scientific director, came upon George Rosenkranz, a Jewish émigré who had worked with the best steroid chemists in Switzerland before fleeing the Nazis. The advice Rosenkranz was given about steroids, according to Bernard Asbell, author of *The Pill*, was, "Don't touch a steroid with a ten foot pole. Everything that can be done has already been achieved." Fortunately, Rosenkranz ignored that advice.

After reinstating Marker's process for producing progesterone (without any notes or even labeled reagents to guide him), he moved on to manufacture testosterone and estrogen as well. But his object now was cortisone. In order to attain it, Rosenkranz recruited a young hot shot Carl Djerassi. At least five major pharmaceutical firms were racing to realize the cortisol patent. In 1951, using Marker's leftover diosogenin, Djerassi led the Syntex team to capture the flag.

But the festivities were short-lived. Within months, two scientists from Upjohn had filed a patent to produce cortisol in a single step through a process of bacterial fermentation from progesterone. The elegant work of chemical synthesis had been overshadowed by a bunch of microorganisms. Yet this new process had an unintended consequence. Now an intense demand arose for cortisol's precursor, progesterone. Big pharma was looking for not kilograms, but tons. Djerassi needed a more potent form of progesterone.

Back in 1944, Maximillian Ehrenstein, at the University of Pennsylvania, had shattered a previous assumption about progesterone, which was that any chemical alteration of its core structure would destroy its biological activity. A compound that he created by manipulating progesterone, called 19-norprogesterone, had not lost its efficacy—in fact, its progesterone activity in animals was heightened. The 19-nor stood for the removal of a carbon and its replacement with a hydrogen between the first and second rings of the four ring backbone. Ehrenstein had produced only a miniscule quantity of the 19-nor with great effort. Djerassi now successfully applied newer methods to obtain much larger quantities. Like Ehrenstein, Djerassi found that the modified hormone had activity four to eight times greater than the original progesterone. The dogma that one could not improve on nature was disproven.

Potent progesterone provided a commercial source for cortisol, but Djerassi realized that it also had another potential use. Menstrual disorders were increasingly being treated with progesterone. But the fragility of progesterone caused it to disintegrate in the stomach. Thus menstrual disorder treatment required painful injections. What was needed was an oral progesterone. As it turned out Djerassi achieved that goal as well by tapping into another unexpected source—testosterone. A German chemist named Hans Herloff Inhoffen had found that if a group of carbons (called an acetyl group) was added to one of the steroid rings of testosterone at a position called 17-α, the change made testosterone weakly progesterone-like. Equally important, the new compound could be given orally. On October 15, 1951, Djerassi, supervising a Mexican chemist named Luis Miramontes, combined their 19-nor form with Inhoffen's 17-α compound. The result was 19-nor-17-α-ethynyltestosterone, shortened to norethindrone. It had the progesterone potency of 19-nor and the oral availability of the 17-α. Djerassi, Miramontes, and Rosenkrantz patented the first orally potent form of progesterone. Never did they imagine that its use would ultimately elicit fame and infamy.

How did this essential ingredient find its way into the Pill? The answer lies at the intersection of science and feminist politics. Margaret Sanger was an Irishwoman who, in the words of a PBS documentary, "devoted her life to legalizing birth control and making it universally available to women." She opposed state laws that outlawed the distribution of contraceptive methods, opened the first birth control clinic in the country, and, in 1921, founded the precursor to Planned Parenthood. By 1951, then 72 years old, Sanger had been scouring the country for a scientific champion to provide a "magic pill" that would relieve women of the burden of conception. At a dinner party, Sanger met Gregory Pincus, a biologist and cofounder of the Worcester Foundation for Experimental Biology. Pincus's "Foundation" was actually a small, struggling private laboratory. Pincus had lost his position at Harvard in the mid-1930s when his work on in vitro fertilization in rabbits, characterized by the press as creating "fatherless" test tube babies, could not be replicated. During his accidental encounter with Sanger, Pincus knew he was getting his second chance. He immediately agreed to deliver a chemical contraceptive. Together with reproductive physiologist Min Chueh Chang and financially supported by International Harvester heiress Katherine McCormick, Pincus replicated earlier rabbit experiments that showed that progesterone injections halted ovulation.

It was then that Pincus and Chang stumbled upon Djerassi's nore-thindrone, as well as a similar oral progesterone that had subsequently been synthesized, called norethynodrel. Although norethynodrel had been submitted for patent by Frank Colton at G. D. Searle two years after norethindrone's application, it was the first to be FDA approved and so Pincus evaluated both compounds. Among the nearly 200 chemicals with progesterone activity that Pincus and Chang tested, norethynodrel and norethindrone were the two that perfectly impeded rabbit ovula-tion. They had found the key ingredient and had established at least theoretically that it might work. Now what they needed to develop the Pill was clinical testing in humans. For that they had to add to their team an expert gynecologist.

John Rock, a famed Harvard-trained gynecologist-obstetrician and ardent Catholic, was the most surprising sponsor imaginable for the first oral contraceptive trials. As told in an autobiography by Marsh and Ronner, "He was so well known by the mid-1940s, one story goes, that when 'a famous movie actress'—Merle Oberon we suspect—arrived in Boston to see the 'fertility doctor' and didn't know his name, she was sent directly to Rock. When she told him how she found him, he told her not to feel embarrassed. After all, he said, 'Before we met, I'd never heard of you, either.'" What drove Rock to work on the Pill was thus not recognition—indeed as a prominent Catholic his involvement threatened his high social stature. What motivated him was empathy for women and a passion for science.

Ironically, two of Rock's scientific triumphs were perfecting in vitro fertilization, which allowed infertile women to become pregnant, and testing the Pill, which prevented women from becoming pregnant. Even more ironically, Rock's most elegant breakthrough was neither of these. It was a study that was designed to do nothing less than to understand how human embryos come to be. Collaborating with obstetrical pathologist

Arthur Hertig, Rock wanted to fully describe the earliest days in the journey that a human egg takes toward becoming a fetus. In an era before the advent of pregnancy tests, before doctors could time ovulation, the audacity of their goal was staggering.

Hertig had gone to Harvard Medical School and then completed a fellowship at the Carnegie Institution in Baltimore, the nation's premier center for human embryology. There he learned the technical wizardry of using microscopy to find miniscule embryos in the reproductive tracts of primates. He also became familiar with Carnegie's collection of human embryo pathology specimens, the largest in the world. These human embryos, found coincidentally during autopsies or gynecologic surgeries (when the uterus was removed no one imagined that the patient was pregnant), provided a rare, albeit incomplete, peek into the early life of pregnancies.

Hertig and Rock's query of how ovulation turns into a developing baby was a *big question*. It contrasted to much more discrete questions that others had been asking, such as when during the menstrual cycle ovulation occurs, or what hormones the corpus luteum secretes.

The idea for the Hertig and Rock experiment came from an *analogy*. In humans, hints about the life course of the embryo had occurred when a pathologist examined a uterus removed to treat disease and was lucky enough to detect an unsuspected embryo. In contrast, animal experiments were based on a *reversal* of this design. Monkeys were mated to purposefully produce a pregnancy, then the reproductive organs were removed in order to find it. Now Hertig and Rock *combined* the approaches.

Two hundred eleven women whose medical conditions required them to have a non-emergency hysterectomy were enrolled. All were married and were known to be fertile by virtue of having at least three prior deliveries. Each subject agreed to mail back postcard calendars in which she tracked her menstrual cycles. In the month before her scheduled surgery, she was instructed to go home and have intercourse at the time that the medical team had determined (using these calendars) she was most fertile. This, as every aspect of the study, had been *dissected* to maximize the likelihood that each woman would conceive before the planned removal of her uterus and fallopian tubes. Once removed, Hertig with his micro-scope painstakingly sought a fertilized egg or embryo—jewels no larger than the size of a pencil point.

In a series of papers published over the course of two decades, Hertig and Rock did what they had set out to do—they introduced the equiva-lent of a stop-action camera into the reproductive tract. Perfectly intact embryos were found within fallopian tubes, suggesting that fertiliza-tion and early cell division both take place within that thin, hollow structure. The youngest embryos ever seen, only seven days old, were detected nestling themselves into the bedding-like lining of the uterus. The work was fundamental, groundbreaking, and it produced tangible meaning for medicine. In vitro fertilization credits this study with lay-ing its foundation.

Indeed, the Hertig and Rock study did even more. It demonstrated that conception occurs only a third or so of the time. It also revealed that women miscarry fully half of their earliest embryos. These esti-mates reveal an unforseen truth about human reproduction: only about 15–30 percent of sexual pairings will lead to a successful pregnancy. Humans turn out to be the least successful reproducers in the animal kingdom.

Rock was drawn into working on the Pill through a chance meeting with Pincus at a scientific conference in 1952. While Pincus had been injecting progesterone to prevent ovulation, Rock had been injecting progesterone and estrogen into infertile women to enhance their abil-ity to conceive. Rock's hormonal treatment posited that some infer-tile women might, when primed with hormones, become pregnant. The method showed some success and came to be called the "Rock rebound." But the kicker was that *during* the hormone injections, pregnancy almost never occurred. Thus, although contrary to Rock's purpose, he had attained Pincus's desired result—the prevention of pregnancy.

In 1954, when Rock began the first clinical trials of the Pill, he did so under cover of his infertility protocol. Fifty women volunteers were told that they were taking the Pill in the hopes of achieving a pregnancy rebound. Both norethindrone and norethynodrel were tested and performed similarly but norethynodrel went into the first Pill formulation, likely because G. D. Searle, its developer, sponsored the first trials.

Rock's results were encouraging. In the five months after the end of the protocol, 14 percent of the women achieved pregnancy. But more true to the trial's intent, while on norethynodrel and norethindrone, none of the women ovulated. Breakthrough bleeding was a problem for a sizable proportion (20 percent) of women on 5 milligram (mg) doses but the side effect was alleviated with 10 mg doses. Progesterone looked to be 100 percent effective in preventing ovulation.

Now Pincus and Rock were ready for bigger things. To prove safety and efficacy on a large scale they took the nascent Pill to a place where the dispensing of contraception was not illegal, as it was in Massachusetts, a consideration that landed them in Puerto Rico. Puerto Rico had a constructive view of contraception, an established network of family planning clinics which could refer subjects, and one of the world's densest populations. In the course of their Puerto Rico trial, conducted in the mid-1950s, the Pill would take its modern, familiar form. Pincus would suggest to Rock that the Pill be taken for 21 days, followed by 7 days off for "natural" menstruation. Rock was delighted with this idea, hoping it would placate the Catholic Church. Although the 21/7 Pill became the standard formulation, its acceptance as "natural" was never accepted by the Church. Rock and Pincus would also trip over estrogen as a beneficial addition to progesterone. During the Puerto Rico trials, they discovered that Searle's norethynodrel was contaminated with about 4–7 percent of an estrogen called mestranol. Panic overtook the research team—would all of their previous results be worthless? But the error turned out to be a serendipitous gift. When Searle removed the mestranol, the pure progesterone formulation caused unacceptably high rates of breakthrough bleeding and the small mestranol impurity was recognized as beneficial. All subsequent Pills have been combinations of progesterone and estrogen.

In 1957, the FDA approved Searle's application for the norethynodrel/ mestranol Pill, giving it the trade name "Enovid 10 mg." The indication was for the treatment of severe menstrual disorders. But few were fooled. Women's magazines spread the word that the new medicine prevented pregnancy. By 1959, severe menstrual disorder, a previously rare condition, was being diagnosed and treated with the Pill in half a million American women. Searle got the message—there was money in the Pill. In 1960, the FDA approved Searle's application for Enovid 5 mg as the first widely prescribed oral contraceptive.

The Pill's popularity grew, despite immediate and continued antagonism from the Catholic Church, but it was far from smooth sailing. In the early 1970s, after use by millions of women, the Pill was linked to the unexpected adverse events blood clots, heart attacks, and strokes. Congressional hearings in response to feminist Barbara Seaman's book *The Doctors' Case Against the Pill* accused the Pill of being a devious experiment thrust upon women by the male medical establishment. Fortunately subsequent studies showed that these clot-related risks were mostly limited to older smokers. Moreover, as lower dose Pills were formulated, adverse outcomes became exceedingly rare. In the end, the Pill survived and flourished. The Congressional Pill Hearings, moreover, had an important benefit in that they led to the inclusion of patient package inserts about medication side effects, now accompanying every prescribed medication.

Modern Pills typically contain about one-third of Enovid's estrogen dose. A modern user's risk of blood clots is only 1 per 100,000 women years. Subsequent Pill scares suggested a link to breast cancer risk, but the most definitive systematic review to date, conducted in 2010, showed that breast cancer rates are no higher among Pill users than non-users. Instead, the Pill has been consistently shown to reduce the risk of ovarian, endometrial, and colorectal cancers. The most common reason that women today discontinue the Pill is because of breakthrough bleeding and concerns about weight gain. There is, however, no consistent scientific evidence that the Pill increases weight.

Today, use of the Pill and other forms of contraception has become routine. In 1972, the Supreme Court struck down the Massachusetts law prohibiting the sale of contraceptives. By 1973, 10 million women were using oral contraception. By the early 2000s, an estimated 100 million women used the Pill worldwide; 19 percent of American women of reproductive age and over 30 percent of 20–24-year-olds are on the Pill at any given time.

Nonetheless, questions remain about whether the Pill was prematurely rushed to market. First, in the Puerto Rican studies, the high-dose norethynodrel that Pincus and Rock tested produced nausea, vomiting, headaches, and dizziness so widespread that Edris Rice-Wray, Puerto Rican medical director of the trial, believed that the Pill was not "generally acceptable." Had a broader range of doses been initially tested, could a safer early Pill have been brought to market?

A second concern about the trials was that women were not informed that the medications were experimental, with unknown side effects. To be sure, the government had not yet formalized regulations protecting human subjects; lack of consent was the norm. But these human subjects' protection concerns pale in comparison to those raised by the experiment by Hertig and Rock. In those studies, reproductive organs were removed which might (or might not) have contained a human embryo. Were these abortions? Did the study design purposefully create human embryos in order to destroy them? In statements by Rock at the time and by Hertig thereafter, the scientists appeared to be shocked when asked about such a possibility. But it is hard to ignore these questions. As with Milgram, did scientific geniuses blind them to ethics in their pursuit of transformational science?

While these concerns may never be resolved, the benefits from the Pill are clear. The world's population growth rate has dropped by half since the 1960's. Although fertility rates in Africa and the Middle East remain high, the most populous countries in the world, China and India, have dramatically reduced their fertility rates. Popular forms of contraception also include sterilization and the use of intrauterine devices (IUDs), but it was the Pill that transformed the discussion about family planning. It put contraceptive decisions into the hands of women. It changed the role of women in society in a most surprising way. But first and foremost, along with the Green Revolution, it has, for now, averted the Malthusian disaster.

MARKER, HERTIG, AND ROCK ANNOTATED:
THE USE OF TOOLS OF INNOVATION

The Contraceptive Revolution was much like the Green Revolution, both springing from the need to avoid a Malthusian apocalypse. Neither was a scientific revolution. Once again, the critical paradigms had been revealed long before. Once again, social transformation was achieved without the underlying science ever needing to be disrupted.

Since the same set of tools of innovation was used by Russell Marker and by Hertig and Rock, the annotation here focuses on the former. Marker personified perseverance in his search for a process to commercialize progesterone. In this pursuit, he was the ultimate *observer* and *dissector*. His meticulous conduct of chemical syntheses and his exertions detailing plant sources created step-by-step advances. One parameter was altered, and then another. One supply was found, and then a better one. There was no end to the search until clarity and perfection were attained.

But Marker was no plodder. The key to efficient synthesis of progesterone, he believed, was the plant sterols, sapogenins. It was pure *deduction*, perhaps fed by the chemical similarity between sapogenins and cholesterol, both of which have a long side chain and a steroid backbone. Or perhaps he was relying on *analogies* to the medicinal use of plants as contraceptives throughout the ages. Whatever the source, he constructed empirical evidence on a foundation of logic.

Perhaps Marker's most creative stroke of genius was in the way that he constructed his *question*. Marker's question was, What is the best way to make progesterone? To ask this "right" question required using the tools of *reversal* and *expansion*. The question others had asked was, How do we maximize the efficiency of changing cholesterol into progesterone? Marker's *enlargement* of the question, removing the assumption that cholesterol must be involved, focused not on how to get to the end, but how to find the beginning. This *reversal*—a focus on finding the starting material within the kingdom of plants—was where Marker focused his intensity.

To say that oral contraception was the work of Marker or of Hertig and Rock or of any other limited set of geniuses would be simplistic, however. The process wherein contraception became available to women of the world was the work of *many*. To provide even an incomplete listing of the leading contributors, one would have to mention Starling, Bayliss, Haberlandt, Corner, Butenandt, Rosenkranz, Djerassi, Ehrenstein, Pincus, Sanger, Chang, Rice-Wray, and Colton. Each contributed their piece to a scientific evolutionary. The "Contraceptive Revolution" was evolutionary science and revolutionary social transformation.

	Question	Groups	Analogy	Rearrange	Observation	Deduction / Induction	Change Point of View	Expand	Narrow/ Dissect	Reverse	Break Frames	Autonomy	Openness	Persistence
Marker	✓	✓	✓		✓			✓	✓	✓		✓		✓
Rock & Hertig	✓	✓	✓		✓			✓	✓	✓		✓	✓	✓

Figure 14.1. Marker, Hertig, and Rock: Tools and Characteristics

15

A Way to Die

Students of Innovation

W hat would Terri Schiavo want? Propped in a wheelchair, her head askew, her eyes wandering aimlessly—Terri Schiavo became the unwitting cause célèbre of a seven-year legal battle over the continuance of her life. Relentless armies amassed on both sides of a question that could never be put to her directly: Should she continue to live with life support, or should she die? Since she had left no end-of-life directives, we will never know what she herself wanted, just as the vast majority of Americans have no advance directives so that when we become too ill to make decisions, we, too, will enter a decision-making gray zone.

Terri, the raven-haired beauty with a lovely smile, was found unconscious by her husband Michael in their St. Petersburg, Florida, apartment at the promising age of 26. Having embarked on a fad diet consisting entirely of large quantities of iced tea, she was later discovered to have a critically low potassium level, presumably triggering a cardiac arrest. When the EMTs arrived in February 1990, their vigorous resuscitation reestablished breathing and a pulse, but the woman remained in coma. For 15 years, her grieving husband and frantic parents worked to awaken their sleeping beauty. Doctors tried experimental thalamic nerve stimulation in San Francisco and state-of-the-art rehabilitation in Florida, but to no avail. Terri had progressed to a permanent vegetative state.

Unlike brain death, which is legally recognized as an indication for termination of life support, persistent vegetative state does not equate to death under the law. Terri had no living will. Thus, her presumed wishes in the Neverland between intellectual functioning and death devolved to petitions by her husband to withdraw the feeding tube versus opposition by her parents on the grounds that, as a devout Roman Catholic, Terri would not have wanted to violate the Church's teachings against euthanasia. Ultimately, Judge George Greer granted Michael's petition and ordered discontinuation of artificial life support. Seven years of court battles followed, with attempted intercession on the part of the governor of Florida, the president of the United States, and both the U.S. House and Senate. On the day that Terri's feeding tube was finally removed, a Florida police officer quipped, "We discussed...whether we had enough (Florida state) officers to hold off the National Guard."

Perhaps the most useful message that arises from the Schiavo debacle is the imperative for all of us to prepare to die with dignity. As Benjamin Franklin famously said, "Nothing in life is sure except death and taxes." Even the few of us who can outwit the tax man cannot outfox the grim reaper. Death—experienced every year by about 2.5 million Americans—is inevitable. The vast majority of deaths come after a struggle with some chronic illness. So, unlike Terri Schiavo's rare case of acute collapse, most of our deaths will occur after we have had some warning.

Each of us can avoid becoming a Terri Schiavo by documenting how we want to die. A quick Internet search brings up forms wherein we can write out our preferences for the use of end-of-life-saving procedures, designate someone to make health care decisions for us should we become incapacitated, and opt in or out of organ donation. These documents are called a living will, a health care durable power of attorney, and an organ donation card. Together, they are termed "advance directives." If we neglect to have advance directives on hand, physicians will typically administer all interventions necessary to sustain life, even if that medical care goes against what family or friends say we have previously expressed. Unless we write down our wishes at a time when we can still make them thoughtfully, our decisions will be made for us.

This is not what most people want. The great majority (65–82 percent) of people in long term care institutions say that they would not want to be intubated, and a similar percent say that they would decline CPR at the end of life. This suggests that much of invasive medical care among the terminally ill is unwarranted. Yet fully one-quarter of all Medicare expenditures—$100 billion annually—is spent in the last year of patients' lives, the majority in the final 60 days. Providing unwanted end-of-life care is a painful burden to the elderly and a staggering waste of resources.

Few Americans are prepared for their final medical encounter. In a population study in Sioux Falls, South Dakota (2009), respondents age 50, on average, often had a last will and testament (50 percent), and even more often had discussed end-of-life preferences with family or friends (80 percent). However, only 30 percent had a written living will or health care power of attorney. Another survey found that, even among patients who have terminal illnesses, only half have written directives. Worse, up to three-quarters of doctors do not know what their patients' directives are, even if the documents exist.

Advance directives affect the care patients receive and the costs they incur at the end of life. Among patients whose advance directives were to have all care possible, a study by Silveira and colleagues (2010) showed that the likelihood of receiving more aggressive care was 20-fold higher than for patients requesting more limited end-of-life care. Conversely, patients requesting limited care in their living wills were only one-third as likely to receive aggressive care. Not surprisingly, lower spending at the end of life accrues to patients who have prepared advance directives. Programs to increase documentation of advance directives within nursing homes have been shown to reduce costs in the last weeks of life. A back-of-the-envelope calculation suggests that getting 10 percent more people to write out their wishes could save $8–10 billion per year in the United States.

How then do we increase the number of Americans who have advance directives? A team of students from the Innovative Thinking class that I teach at the University of Texas School of Public Health attempted to answer this question using the tools of innovation. Nancy Tucker, Robert Reynolds, Stephen Jones, and John D'Amore attempted to emulate the thinking process of great innovators. Stephen is a physician, John a computer informatics geek, Robert a public health educator, and Nancy a professional student.

Their first step was to observe by listening to an array of stakehold-ers: doctors caring for terminal patients, families, and the patients them-selves. These conversations, although informal and open, were designed to understand the barriers to people's discussing and documenting advance directives.

The team's first question was: Why do so many of us put ourselves and our families in this kind of moral hazard? What they learned is that families are markedly uncomfortable conversing about death because it invokes guilt, fear, and denial. Cultural beliefs are a factor. Among many Hispanics, talking about something is equivalent to making it happen. Members of other groups, although they may consider that belief "quaint" or "quirky," behave in the same guilt-ridden way. Surely we do not want to wish death on a loved one, so why discuss it?

The fear that death invokes is as palpable as the visceral reaction to touch-ing a dead animal. Our metaphors for death include the grim reaper; six feet under; when death comes knocking; the void; and judgment day. It is a frame of the unknown, filled with fright and darkness. Indeed, death is so terrifying that the first stage of dealing with a terminal illness, as described by Elizabeth Kubler-Ross in her 1969 book *On Death and Dying*, is denial.

Doctors, too, express guilt and denial when confronting the end of life. Modern-day medicine prides itself on accomplishing miracles. Death rep-resents a shameful inadequacy, represented by the typical statement, "I am sorry we couldn't do more." In other words, "We failed." Indeed, when asked to comment on a New York State law requiring that health care practitioners to offer counseling to patients who have a terminal condition about appropriate palliative and hospice options, an oncologist at a major teaching hospital in that state said, "The new law is going to have a direct negative effect on too many cancer patients." He feared that his patients' reaction to the discussion would be, "What, are they trying to kill me?"

These frames of guilt, fear, and denial, once uncovered by the University of Texas students, clearly explained why so few of us have advance direc-tives. Now the question became how to create a frame break. Their first approach was to expand the question in time. Over the course of history, they asked, how did people consider death?

Prior to the thirteenth century, the Christian philosophy toward death was *et morie mur*, meaning "and we shall all die," a reflection of the certitude of an (often premature) death. At a time when about one-third of children did not survive past the first year of life, when war, poverty, pestilence, and famine were routine, death was as familiar as life. Mourning death was a public occasion involving family, friends, and neighbors. As a matter of course, children were involved, and as a matter of practicality, funeral ceremonies were simple and efficient.

Philippe Ariès, who made a life's work of understanding mankind's collective consciousness toward death, suggests that as the Church moved toward a philosophy of divine judgment, attitudes toward death shifted to *la mort de soi*, or "the death of the self." Insofar as the soul was now thought to hang in the balance between heaven and hell, death became a moment of personal reckoning. Intercession by clergy at the end of life became paramount. Indeed, the way to salvation became an overriding public preoccupation. To pave the way to salvation, the Church required parishioners to engage in regular confession, absolution, and penance. When, by the sixteenth century, indulgences, granted as a kind of entry ticket to heaven, became a major source of revenue for the Catholic Church, the practice triggered Martin Luther's opposition and thus the Protestant reformation.

According to Ariès, the next era of thinking toward death was characterized by *la mort de toi*, or "thy death," that is, the death of a loved one. As the preeminence of individuality replaced that of the Church, the role of family replaced the role of clergy at the deathbed. In the nineteenth century, dying was characterized by the emotional pain of loved ones.

In the modern era, Ariès believes, science reigns supreme, and medicine offers the hope of an ever longer life. Death occurs at the edge of medicine's power. It is the dishonorable limit of our achievements. The dying are patients who end their days in hospitals, hospices, and nursing homes. Their bodies are disposed of by strangers.

All of this acknowledges that our frames for death are modern and not predetermined. Is there a way to turn back the clock to the time when feelings for family were paramount—when decisions were weighted by the desire to spare loved ones from having to make heart-wrenching decisions?

What if death—especially the death that comes after a long life —were considered in the opposite way from its usual conception—as a blessing rather than a curse? The students, in other words, considered a reversal. J. R. R. Tolkien, in his book *The Silmarillion*, describes the creation of the races that populate the world of *The Lord of the Rings*. Elves, Tolkien explains, were given great wisdom, strength, and beauty to match their eternal life. Humans were given the gift of death. At first glance, this seems like anything but fair. But Tolkien explains that, as time wears ever onward, even the gods themselves will envy the gift of limited life. How fulfilling would events be in a life without end? Would people with pain suffer far longer? Would older people, after a long and rewarding life, be unable to say that they have made their peace—they are ready for death? Perhaps death can be a gift or at least a necessity for enjoying life.

When the students changed their point of view to put themselves in the place of a person considering the components of advance directives—for example, deciding about various components of life support, designating a health care proxy, and organ donation—they realized that organ donation is handled differently from other aspects of advance directives. Many states ask citizens to make a decision about donating organs when they get a driver's license. That license then displays their decision so that, if they are in a fatal car crash, health care workers can save their organs. Such programs have had some success in increasing rates of organ donation. Could such a model be used for other end-of-life decisions?

All of these insights were mind-expanding. But they didn't seem to trigger any innovation, that is, any useful way to help more people to think through and write down advance directives.

So, the students turned to the linguistic mechanism by which we express our frames—metaphors. As they had already learned from their interviews with patients and families, most metaphors around death are dark and frightening. But not all. Consider these: die laughing; dressed to kill; lady killer; kill off a martini. Somehow our metaphors, particularly around killing, can be lively and even sexy. During one of their group brainstorms, they found themselves laughing at Benjamin Franklin's aphorism, "Nothing in life is sure except death and taxes."

And viola! It all came together—a rearrangement of death and taxes. Advance directives could be handled like taxes—disagreeable but necessary. In fact, advance directives could be completed on a form looking much like a tax form, consisting of easy-to-use check-off boxes. "I designate such-and-such as my health care representative," or "I do not wish to designate a health care representative." "I wish to be resuscitated under the following circumstances (choose from list)" or "I do not wish to be resuscitated." The *Individual Advanced Directives Claim Form* could be updated with each annual tax submission. The government might even incentivize citizens to turn in the advance directive form by providing a small tax rebate for doing so.

It seems like a great idea. Why don't we actually do this? During the debate on the Affordable Care Act, or ACA (sometimes called "Obamacare"), a proposed component to incentivize physicians to discuss end-of-life care was reframed as "Death Panels." Until the rider was removed, it became a lightning rod for opponents of the ACA. Discussions of death (and taxes) are always controversial. But, who knows? Perhaps some advocacy group will get behind the idea of death as a bureaucratic obligation and start a movement. Wouldn't it be wonderful if a group of students could get a really innovative idea adopted and change the world?

STUDENTS ANNOTATED: THE USE OF TOOLS OF INNOVATION

Since this last story is not about genius but about students and is not about characters from history but about contemporaries, it seems only fair to offer up a challenge. We have seen the tools used by a dozen iconic minds. Now we have seen their worth in the hands of people just like us. Consider the elements of Figure 15.1 as hints in a treasure hunt. Can you identify the tools the students used? How were these tools used? Can you imagine adding other tools or using the tools differently to find alternative solutions?

Students	Question	Groups	Analogy	Rearrange	Observation	Deduction / Induction	Change Point of View	Expand	Narrow/ Dissect	Reverse	Break Frames	Autonomy	Openness	Persistence
Students	🔧	🔧	🔧	🔧	🔧		🔧		🔧	🔧	🔧		N/A	

Figure 15.1. Students: Tools and Characteristics

16

Steering the Craft

n advice to would-be fiction writers, the widely recognized author Ursula Le Guin compares the writing of stories to steering a vessel: "I like my image of 'steering the craft,'" she says. "But in fact the story boat is a magic one. It knows its course. The job of the person at the helm is to help it find its own way to wherever it's going."

When I set out to write this book about how great innovators think, my plan was relatively unformed. I had one belief, in truth a bias, that creativity and innovation can be taught and that a powerful method of teaching is by example.

Dean Simonton, a noted scholar on creative genius, has argued that eminent creative minds are distinguished by the very number of ideas that they generate. But the mechanisms that produce genius have been sealed inside a black box. Ingenuity has been viewed as cryptic, rather than systematic. My goal was to see whether scientific genius is some unfathomable ability—or not. I hoped to unmask genius.

Having spent the last many pages navigating around a few minds, I am convinced that innovation, even of such greatness as to be considered genius, can be mapped. My story craft alighted upon a pattern that was discernible and predictable. To generate useful ideas, virtually all innovators used a common set of tools. But my craft also landed at some sites that were unexpected. These surprises included the extent to which tools constitute a creative hierarchy, and the slippery slope between creativity and duplicity.

Idea generation has been considered the hallmark of creativity since creativity became an attribute first measured by J. P. Guildford in 1950 and the tools for innovation are means for generating a diversity of original ideas. Guildford described the notion of divergent thinking—the spawning of a wide array of ideas. Convergent thinking, in contrast, is the determination of a single best answer. Widening the circle of ideas is achieved by all of the cognitive strategies discussed in this book—the right question, working in groups, analogy, observation, rearrangement, and so on.

Analogy, in particular, one of the most common tools used by the iconic scientists surveyed here, may also be a marker for divergent thinking. According to Sarnoff Mednick's theory of remote associations, creative minds find analogies through associations. Mednick proposed that the more creative the individual, the more facile they are at making what he called "flat associations." Flat associations, which are abundant and loose—provide wider matrices that are more likely to overlap than do "steep associations," which are limited and rigidly interlinked. Overlaps then form analogies.

Consider the word "dog." Asked to elicit associates, a person with a steep hierarchy of associations might say, "mutt," "Fido," "cat," and "bark." Similarly, the same person given the word, "beauty" may say, "pretty," "model," "hair," and "woman." In contrast, a person with a flat associative hierarchy might respond to "dog" with the above list plus the additional words "collar," "hair," "couch," "house," "bone," "beast," "friend," "walk," "pound," "grooming," "parlor," and "trainer." For the word "beauty," the steep associative list might be expanded to "actress," "vanity," "conceit," "attractive," "desired," "aspire," "parlor," "clothes," "shopping," "beast," and "best." The point is that flat associations are more wide-ranging but also that they are overlapping. Thus, for the remote words "dog" and "beauty," the flat hierarchical association lists yielded three overlapping words: "parlor," "hair," and "beast."

Flatter associative hierarchies yield more numerous and more unpredictable or idiosyncratic lists—more divergence. Mednick's theory implies that, as a by-product of divergence, highly creative people find more analogies, including ones that are remote and therefore original. Analogy is thus a marker of the ability to generate associations—to generate ideas.

A second tool, the power of groups, was also universal. To learn that great innovators stood on the shoulders of giants was no great surprise.

Ascending to the fiftieth floor is far easier if one is starting on floor forty-nine. Surely reaching higher is easier when the goal is only a short distance away.

Because knowledge acquired from others is not specific to a single innovator, scientists were often poised to ask the same question. Baran is given credit for the discovery of packet switching, but Davies was having the same thoughts at about the same time. Darwin scurried to publish *On the Origin of Species* because he was on the verge of being scooped by Alfred Russell Wallace. In many cases, renowned innovators were not the only and arguably not even the first to invent. They were, however, the first to publish or to patent, or to be recognized. Is it possible, then, that beyond their imposing creative prowess, the thing that made innovators famous was their drive and their speed?

In addition to analogy and the power of groups, asking the right question and dissecting the question were tools used by all these greats. Beyond that, however, the cognitive tools used by innovators tended to divide into two patterns. One pattern was common to revolutionary innovators and the other to evolutionary innovators. Revolutionary innovators shifted frames and, as it turns out, used a wider array of tools. Of the 14 innovators considered in some detail here, 10 were revolutionary (frame breakers); on average, these men and women used 10.3 of the 11 innovation tools. In contrast, the four evolutionary innovators used 5.5 of the 11 innovation tools. This is not meant to represent a meaningful statistical comparison but instead to reveal a general pattern. Put simply, more is more.

The observation that more radical innovators used a more diverse set of tools is similar to the theory that the most creative minds generate the most ideas. David Campbell and subsequently Dean Simonton have proposed that creativity is Darwinian in the sense that its basis is the generation of variation. Creative minds, like reproductive assortment in nature, produce large numbers of "blind" ideas. Although this abundance necessarily involves many alternatives, any given idea may or may not be beneficial in solving the creator's problem. Similarly, some mutations in nature are adaptive but most are not; both creative generation and evolution are failure-prone. Nonetheless, the more ideas that eminent creators hatch and the more genetic variants that species produce, the more likely there are to be successes. Revolutionary innovators, I postulate, because they used more and more diverse tools, generated the greatest variety of ideas and had the most radical achievements. Taking the evolutionary analogy one step further, we might say that revolutionary insights were the most likely to generate variants that endured "survival of the fittest."

Revolutionary innovators, that is, frame shifters, were more likely to use reversal, to change their point of view, to switch between opposite modes of thinking, and to rearrange previous insights to meet their aims. These are cognitive strategies that go well beyond the production of associations. These tools not only amass divergent ideas but produce thoughts both original and flexible. Guildford defined "originality" as responses that are unusual while still appropriate. Flexibility implies an ability to think across conceptual categories. For example, a paper clip is typically used to hold papers together. The recognition that a paper clip can also pick a lock or tighten the tiny screw on the hinge of a pair of glasses is flexible thinking.

Associations are consistent with our daily experience. When we put on a shoe, we do so over a foot and a sock. Shoe, foot, and sock are natural associations. On the other hand, processes such as reversal, changing point of view, rearrangement, and induction/deduction are less than natural. Our habitual experience does not lead us to think like a plant, as Darwin did, or to imagine ourselves as a bulb within a system of lighting, as Edison did, or to guess how a packet of information would flit between computer nodes, as Baran did. We do not think in reverse naturally. We may have seen a dog bite a cat, but we do not ordinarily jump from this experience to envisioning a cat biting a dog.

An experience from my class Innovative Thinking provides further evidence that higher level innovation tools produce more surprising ideas. In a group assignment, students sought to generate ideas as to why America is experiencing increasing rates of adolescent hearing loss. In 2005–2006, the prevalence of hearing loss in 12–19-year-olds in the United States was about 20 percent, up from 15 percent in 1988–1994. Some of the causes that have been associated with hearing loss in youth are ear infections, head injury, birth defects, and noise. Using analogy, the class proposed any number of associative questions. Students suggested experiments to understand how physiologic damage occurs to the outer/middle ear, the neurosensory system, and the cochlea, all of which are involved in hearing. They asked how much ambient noise is delivered through headphones; how often adolescents are subjected to excessive volumes; and the rates over time of ear infections. Their more peripheral associations included questions such as whether personal headgear could limit the intrusion of sound.

Then the students turned to tools such as reversal and changing point of view. Instead of asking how hearing loss might be the result of noise, the students suggested testing questions such as, Is silence necessary for auditory health? Can the sounds of nature counteract louder and less naturalistic clamor? Are there benefits to noise—hearing or otherwise? Using the tool of changing point of view, students got into the heads of teenagers. Through unstructured interviews with adolescents, they learned that raucousness is equated with parties and concerts, whereas silence occurs during tests and while a teen is grounded. Adults may fear the damaging effects of noise, but adolescents dread the correlates of silence. Students thus devised an experiment asking how to make quiet environments socially attractive to teens. On the face of it, this set of queries was simply more original.

One of the surprises from the stories of genius scientists, then was the concept that the tools of innovation may represent a hierarchy. Associative tools such as working in groups, observation, dissection, and analogy are lower level and more commonly used tools. Reversal, rearrangement, changing point of view, and, of course, frame breaking, are more unusual and more unnatural. Because the latter set of tools represents a kind of thinking that is aberrant, their use takes more practice. The mind cannot simply wander but must be forced to work in such ways.

Perhaps the most unexpected pattern uncovered in the stories of these scientific geniuses was that, though the character traits of great creators enhance their scientific contributions, those same traits can have an underbelly. A long tradition of behavioral research has linked genius to mental disorders. For instance, Arnold Ludwig, in his book *The Price of Greatness*, examined evidence of psychiatric conditions among over a thousand prominent artists, scientists, and leaders. He found that conditions such as mania, depression, personality disorders, and schizophrenia were more common than in the general population. Although scientists were the least affected group (28 percent as compared to poets at 87 percent), Ludwig noted that the greater the achievement, the more likely the presence of pathological features.

Hans Eysenck, a leader in the study of personality, has argued that psychopathology is simply an extreme manifestation of the innate ability of creative individuals to produce large quantities of unusual, even bizarre ideas. Individuals who score high on Eysenck's test for psychoticism seem to be more likely to produce random or incongruous associations. That is, they lack a strong "filter mechanism" that keeps ideas separated by conceptual bounds. Mednick would call these associations "flat," allowing richer analogies and insights. Eysenck might argue that when dialed to a slightly higher level of chaos, such ideation may become pathological.

What do people look like who are autonomous and tenacious to the point that they consistently reject normal social constraints? Of course, they may look like model creators. However, more extreme or less balanced nonconformists may look like schizophrenics or sociopaths. Audacious ambitions, feverish motivation, and exuberant optimism can appear as mania.

One wonders why such traits would be maintained in the genetic pool. Is creativity so beneficial that it overcomes the tendency to isolate oneself or even to try to kill oneself? Geoffrey Miller put forth a provocative theory as to the benefit of extreme nonconformity, calling it "Machiavellian intelligence." In a world consisting of a complex web of cooperation and competition, Miller claims that persons whose behavior is unpredictable will succeed in outsmarting adversaries. Social dominance goes to those individuals whose next move cannot be anticipated. Thus, even if it sometimes borders on the unstable, the ability to think originally and flexibly, within the pecking order of complex social groups, becomes a competitive evolutionary advantage.

Previous commentaries on the link between creativity and mental health have generally taken a sympathetic view of the creative personality, even when it traverses into psychopathology. But the geniuses in this book sometimes crossed boundaries that involved an unsavory disregard for others. Of course, the most infamous example is Milgram. The ethicalness of his obedience experiments remains unresolved but Milgram's willingness to deceive demonstrates social indifference or even social contempt in the name of scientific absorption.

The Hertig and Rock experiment that tracked the development of embryos is another example. Remarkably, science has been discrete in its judgment. But the work involved advising women to become pregnant directly before a therapeutic hysterectomy. Surely, some women must have intuited the purpose of the instructions, but the consent procedure was not explicit. When interviewed later, Hertig adamantly rejected the pejorative perspective that he and Rock were engaging in abortion. The context that Rock was an active Catholic makes the issue all the more enigmatic. Hertig and Rock's very purpose was to create human embryos and then to remove them for study.

Ancel Keys's starvation experiments—again, never admonished—are another example of the application of questionable ethics. Participants duly consented and were allowed to withdraw at any time. However, the circumstances reek of coercion. Participants were conscientious objectors who, while refusing to fight and die for America, were instead "allowed" to give to science. Keys and his military sponsors reasoned that knowing the best approach to re-feeding was a greater benefit than the risk to participants from starvation. But was their design for answering this question defensible? Europe was starving. Wouldn't a more humane way to answer the question simply have been to intervene with various nutrition supplements within a program of foreign aid? One can only imagine that Keys's ambition to exercise novelty overtook his ability to envision more sympathetic alternatives.

Finally, even the darling of modern innovators, Thomas Edison, became embroiled in unsavory practices. Edison was so intent to promote his own DC current over Tessla and Westinghouse's competing AC current that he initiated the "war of the currents." As depicted in Josephson's biography of Edison, "There on any day in 1887 one might have found Edison and his assistants occupied in certain cruel and lugubrious experiments: the electrocution of stray cats and dogs by means of high tension currents. In the presence of newspaper reporters and other invited guests, Edison and Batchelor would edge a little dog onto a sheet of tin to which was attached wires from an AC generator supplying current at 1000 volts." Despite testimony from trusted associates that AC current was no more dangerous than DC, Edison continued all attempts to squelch Westinghouse's alternative. Indeed, Edison's public statements were so inflammatory that Westinghouse considered bringing a libel suit. Not until 20 years later did Edison admit that he had been wrong. Surely, this was not the result of an overabundance of originality but instead the accumulation of a lifetime of over-confidence. In the case of some geniuses, the most radically original thinking and the most surprising and useful contributions may go hand in hand with the greatest blind spot for human interactions.

Both expected and unexpected lessons came from the voyage of our story craft. What was expected was that, when it came to their thinking, the talents of these geniuses were magnificent. But their cognitive approaches were not mystical. All of these iconic scientists were masterful users of the tools of innovation. What was less expected about their thinking was that frame shifters used tools that are more unusual and unnatural. Even through both evolutionary and revolutionary innovators produced surprising outcomes, the twists of the minds of the latter went beyond that of the former. When it came to geniuses' personalities, what was expected was that "creative personalities," like their accomplishments, were larger than life. What was less expected about these characteristics was that they had an upside and a downside. Society benefited from geniuses' accomplishments, but their actions were not always benign. It is no surprise that the most creative do not always fit comfortably among us.

With any luck, these stories have demystified genius. Appreciating the use of the tools of innovation brings us one step closer to following in their footsteps. Returning to the question that opened this book, How can each of us learn to become better innovators? we may be guided by the adage in medicine to "see one, do one, teach one." We have unmasked the thinking of celebrated scientists. With our newfound tools, we are primed to engage in greater feats of creativity and to transmit our insights. I hope you use the innovation tools with great success and joy. I hope too that by passing onto children the tools of innovation we together prepare a next generation full of genius scientists.

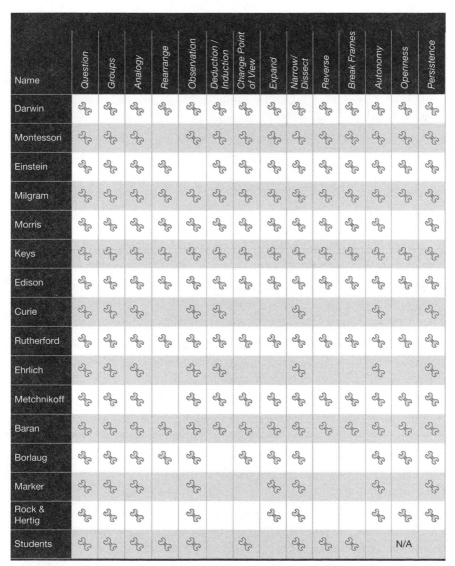

Figure 16.1. All Innovators: Tools and Characteristics

Hero Worship

Goldfrank: Graham ME, Tunik MG, Farmer BM, Bendzans C, McCrillis AM, Nelson LS, Portelli I, Smith S, Goldberg JD, Zhang M, Rosenberg SD, Goldfrank LR (2010) Agent of opportunity risk mitigation: People, engineering, and security efficacy. *Disaster Medicine & Public Health Preparedness* 4:291–299; Stroud C, Altevogt BM, Goldfrank LR. (2010) Institute of Medicine's Forum on Medical and Public Health Preparedness for Catastrophic Events: Current initiatives [Editorial]. *Disaster Medicine & Public Health Preparedness* 4:174–177; Raven MC, Billings JC, Goldfrank LR, Manheimer ED, Gourevitch MN (2009) Medicaid patients at high risk for frequent hospital admission: Real-time identification and remediable risks. *Journal of Urban Health* 86(2):230–241; Gourevitch MN, Malaspina D, Weitzman M, Goldfrank, LR (2008) The public hospital in American medical education. Journal of urban health 85:779–786; Goldfrank LR (2009) Call centers, disaster medicine, and public health preparedness [Editorial] *Disaster Medicine & Public Health Preparedness* 3(1):136–137.

Effectiveness of creativity training programs: Ness RB (2012) *Innovation generation: How to produce creative and useful scientific ideas*. New York: Oxford University Press; Scott G, Leritz LE, Mumford MD (2004) The effectiveness of creativity training: a quantitative review. *Creativity Research Journal* 16:361–388; Clapham MM (2003) The development of innovative ideas through creativity training. *The International Handbook on Innovation*, ed. Larisa V. Shavinina, Oxford: Elsevier, pp. 366–374; Basadur MS, Graen GB, Scandura TA (1986). Training effects on attitudes toward divergent thinking among manufacturing engineers, *Journal of Applied Psychology* 4:612–617; Basadur MS, Finkbeiner CT (1985) Measuring preference for ideation in creative problem solving training. *Journal of Applied Behavioral Science* 21:37–49.

Innovation slow-down: Members of the 2005 "Rising Above the Gathering Storm" Committee; Prepared for the Presidents of the National Academy of Sciences, National Academy of Engineering, and Institute of Medicine. *Rising above the gathering storm revisited: Rapidly approaching category 5*. Washington, DC: The National Academies Press; 2010; Brooks D. (2011) Where are the jobs? New York Times Opinion Pages. http://www.nytimes.com/2011/10/07/

opinion/brooks-where-are-the-jobs.html (accessed 12/23/11); Tyler C. (2010) *The great stagnation: How America ate all the low hanging fruit of modern history, got sick and will (eventually) feel better.* New York: Penguin; Mandel M. (2009) The failed promise of innovation in the U.S. Bloomberg Business Week. http://www.businessweek.com/magazine/content/09_24/b4135000953288. htm?chan=magazine+channel_top+stories (accessed 12/23/11); Salam R. (2011) Peter Thiel and the Why things have slowed-down question. National Review Online. http://www.nationalreview.com/agenda/279171/peter-thiel-and -why-things-have-slowed-down-question-reihan-salam (accessed 12/23/11).

Creativity in modern art: Varnedoe K. (1990) *A fine disregard: What makes modern art modern.* New York: Harry N. Abrams.

Nature versus God

Gallup Poll on evolution: Gallup: Evolution, Creationism, Intelligent Design. http://www.gallup.com/poll/21814/evolution-creationism-intelligent-design. aspx (accesssed 12/23/11).

Darwin's life and works: Ridley M. (ed) (1996) *The Darwin reader* (2nd ed). New York: W W Norton; Quammen D (2006) *The reluctant Mr. Darwin: An intimate portrait of Charles Darwin and the making of his theory of evolution.* New York: W W Norton; Simonton DK (1999) *Origins of genius: Darwinian perspectives on creativity.* New York: Oxford University Press.

Darwin's *Origin of Species*, supporters and detractors: Darwin C (Foreword copyright 1979) *On the origin of species.* New York: Random House. Originally published 1859 by J Murray London under the title: *On the origin of species by means of natural selection;* Dawkins R (2009) *The greatest show on earth: The evidence for evolution.* New York: Simon & Schuster; Coyne JA. (2009) *Why evolution is true.* New York: Penguin; Zimmer C (2001) *Evolution: The triumph of an idea.* New York: Harper Collins; Coffin HG, Brown RH, Gibson RJ (2005) *Origins by design.* Hagerstown, MD: Review and Herald Pub; Milton R (1997) *Shattering the myths of Darwinism.* Rochester, VT: Park Street Press; Wells J (2000) *Icons of evolution: Science or myth? Why much of what we teach about evolution is wrong.* Washington, DC: Eagle.

Darwin's *Descent of Man*: Darwin C (Penguin Classic copyright 2004) *The descent of man.* Originally published 1879 by J Murray London.

Malthus essay: Malthus TR. *An essay on the principle of population: Or a view of its past and present effects on human happiness; with an inquiry into our prospects respecting the future removal or mitigation of the evils which it occasions.* Library of Economics and Liberty. Originally published 1798 by J Murray,

London. http://www.econlib.org/library/Malthus/malPlong1.html (accessed 12/23/11)

Creationists at the time of Darwin: Paley W (1809) *Natural theology: or, evidences of the existence and attributes of the deity* (12th ed). London: Printed for J. Faulder. The Complete works of Charles Darwin on-line. http://darwin-online. org.uk/content/frameset?itemID=A142&viewtype=text&pageseq=1 (accessed 12/23/11).

Whewell W. *History of the inductive sciences, from the earliest to the present times.* 3 vols, London: Appleton (2nd ed). 1869.

Darwin Annotated

Diderot: Adams D, ed. (1999) *Thoughts on the interpretation of nature and other philosophical works* (1753). Manchester, England: Clinamen Press Ltd. p 42.

Tool 1: Finding the right question: Baldwin N (1995) *Edison: Inventing the century.* New York: Hyperion; White M, Gribbin J (1959) *Einstein: A life in science.* New York: Dutton Book (Penguin Group); Josephson M (1959) *Edison: A biography.* New York: McGraw-Hill; Collins J, Porras JI (1994) *Built to last: Successful habits of visionary companies.* New York: Harper Collins; AIESEC—The world's largest student-driven organization. http://www.aiesec.org/ (accessed 12/29/11); Schonfeld E. (2009) Twitter's international strategy laid bare: to be "the pulse of the planet." Tech Crunch. http://techcrunch.com/2009/07/16/tw itters-internal-strategy-laid-bare-to-be-the-pulse-of-the-planet-2/ (accessed 12/29/11).

Tool 2: Observation: Darwin C (Foreword copyright 1979) *On the origin of species.* New York: Random House. Originally published 1859 by J Murray London under the title: *On the origin of species by means of natural selection*; Rose JK, Rankin CH (2001) Analyses of habituation in *Caenorhabditis elegans, Learning and Memory* 8:63–69; Ness RB (2012) Innovation generation: How to produce creative and useful scientific ideas. New York: Oxford University Press; Heilbron JL (2003) Ernest Rutherford and the explosion of atoms. Oxford: Oxford University Press.

Tool 3: Analogy: Simonton DK (1999) *Origins of genius: Darwinian perspectives on creativity.* New York: Oxford University Press; Darwin C (Foreword copyright 1979) *On the origin of species.* New York: Random House. Originally published 1859 by J Murray London under the title: *On the origin of species by means of natural selection*; Abbate J (1999) *Inventing the Internet.* Cambridge, MA: The MIT Press; Tauber AI (2003) Metchnikoff and the phagocytosis theory. *Nature Reviews* 4:897–901; Kaufman SHE (2008) Immunology's foundation:

The 100-year anniversary of the Nobel Prize to Paul Ehrlich and Elie Metchnikioff. *Nature Immunology* 9:705–712.

Tool 4: Induction and deduction: Kwa C (2011) *Styles of knowing: A new history of science from ancient times to the present.* Pittsburgh, PA: University of Pittsburgh; Henig RM (2000) *The monk in the garden: The lost and found genius of Gregor Mendel, father of genetics.* Boston: Houghton Mifflin; Eysenck HJ (1947) *The structure of human personality.* New York: John Wiley and Sons; Einstein A (1949) Autobiographical notes. In Schilpp PA (ed) *Albert Einstein: Philosopher scientist* (pp. 2–17). New York: Harper & Row.

Tool 5: Changing point of view: Banerjee AV, Duflo E (2011) *Poor economics.* New York: Public Affairs; Associated Press. (2005) Judge rules against "intelligent design." "Religious alternative" to evolution barred from public-school science classes. Science on MSNBC.com. http://www.msnbc.msn.com/id/10545387/ns/technology_and_science-science/t/judge-rules-against-intelligent-design/ (accessed 12/29/11); Darwin C (Foreword copyright 1979) *On the origin of species.* New York: Random House. Originally published 1859 by J Murray London under the title: *On the origin of species by means of natural selection*; Einstein A (1961) *Relativity: The special and general theory.* New York: Crown Publishers; Montessori M (1970) *The child in the family.* Translated by Nancy Rockmore Cirillo. New York: Avon.

Tool 6: Broadening perspective. Till BD, Heckler D (2009) *The truth about creating brands people love.* Upper Saddle River, NJ: Pearson Education; How "Just Do It" was conceived by Wieden and Kennedy for Nike. You Tube. http://www.youtube.com/watch?v=yTkVma4JFmE&noredirect=1 (accessed 12/29/11); Keys A, Mienotti A, Karvonen MJ, et al. (1986) Diet and 15 year death rate in the Seven Countries Study. *American Journal of Epidemiology* 124:903–915; Marker RE, Wagner RB, Ulshafer PR, Wittbecker EL, Goldsmith DPJ, Ruof CH (1947) Sterodial sapogenins. *Journal of the American Chemical Society* 69:2167–2230.

Tool 7: Dissecting the problem: US Department of Transportation National Highway Traffic Safety Administration (2009) Lives saved calculations for seat belts and frontal airbags. www-nrd.nhtsa.dot.gov/pubs/811206.pdf (accessed 12/29/11); Nader R (1965) *Unsafe at any speed: The designed-in dangers of the American automobile.* New York: Grossman Publishers; Chase B (2009) *Still unsafe at any speed: Auto defects that cause wrongful deaths and catastrophic injuries.* Newport Beach, CA: Equalizer Books; Quammen D (2006) *The reluctant Mr. Darwin: An intimate portrait of Charles Darwin and the making of his theory of evolution.* New York: W W Norton; Blass T (2004) *The man who shocked the world: The life and legacy of Stanley Milgram.* New York: Basic Books.

Tool 8: Reversal: Brad Paisley Lyrics. "Flowers." http://www.azlyrics.com/lyrics/bradpaisley/flowers.html (accessed 12/29/11); Brown K (2005) *Penicillin man: Alexander Fleming and the antibiotic revolution*. London: BMJ Publishing Group; Mukherjee S (2010) *The emperor of all maladies: A biography of cancer*. New York: Simon & Schuster.

Tool 9: Recombination and rearrangement: German TP, Barrett HC (2005) Functional fixedness in a technologically sparse culture. *Psychological Science* 16:1–5; Adamson RE (1952) Functional fixedness as related to problem solving: A repetition of three experiments. *Journal of Experimental Psychology* 44:288–291; Baldwin N (1995) *Edison: Inventing the century*. New York: Hyperion; Science Daily (2011) Mapping urban food deserts. http://www.sciencedaily.com/releases/2011/03/110303141557.htm (accessed 12/29/11).

Tool 10: The power of groups: Maddox B (2002) *Rosalind Franklin: The dark lady of DNA*. New York: Harper Collins; Franklin RE, Gosling RG (1953) Evidence for 2-chain helix in crystalline structure of deoxyribonucleate. *Nature* 172:156–157; Gamow G (1961) *The great physicists from Galileo to Einstein*. New York: Dover; Ryan J (2010) *A history of the Internet and the digital future*. London: Reaktion Books.

Tool 11: Frame shifting: Ness RB (2012) *Innovation generation: How to produce creative and useful scientific ideas*. New York: Oxford; Thibodeau PH, Boroditsky L (2011) Metaphors we think with: The role of metaphor in reasoning. PLoS One. 6:e16782; McGraw Hill. Online Learning Center. Interactive Time Line. Discovering the microbial world. http://highered.mcgraw-hill.com/sites/0072320419/student_view0/interactive_time_line.html (accessed 9/12/11); Kuhn TS (1962) *The structure of scientific revolutions*. Chicago: University of Chicago Press: Toulmin S (1972) Human understanding: The collective use and understanding of concepts. Princeton, NJ: Princeton University Press.

The Miracle Worker

About Montessori: Inner Sydney Montessori Association (2009) About Montessori: Maria Montessori. http://esvc000664.wic057u.server-web.com/about-montessori.aspx (accessed 8/31/11); Enright M (2011) Foundations study guide: Montessori education. *The Atlas Society*. http://www.atlassociety.org/guide-montessori (accessed 8/31/11); Standing EM (1957) *Maria Montessori: Her life and work*. London: Hollins & Carter; Park Road Montessori. What is Montessori? Charlotte-Mecklenburg Schools. http://schools.cms.k12.nc.us/parkroadES/Pages/WhatisMontessori.aspx (accessed 8/31/11).

By Montessori: Montessori M (1970) *The child in the family.* Translated by Nancy Rockmore Cirillo. New York: Avon; Montessori M (1936) *Secret of childhood.* Translated by M. Joseph Costelloe. New York: Ballantine Books; Montessori M (1989) *The discovery of the child.* Oxford, UK: Clio Press; Montessori M (1912) *The Montessori method.* Translated by Anne Everett George. New York: Frederick A. Stokes; Montessori M (1967) *The absorbent mind.* New York: Holt, Rinehart and Winston.

Montessori method adapted to the Web: Kahn S (2011). Let's use video to reinvent education. *TED.* TED Conferences, LLC, http://www.ted.com/talks/salman_khan_let_s_use_video_to_reinvent_Education.html (accessed 8/31/11);

Bending Time

About Einstein: White M, Gribbin J (1959) *Einstein: A Life in science.* New York: Penguin; Kakalios J (2010) *The amazing story of quantum mechanics: A math-free exploration of the science that made our world.* New York: Gotham Books; Gamow G (1966) *Thirty years that shook physics: The story of quantum theory.* New York: Dover; Gamow G (1961) *The great physicists from Galileo to Einstein.* New York: Dover; Gardner H (1993) *Creating minds: An anatomy of creativity seen through the minds of Freud, Einstein, Picasso, Stravinsky, Eliot, Graham, and Gandhi.* New York: Perseus; Isaacson W (2007) Einstein: His life and universe. New York: Simon & Schuster; Folsing A, Osers E (1997) *Albert Einstein: A biography.* New York: Penguin.

By Einstein: Einstein A (1961) *Relativity: The special and general theory.* New York: Crown Publishers; Einstein A (1949) Autobiographical notes. In Schilpp PA (ed) *Albert Einstein: Philosopher scientist* (pp. 2–17). New York: Harper & Row; Einstein A, Infeld L (1938) *The evolution of physics: From early concepts to relativity and quanta.* New York: Simon & Schuster.

Pick the Innovator

Adelson B (2003) Issues in scientific creativity: Insight, perseverance and personal technique profiles of the 2002 Franklin Institute laureates. *Journal of the Franklin Institute* 340:163–189; Choi JN (2004) Individual and contextual predictors of creative performance: The mediating role of psychological processes. *Creativity Research Journal* 16:187–199; Dellas M, Gaier EL (1970) Identification of creativity: The individual. *Psychological Bulletin* 73:55–73; Dollinger SJ, Urban KK, James TA (2004) Creativity and openness: Further validation of two creative product measures. *Creativity Research Journal*

16:35–47; Dowd ET (1989) The self and creativity: Several constructs in search of a theory. In JA Glover, RR Ronning, CR Reynolds (eds), *Handbook of creativity* (pp. 233–242) New York: Basic Books; Eysenck HJ (1997) Creativity and personality. In MA Runco, RS Albert (eds), *The creativity research handbook* (Vol. 1, pp. 41–66) Cresskill, NJ: Hampton Press; Feist GJ (1998) A meta-analysis of personality in scientific and artistic creativity. *Personality and Social Psychology Review* 4:290–309; Gardner H (1994) The creators' patterns. In MA Boden (ed) *Dimensions of creativity* (pp. 143–158) Cambridge, MA: MIT Press; George JM, Zhou J (2001) When openness to experience and conscientiousness are related to creative behavior: An interactional approach. *Journal of Applied Psychology* 102:133–142; Martindale C (1989) Personality, situation, and creativity. In JA Glover, RR Ronning, CR Reynolds (eds), *Handbook of creativity* (pp. 211–232). New York: Basic Books; McCrae RR, Costa PT (1997) Conceptions and correlates of openness to experience. In R Hogan, J Johnson, S Briggs (eds), *Handbook of personality psychology* (pp. 825–847) San Diego, CA: Academic Press; Oldham GR, Cummings A (1996). Employee creativity: Personal and contextual factors at work. *Academy of Management Journal* 39:607–634; Prabhu V, Sutton C, Sauser W (2008). Creativity and certain personality traits: Understanding the mediating effect of intrinsic motivation. *Creativity Research Journal* 20:53–66; Sternberg RJ (1988) A three-facet model of creativity. In RJ Sternberg (ed), *The nature of creativity* (pp. 125–147) New York: Cambridge University Press; Tardif TZ, Sternberg RJ (1988) What do we know about creativity? In RJ Sternberg (ed) *The nature of creativity* (pp. 429–440) New York: Cambridge University Press; Wolfradt U, Pretz JE (2001) Individual differences in creativity: Personality, story writing, and hobbies. *European Journal of Personality* 15(4):297–310; Feynman RP (1999) *The pleasure of finding things out*. Cambridge, MA: Perseus.

Is Psychology All in Your Head?

About Milgram: Blass T (2004) *The man who shocked the world: The life and legacy of Stanley Milgram*. New York: Basic Books; Korn J (1997) Illusions of reality: A history of deception in social psychology. Albany: State University of New York Press; Patnoe S (1988) *A narrative history of experimental social psychology: The Lewin tradition*. New York: Springer-Verlag; Rosnow R (1981) *Paradigms in transition: The methodology of social inquiry*. New York: Oxford University Press; Burger JM (2009) Replicating Milgram: Would people still obey today? *American Psychologist* 64:1–11; Elms AC (2009) Obedience lite. *American Psychologist* 64:32–36; Packer DJ (2008) Identifying systematic disobedience in Milgram's obedience experiments: A meta-analytic review. *Perspectives on Psychological Science* 3:301–304.

By Milgram: Milgram S (1974) *Obedience to authority: An experimental view.* New York: Harper & Row; Milgram S (1963) Behavioral study of obedience. *Journal of Abnormal and Social Psychology* 67:371–378; Milgram S (1965) Some conditions of obedience and disobedience to authority. *Human Relations* 18:57–76; Milgram S (1983) Reflections on Morelli's "Dilemma of Obedience." *Metaphilosophy* 3–4:190–194.

Inspirations from the Heart

About heart disease, reduced fat, and exercise: Blackburn H (2007) Cardiovascular disease epidemiology. In Holland WW, Olsen J, Florey C du V(eds). *The development of modern epidemiology: Personal reports from those who were there.* Oxford: Oxford University Press; Ergin A, Muntner P, Sherwin R, He J (2004) Secular trends in cardiovascular disease mortality, incidence, and case fatality rates in adults in the United States. *The American Journal of Medicine* 117: 219–227; USDA Choose My Plate.gov. U.S. Department of Agriculture. http://www.choosemyplate.gov/guidelines/index.html (accessed 8/19/11); Hooper L, Summerbell CD, Thompson R, Sills D, Roberts FG, Moore H, Davey Smith G (2011). Reduced or modified dietary fat for preventing cardiovascular disease. *Cochrane Database of Systematic Reviews* Issue 7. Art. No: CD002137; Sofi F (2009) The Mediterranean diet revisited: evidence of its effectiveness grows. *Current Opinion in Cardiology* 24:442–246; Shiroma EJ, Lee I-M (2010) Physical activity and cardiovascular health: Lessons learned from epidemiological studies across age, gender and race/ethnicity. *Circulation* 122:743–752.

About Keys: Tucker T (2006) *The great starvation experiment: Ancel Keys and the men who starved for science.* Minneapolis: University of Minnesota.; Blackburn H (2007). Cardiovascular disease epidemiology. In Holland WW, Olsen J, Florey C du V(eds) *The development of modern epidemiology: Personal reports from those who were there* (pp. 71–93). Oxford: Oxford University Press; Brody JE (2004) Dr. Ancel Keys, 100, promoter of Mediterranean Diet, dies. *New York Times.* http://www.nytimes.com/2004/11/23/obituaries/23keys.html (accessed 7/26/11); Macini M, Stamler J (2004) Diet for preventing cardiovascular diseases: Light from Ancel Keys, distinguished centenarian scientist. *Nutrition, Metabolism, and Cardiovascular Diseases* 14:52–57.

By Keys: Keys A, Brozek J, Henschel A et al. (1950) *The biology of human starvation.* Minnneapolis: University of Minnesota Press; Keys A (1957). Diet and the epidemiology of coronary heart disease. *Journal of the American Medical*

Association 164:1912–1919; Keys A, Keys M (1975) *Eat well and stay well the Mediterranean Way*. New York: Doubleday; Keys A, Aravanis C, Blackburn H et al. (1972) Probability of middle-aged men developing coronary heart disease in five years. *Circulation* 45:815–828; Keys A, Taylor HL, Blackburn H, Brozek J, Anderson JT, Simonson E (1963) Coronary heart disease among Minnesota business and professional men followed fifteen years. *Circulation* 28:381–395; Keys A, Mienotti A, Karvonen MJ, et al. (1986) Diet and 15 year death rate in the Seven Countries Study. *American Journal of Epidemiology* 124:903–915.

About Morris: Hevesi D (2009) Jeremy Morris, who proved exercise is heart-healthy, dies at 99½. *New York Times:* Research. http://www.nytimes.com/2009/11/08/health/research/08morris.html. (accessed 7/25/11);

Kuper S. (2009) The man who invented exercise. *Financial Times Magazine*. **http://www.ft.com/intl/cms/s/0/e6ff90ea-9da2-11de-9f4a-00144feabdc0.** html#axzz1hNTpqeNe (accessed 7/25/11); Paffenberger RS, Blair SN, Lee I-M (2001) A history of physical activity, cardiovascular health and longevity: The scientific contributions of Jeremy N Morris, DSc, DPH, FRCP. *International Journal of Epidemiology* 30:1184–1192; Kohl HW, Blair SN (2010) Lessons from a life well-lived. *Journal of Physical Activity and Health* 7:1–2.

By Morris: Morris JN (1964). *Uses of epidemiology*. Baltimore MD: Williams & Wilkins; Morris JN, Heady JA, Raffle PAB, Roberts CG, Parks JW (1953) Coronary heart-disease and physical activity of work. *Lancet* 265:1053–1057 and 1111–1120.

It's Electric

About Edison: Jehl F (2002) *Menlo Park reminiscences*. Part 1. Whitefish, MT: Kessinger Publishing; Josephson M (1959) *Edison: A biography*. New York: McGraw-Hill; Baldwin N (1995) *Edison: Inventing the century*. New York: Hyperion; Israel P (1998) *Edison: A life of invention*. New York: John Wiley & Sons; Gorman ME (1990) Interpreting invention as a cognitive process: The case of Alexander Graham Bell, Thomas Edison, and the telephone. *Science, Technology & Human Values* 15:131–164; Dyer FL, Martin TC (2010) *Edison: His life and inventions: The complete Work*. Timeless Classic Books. Timeless classic books.net; Stross R (2007) *The Wizard of Menlo Park: How Thomas Alva Edison invented the world*. New York: Three Rivers Press.

Michalko M. The creative thinking habits of Thomas Edison. Creativity Portal. http://www.creativity-portal.com/articles/michael-michalko/creative-thinking-habits-thomas-edison.html (accessed June 28, 2011).

By Edison: Edison TA (1878) The phonograph and its future. *The North American Review* 126:527–536.

Quotes: "Discovery is not just invention." Edison quoted by EH Johnson article in *Electrical World*, February 22, 1890; "He who makes two blades of grass grow..." Rowland quoted in Josephson M (1959) *Edison: A biography*. New York: McGraw-Hill; "I was always at the foot of the class..." Edison quoted in *New York Herald Tribune* article, October 19, 1931; "I haven't heard a bird sing..." "My refuge was the Detroit Public Library..." Quotes from Edison's diary in: Josephson M (1959) *Edison: A biography*. New York: McGraw-Hill; "A minor invention every ten days..." 2002 National Inventors Hall of Fame. http://www.invent.org/hall_of_fame/50.html. (accessed 9/11/11); "It has been just so..." Thomas Alva Edison, Inventor in: Today in Science History. http://www.todayinsci.com/E/Edison_Thomas/EdisonThomas-Quotations.html. (accessed 9/11/11); "The machine must talk." "I was never so taken aback..." Jehl F (2002) *Menlo Park reminiscences*. Part 1. Whitefish, MT: Kessinger Publishing; "Besides I am so deaf..." Edison quoted in: Josephson M (1959) *Edison: A biography*. New York: McGraw-Hill (p 146).

Two Luminous Lives

About Curie: Quinn S (1995) *Marie Curie: A life*. Cambridge, MA: Perseus; Curie E (1937) *Madame Curie: A biography*. Cambridge, MA: Perseus; Curie P (1905) Radioactive substances, especially radium. Nobel lecture, June 6, 1905. http://www.nobelprize.org/nobel_prizes/physics/laureates/1903/pierre-curie-lecture.pdf (accessed 12/31/11).

About Rutherford and physics concepts: Reeves R (2008) *A force of nature: The frontier genius of Ernest Rutherford*. New York: W W Norton; Einstein A, Infeld L (1938) *The evolution of physics: From early concepts to relativity and quanta*. New York: Simon & Schuster; Gamow G (1961) *The great physicists from Galileo to Einstein*. New York: Dover; Heilbron JL (2003) Ernest Rutherford and the explosion of atoms. Oxford: Oxford University Press.

By Curie: Curie M. *Radioactive substances*. English translation (2002). New York: Dover; Curie M, Debierne A, Eve AS, Geiger H, Hahn O, Lind SC, Meyer S, Rutherford E, Schweidler E (1931) The radioactive constants as of 1930. Report of the International radium-standards commission. *Journal of the American Chemical Society* 53:2437–2450; Curie M. Radium and new concepts in chemistry. Nobel lecture December 11, 1911. http://www.nobelprize.org/nobel_prizes/chemistry/laureates/1911/marie-curie-lecture.html (accessed 12/31/11).

By Rutherford: Rutherford E. The chemical nature of alpha particles from radioactive substances. Nobel lecture December 11, 1908. http://www.nobelprize. org/nobel_prizes/chemistry/laureates/1908/rutherford-lecture.html (accessed 12/31/11); Rutherford E, Chadwick J, Ellis CD (1930) *Radiations from radioactive substances*. Cambridge: Cambridge University Press; Rutherford E (1920) Bakerian Lecture: Nuclear constitution of atoms. *Proceedings of the Royal Society of London. Series A: Containing Papers of a Mathematical and Physical Character* 97:374–400.

Immunology and the Uncommon Man

About Metchnikoff and Ehrlich: Paul Ehrlich. Nobel lecture. Partial cell functions. December 11, 1908. http://www.nobelprize.org/nobel_prizes/medicine/ laureates/1908/ehrlich-lecture.html?print=1 (accessed 12/23/11); Tauber AI (2003) Metchnikoff and the phagocytosis theory. *Nature Reviews: Molecular Cell Biology* 4:897–901; Kaufman SHE (2008) Immunology's foundation: The 100-year anniversary of the Nobel Prize to Paul Ehrlich and Elie Metchnikioff. *Nature Immunology* 9:705–712; Schmalsteig FC, Goldman AS (2008) Ilya Ilich Metchnikoff (1845–1915) and Paul Ehrlich (1854–1915): The Centennial of the 1908 Nobel Prize in physiology or medicine. *Journal of Medical Biography* 16:96–104; Schmalsteig FC, Goldman AS (2010) Birth of the science of immunology. *Journal of Medical Biography* 18:88–98.

By Metchnikoff: Metchnikoff E, Metchnikoff II, Mitchell PC. (2004) *The prolongation of life: Optimistic studies*. New York: Springer (from original: 1908 New York: Putnam); Metchnikoff E (1893) *Lectures on the comparative pathology of inflammation: Delivered at the Pasteur Institute in 1891*. Translated by FA Starling and EH Starling. London: Kegan Paul, Trench, Trubner; Mechnikov I. Nobel lecture. On the present state of the question of immunity in infectious diseases. December 11, 1908. http://www.nobelprize.org/nobel_prizes/medicine/laureates/1908/mechnikov-lecture.html (accessed 12/23/11); Metchnikoff E (1984) Classics in infectious disease. Concerning the relationship between phagocytes and anthrax bacilli. *Clinical Infectious Disease* 6:761–770.

Connectivity

About the creation of the Internet and Paul Baran: Gleick J (2011) How Google dominates us. *The New York Review* August 18. 24–27; Griffin S. Internet pioneers. http://www.ibiblio.org/pioneers/index.html (accessed 12/23/11); Ryan J (2010) A history of the Internet and the digital future. London: Reaktion

Books; Abbate J (1999) *Inventing the Internet.* Cambridge, MA: The MIT Press.; Hafner K, Lyon M (1996) *Where wizards stay up late: The origins of the Internet.* New York: Simon & Schuster; Paul Baran, Internet pioneer dies at 84. *New York Times.* http://www.nytimes.com/2011/03/28/technology/28baran.html (accessed 1/1/12). History of Internet and computing, Internet dreamers, Paul Baran. http://history-computer.com/Internet/Birth/Baran.html (accessed 1/1/12).

By Baran: Baran P. On distributed communications networks. The RAND Corporation. http://www.attivissimo.net/timeline/paul-baran-on-distributed-comms. pdf (accessed 1/1/12);

Baran P (2002) The beginnings of packet switching: Some underlying concepts. *Communicatins Magazine, IEEE.* 40:42–48; Baran P (1977) Some perspectives on networks—Past, present, and future (B. Gilchrist, ed) *Information Processing.* Amsterdam: North-Holland Publishing.

A Modest Proposal for Saving Mankind

Population: Malthus TR. *An essay on the principle of population: or a view of its past and present effects on human happiness; with an inquiry into our prospects respecting the future removal or mitigation of the evils which it occasions.* Library of Economics and Liberty. Originally published 1798 by J Murray, London; Ehrlich PR (1968) *The population bomb.* Cutchogue, NY: Buccaneer Books.

Vavilov: Encyclopedia of World Biography (2004) Nikolai Ivanovich Vavilov. http://www.encyclopedia.com/topic/NikolaI_Ivanovich_Vavilov.aspx. (accessed 8/11/11).

Borlaug and the Green Revolution: Hessler L (2006). *The man who fed the world: Nobel Peace Prize Laureate Norman Borlaug and his battle to end world hunger.* Dallas: Durban House; Conway G (1997) *The doubly green revolution: Food for all in the twenty-first century.* Ithaca, NY: Cornell University Press; Randhawa MS (1974) *Green revolution: A case study of Punjab.* Uttar Pradesh, India: Vikas Publishing House; Agribusiness Council (1974) *Agricultural initiative in the third world: A report on the conference "Science and Agribusiness in the Seventies."* Washington, DC: Agribusiness Council; Paarlberg D, Paarlberg P (2000) *The agricultural revolution of the 20th century.* Ames: Iowa University Press; Borlaug N. The Green Revolution, peace, and humanity. Nobel Lecture December 11, 1970. http://www.nobelprize.org/nobel_prizes/peace/laureates/1970/borlaug-lecture.html (accessed 12/31/11); The Norman Borlaug Heritage Foundation. http://www.normanborlaug.org/ (accessed 12/31/11).

Nitrogen fertilizers: Mosier A, Syers JK, Freney JR (2004) *Agriculture and the nitrogen cycle: Assessing the impacts of fertilizer use on food production and the* *environment.* Washingotn, DC: Island Press; Bothe H, Ferguson SJ, Newton WE (eds) (2007) *Biology of the nitrogen cycle: COST edition.* Oxford: Elsevier; Biographybase. Kristian Birkeland biography http://www.biographybase.com/biography/Birkeland_Kristian.html (accessed 8/12/11)

By Haber: Haber F. Nobel lecture, June 2, 1920. The synthesis of ammonia from its elements. http://www.nobelprize.org/nobel_prizes/chemistry/laureates/1918/haber-lecture.pdf. (accessed 8/11/11)

World food statistics: Food and Agriculture Organization of the United Nations. Statistics. http://www.fao.org/corp/statistics/en/ (accessed 5/15/12)

Medications Everywhere But Only One Pill

Facts about population and birth control: CIA World Fact Book. https://www.cia.gov/library/publications/the-world-factbook/geos/us.html (accessed 9/11/2011)

About the Pill: Mosher WD, Martinez GM, Chandra A et al (2004) CDC Advanced data. No. 350 : Use of contraception and use of family planning services in the United States 1982-2002 http://www.cdc.gov/nchs/data/ad/ad350.pdf (Accessed 2/8/2013). Vessey M, Yeates D, Flynn S (2010) Factors affecting mortality in a large cohort study with special reference to oral contraceptive use. *Contraception* 82:221–229.

History of the Pill: Seaman B (1969) *The doctor's case against the Pill.* Alameda, CA: Hunter House; American Experience. The Pill. http://www.pbs.org/wgbh/amex/pill (accessed 8/12/11); Marks LV (2001) *Sexual chemistry: A history of the contraceptive pill.* New Haven, CT: Yale University Press; Asbell B (1995) *The Pill: A biography of the drug that changed the world.* New York: Random House; Marsh M, Ronner W (2008) *The fertility doctor: John Rock and the reproductive revolution.* Baltimore, MD: The Johns Hopkins University Press; Djerassi C (2001) *This man's pill: Reflections on the 50th birthday of the Pill.* Oxford: Oxford University Press; Kline J, Stein Z, Susser M (1989) *Conception to birth: Epidemiology of prenatal development.* Oxford: Oxford University Press; Guillebaud J, McGregor A (2005) *The pill and other forms of hormonal contraception.* 7th ed. New York: Oxford University Press.

By Marker: Marker RE, Wagner RB, Ulshafer PR, Wittbecker EL, Goldsmith DPJ, Ruof CH. (1947) Sterodial sapogenins. *Journal of the American Chemical Society* 69:2167–2230.

By Hertig and/or Rock: Hertig AT (1989) A fifteen year search for first stage human ova. *Journal of the American Medical Association* 216:434–435; Hertig AT, Rock J, Adams EC, Menkin MC (1959) Thirty-four fertilized human ova, good, bad and indifferent, recovered from 210 women of known fertility: A study of biologic wastage in early human pregnancy. *Pediatrics* 23:202–211; Hertig AT, Rock J, Adams EC (1956) A description of 34 human ova within the first 17 days of development. *American Journal of Anatomy* 98:435–493; Pincus G, Rock J, Garcia CR, Ricewray E, Paniagua M, Rodriguez I (1958) Fertility control with oral medication. *American Journal of Obstetrics and Gynecology* 75:1333–1346.

Quotes: "To synthesize something…" Quote by Leonard Engels. Asbell B (1995) *The Pill: A biography of the drug that changed the world.* New York: Random House, page 88; "I drew out of the bank…" Quote by Russell Marker. Djerassi C (2001) *This man's pill: Reflections on the 50th birthday of the Pill.* Oxford: Oxford University Press; "Don't touch a steroid with a ten foot pole." Asbell B (1995) The Pill: A biography of the drug that changed the world. New York: Random House, page 106.

A Way to Die

Terri Schiavo: Fuhrman M (2006) *Silent witness: The untold story of Terri Schiavo's death.* New York: Harper Collins; Eisenberg J (2006) *The right vs. the right to die: Lessons from the Terri Schiavo case and how to stop it from happening again.* New York: Harper Collins; Caplan AL, McCartney JJ, Sisti DA (2006) The case of Terri Schiavo: Ethics at the end of life. Amherst, NY: Prometheus Books.

History of death and dying: Ariès, Philippe. Encyclopedia of death and dying. http://www.deathreference.com/A-Bi/Ari-s-Philippe.html#ixzz1N7b6K2FW) (accessed 1/1/12); ArièNews P (1975) *Western attitudes toward death: From the middle ages to the present.* Baltimore, MD: The Johns Hopkins Press; Lancaster H (1990) *Expectations of life: A study in the demography, statistic, and history of world mortality.* London: Springer-Verlag; Mitford J (1998) *The American way of death revisited.* New York: Random House.

Advance directives ownership and impact: Agency for Healthcare Research and Quality (2003) Advance care planning: Preferences for care at the end of life. AHRQ Research In Action Report Series, Issue 12; Lawrence J (2009) The advance directive prevalence in long-term care: A comparison of relationships between a nurse practitioner healthcare model and a traditional healthcare model. *Journal of the American Academy of Nurse Practitioners* 21:179–185; Resnick H, Schuur J, Heineman J, Stone R, Weissman J (2009) Advance directives in nursing home residents aged >=65 years: United States 2004. *American Journal of Hospice & Palliative Medicine* 25:476–482; Schrader S, Nelson M, Eidsness L (2009) "South Dakota's dying to know": A statewide survey about end of life. *Journal of Palliative Medicine* 12:695–705; Silveira M, Kim S, Langa

K (2010) Advance directives and outcomes of surrogate decision making before death. *New England Journal of Medicine* 362:1211–1218; Beach MC, Morrison RS (2002) The effect of do-not-resuscitate orders on physician decision-making. *Journal of the American Geriatrics Society* 50:2057–2061.

Advanced directives cost savings: Hogan C, Lunney J, Gabel J, Lynn J (2001) Medicare beneficiaries' costs of care in the last year of life. *Health Affairs* 20:188–195; Morrison RS, Penrod JD, Cassel JB, et al. (2008) Cost savings associated with US hospital palliative care consultation programs. *Archives of Internal Medicine* 168:1783–1790.

Steering the Craft

On creativity: Simonton DK (1999) *Origins of genius: Darwinian perspectives on creativity*. New York: Oxford University Press; Robinson A (2010) *Sudden genius? The gradual path to creative breakthroughs*. New York: Oxford University Press; Kahneman D (2011) *Thinking fast and slow*. New York, NY: Farrar, Straus and Giroux. Guilford JP (1967) *The nature of human intelligence*. New York: McGraw-Hill; Mednick SA (1962) The associative basis of the creative process. *Psychological Review* 69:220–232; Campbell DT (1965) Variation and selective retention in socio-cultural evolution. In HR Barringer, GI Blanksten, RW Mack (eds) *Social change in developing areas*. Cambridge, MA: Schenkman (pp. 19–49); Ludwig AM (1995) *The price of greatness: Resolving the creativity and madness controversy*. New York: Gilford Press; Eysenck HJ (1993) Creativity and personality: Suggestions for a theory. *Psychological Inquiry* 4:147–148; Eysenck HJ (1994) Creativity and personality: Word association, origence, and psychoticism. *Creativity Research Journal* 7:209–216.

Hearing loss statistics: Shargorodsky J, Curhan SG, Curhan GC, Eavey R (2010) Change in prevalence in hearing loss in US adolescents. *Journal of the American Medical Association* 304:772–778; Niskar AS, Kieszak SM, Holmes A, Esteban E, Rubin C, Brody DJ (1998) Prevalence of hearing loss among children 6 to 19 years of age: The Third national Health and Nutrition Examination Survey. *Journal of the American Medical Association* 279:1071–1075; Henderson E, Testa MA, Hartnick C (2001) Prevalence of noise-induced hearing-threshold shifts and hearing loss among US youth. *Pediatrics* 127:e39–46.

Milgram, Hertig and Rock, Keys, Edison: See relevant chapter references.